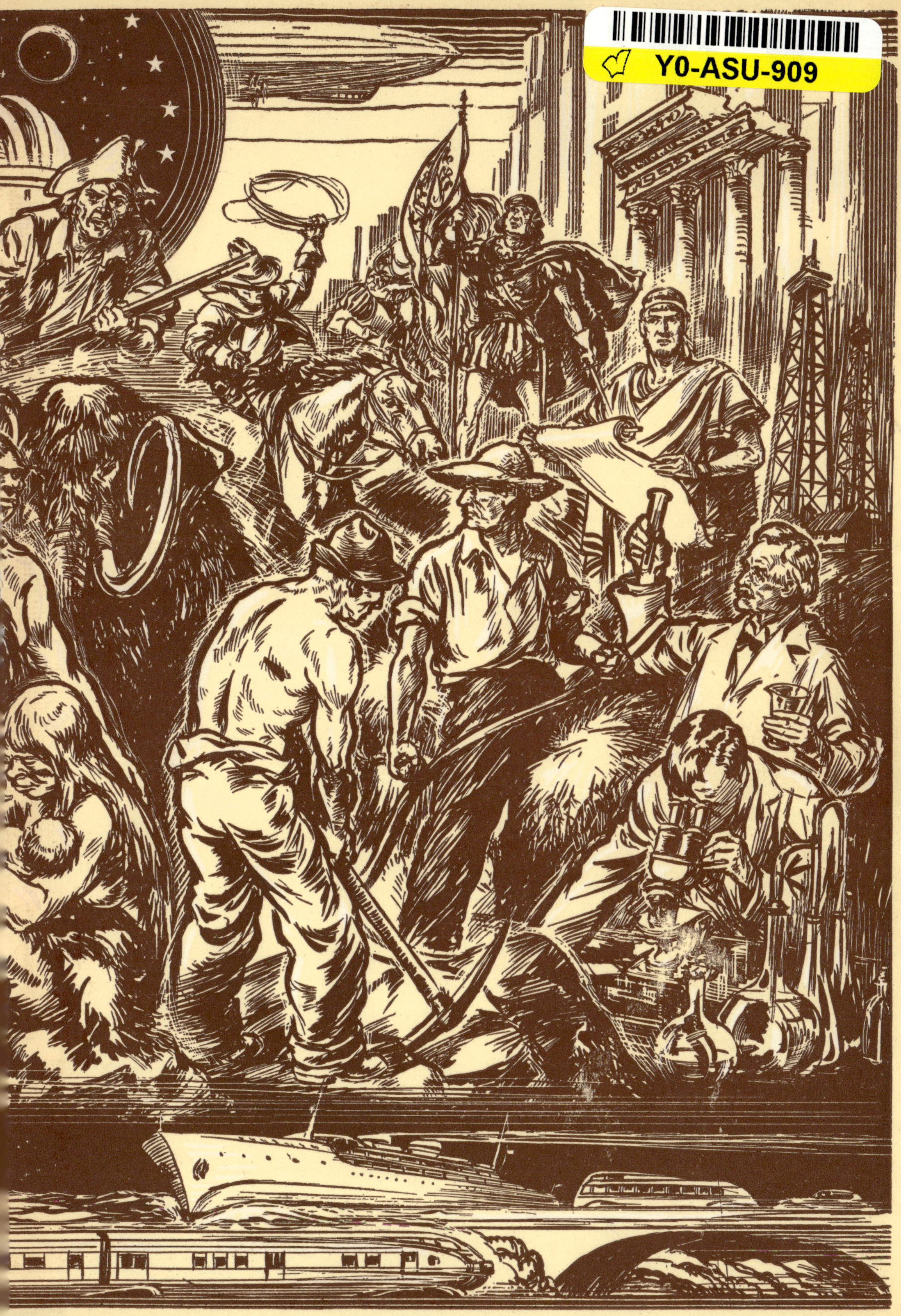

UNIVERSITY OF KNOWLEDGE INCORPORATED
GLENN FRANK, B.A., M.A., Litt.D., L.H.D., LL.D., *Editor-in-Chief*

PRINTED AND BOUND IN THE UNITED STATES
OF AMERICA BY THE CUNEO PRESS, INC.

VIA APPIA ANTICA

The ancient Appian road is in some respects the most famous highway in the world, with its history running back into the dim past. Over this highway mighty kings, emperors, and popes have traveled. Great armies have tramped it, and by it St. Paul made his way to Rome.

UNIVERSITY OF KNOWLEDGE

GLENN FRANK, EDITOR-IN-CHIEF

THE WORLD WE LIVE IN

AND

THE PEOPLE WE LIVE WITH

STILL MORE TRAVEL

Written and compiled by
NUMEROUS WORLD TRAVELERS

under the direction

of

MASON WARNER

World Traveler — Foreign News Correspondent
Member
Adventurers' Club of Chicago

•

UNIVERSITY OF KNOWLEDGE INCORPORATED
CHICAGO

COPYRIGHT 1937
BY UNIVERSITY OF KNOWLEDGE, INCORPORATED, CHICAGO, U.S.A.

ACKNOWLEDGMENT

From revolutionary Spain to war-torn China, and from the islands of the Mediterranean to the islands of the South Seas we have gathered pictures for this volume. Friends, and societies of various kinds, have co-operated with us in a whole-hearted manner.

We desire to express our appreciation for the kind co-operation given to us by:

Intourist Inc., New York
The Art Institute of Chicago
American Museum of Natural History, New York
Nippon, Yusen, Kaisha Steamship Company, Chicago
Chamber of Commerce of Hilo, Hawaii
Italian Tourist Information Office, Chicago
Swiss Federal Railways, New York.

J. BRADFORD PENGELLY
Picture Editor

TABLE OF CONTENTS

	PAGE
ACKNOWLEDGMENT	vii
PORTUGAL	13
SPAIN	23
SWITZERLAND	55
ITALY	89
THE MEDITERRANEAN ISLANDS	123
TURKEY	133
PALESTINE	157
SYRIA	177
ARABIA	187
IRAN	193
AFGHANISTAN	198
SIAM	202
FRENCH INDO-CHINA	205

	PAGE
THE HAWAIIAN ISLANDS	209
THE PHILIPPINE ISLANDS	217
ISLANDS OF THE SOUTH SEAS	225
DUTCH EAST INDIES	243
NEW GUINEA	249
JAPAN	251
CHINA	287
RUSSIA	331
BRITISH MALAYA	373

Drawing by Raeburn Rohrbach

THE WHITE AREAS REPRESENT COUNTRIES DESCRIBED IN THIS VOLUME

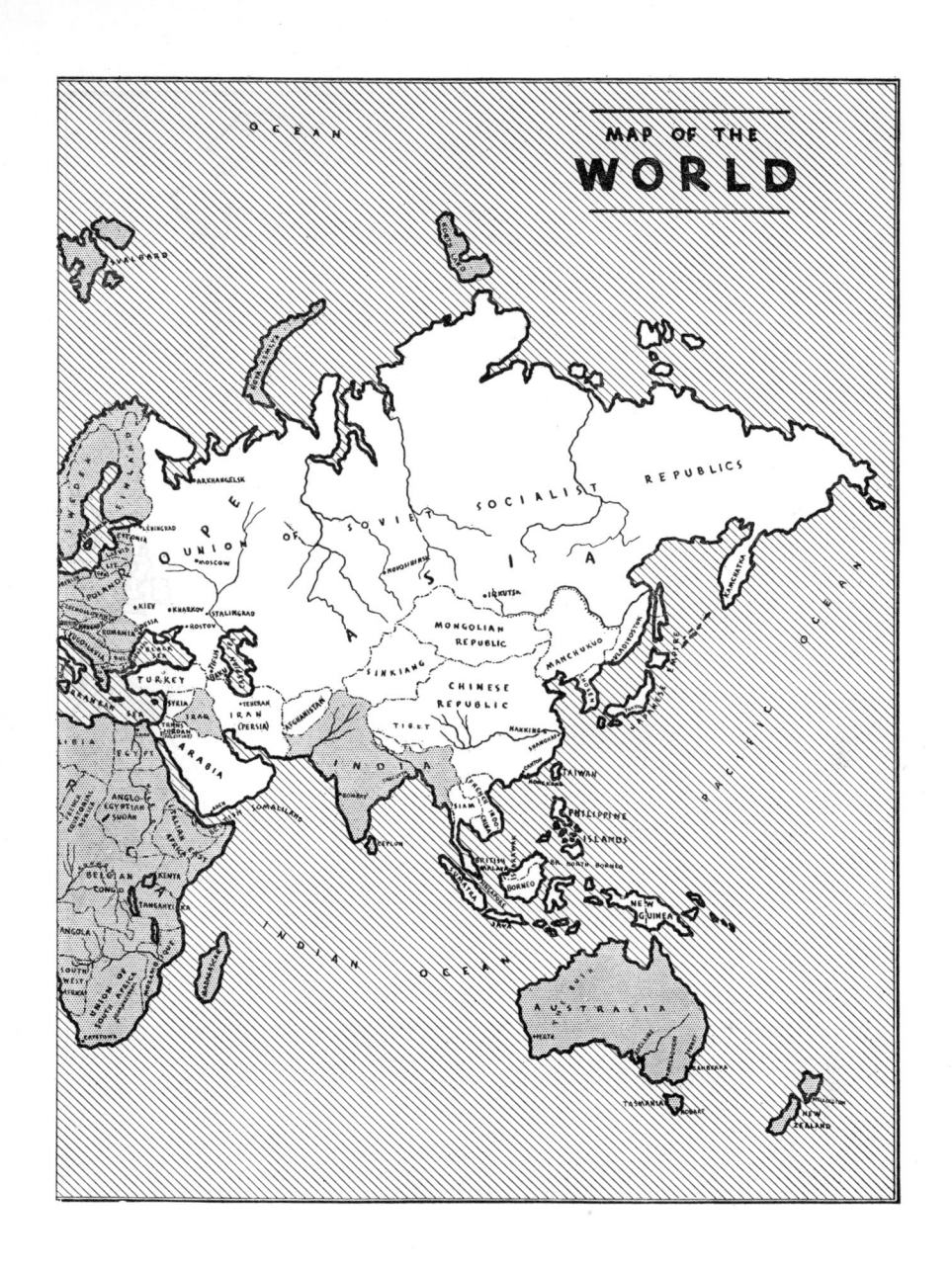

THE SHADED LAND AREAS ARE DESCRIBED IN COMPANION VOLUMES

Black Star photo By Dorien Leigh

WINE BOATS AT THE QUAY, OPORTO, PORTUGAL
The view is from the high bridge, "Ponte de Dom Luizi," over the Douro River.

[XII]

PORTUGAL

MONTE ESTORIL, PORTUGAL

THE LAND AND ITS PRODUCTS

PORTUGAL, a compact little country on the western side of the Iberian peninsula, has an area of 35,490 square miles and a population of more than six million. Several mountain chains, extensions of the Spanish ranges, cross the country. The most important rivers are the Tagus, the Douro, and the Guardiana.

Few European countries have as great a variety of agricultural products as Portugal. The semi-tropical climate and carefully husbanded soil give plentiful yields of nuts, figs, oranges, lemons, and citrons. Small grains are also produced. Grapes form one of the outstanding crops. From bountiful forests come cork, oak, and a species of sea pine. The rivers and ocean yield fish in abundance, and good pasture lands make grazing a leading industry. Iron, marble, and salt are found, as well as limited amounts of gold and silver, though only iron is mined to any great extent. Manufacturing is little developed, with the exception of the silk, woolen, and earthernware industries.

WINDMILLS OF PORTUGAL
Almost every hilltop has its great windmill.

Black Star photo
By Dorien Leigh

FROM ROMAN PROVINCE TO REPUBLIC

Portugal, once an independent region known as Lusitania, was made a Roman province by Augustus. The Visigoths established their control in the fifth century; and in turn, the Moors in the eighth century. Christian princes persisted in efforts to drive their Moorish oppressors back into Africa. Don Alonzo Henriquez succeeded in throwing off the claims of Leon and obtained the recognition of Portuguese independence in 1185. Intermittent warfare was carried on with the Moors and Castile.

John I of the House of Aviz came to the throne in 1385. During his reign Portugal prospered, Ceuta was captured from the Moors, and Prince Henry the Navigator established his remarkable "school" at Sagres. From Prince Henry's efforts later came the circumnavigation of Africa and the discovery of an all-water route to India. By the middle of the sixteenth century, Portugal possessed important colonies in the Far East and in South America.

Portugal was one of the world's great countries until the time of Philip II of Spain, who won the throne in 1580 when the Aviz line died out. This "captivity" lasted until 1640, when John IV of the House of Braganza was established on the throne. International complications continued to weaken Portuguese power, and in 1807 the royal family fled to Brazil to escape Napoleon's invading army. The itinerant king, John VI, returned to Portugal in 1821, and the next year Brazil declared its independence from Portugal.

PORTUGAL'S STORMY REPUBLICAN GOVERNMENT

After the overthrow of the monarchy in 1910, republican constitutional government was adopted. The alliance with England involved Portugal in the World War, but its activities were confined chiefly to the confiscation of German ships, and to fighting in Africa. Following the war, riots and labor troubles kept the government in constant turmoil. But in 1928, the popular military leader, Carmona, was elected president and under his direction, the domestic difficulties were quickly ironed out. The actual power of the government is in the hands of the prime minister, Dr. Salazar, who is virtually a dictator. During the Revolution in Spain, Portugal, while not actually engaged in the arms traffic, allowed Fascist troops and supplies to reach the Franco forces.

PORTUGAL'S PICTURESQUE PEASANTRY

Portuguese peasants are sturdy folk, the men strong and handsome, the women full-bosomed and hardy. At least two-thirds of the work in the fields is done by women. In northern Portugal women serve as hotel porters and stevedores, and, carrying great burdens on their heads, they transport farm produce for long distances.

The peasant women wear long, brightly colored skirts, an abundance of petticoats, and turban-like headpieces, with scarves

VINE CULTURE IN PORTUGAL
Much Portuguese wine is exported.
Black Star photo
By Dorien Leigh

[18] UNIVERSITY OF KNOWLEDGE

Black Star photo
"TORRE DE BELEM," NEAR LISBON
Like a battleship of stone looms this sixteenth-century tower at the mouth of the Tagus River.

with iron trays on their heads; donkeys bear cans of oil, kerosene, gasoline, and vinegar, and even wood is peddled in the streets. The warm southern part of the country produces tropical and semi-tropical fruits such as oranges, lemons, nuts, and figs.

LANGUID LISBON

At the mouth of the Tagus River is Lisbon, a city of six hundred thousand people, and Portugal's capital. Between purple mountains and a variegated waterfront the houses of Portugal's largest city cluster along the sloping, hilly streets, a strange mixture of the old and the new. The newer section is proud of the modern buildings and parks along its great main avenue, the Praça do Commercio; in the older sections are narrow streets, lined with blue and brown houses. One seldom sees a wagon; burdens are carried on people's heads and occasionally on heavily laden donkeys. Peddlers fill the streets with their cries.

PORTUGAL [15]

PORTUGAL'S STORMY REPUBLICAN GOVERNMENT

After the overthrow of the monarchy in 1910, republican constitutional government was adopted. The alliance with England involved Portugal in the World War, but its activities were confined chiefly to the confiscation of German ships, and to fighting in Africa. Following the war, riots and labor troubles kept the government in constant turmoil. But in 1928, the popular military leader, Carmona, was elected president and under his direction, the domestic difficulties were quickly ironed out. The actual power of the government is in the hands of the prime minister, Dr. Salazar, who is virtually a dictator. During the Revolution in Spain, Portugal, while not actually engaged in the arms traffic, allowed Fascist troops and supplies to reach the Franco forces.

PORTUGAL'S PICTURESQUE PEASANTRY

Portuguese peasants are sturdy folk, the men strong and handsome, the women full-bosomed and hardy. At least two-thirds of the work in the fields is done by women. In northern Portugal women serve as hotel porters and stevedores, and, carrying great burdens on their heads, they transport farm produce for long distances.

The peasant women wear long, brightly colored skirts, an abundance of petticoats, and turban-like headpieces, with scarves

VINE CULTURE IN PORTUGAL
Much Portuguese wine is exported.
Black Star photo
By Dorien Leigh

TWO LISBON FISHWIVES DIVIDING THE SARDINES THEY HAVE PURCHASED TOGETHER

flowing down the back. These interesting people live in little stone houses with thatched roofs. They speak a language somewhat similar to Spanish.

RARE OLD WINES AND ARTS

Northern Portugal has been noted for centuries for its rare old wines and fine grapes, shipped from Oporto, second city in size in the country. The country is so carefully maintained that every blade of grass seems to be in its place. Vineyards are kept immaculate, and their trellises are tall granite posts. The vineyards are located on terraced hillsides, whose maintenance requires endless toil because of the heavy seasonal rains. The vines are grown "low-bush" fashion, seldom reaching a height of more than six feet. At harvest time the grapes are gathered in baskets and carried to the presses where bare-footed men trample them in huge granite vats to the tune of peasant folk music. The vats serve as fermenting containers for the juice until the famous port wine, named for the city of Oporto, is put into oak casks to be shipped.

Vianna do Castello was the great port during the twelfth century, as Oporto is today. Brisk trade followed Vasco da Gama's exploits, and at that time the art of Flemish lacemaking, which is still practiced by Portuguese women, was first introduced into the country. Fishing fleets sailed from Vianna to the Newfoundland banks in search of cod, and many boats still make this long voyage to the Grand Banks.

Of the six million inhabitants of Portugal, the greatest number live in the wine-producing region of the Douro River. South of the Douro farming is carried on, though the infrequency of rainfall makes irrigation necessary. Blindfolded donkeys supply power to pump the well water into irrigation ditches. Timber, salt, and rice are the leading products of this region.

MOUNTAINS IN PORTUGAL

Bussaco where, it is said, early Christians fled and hid in caves, is a land of great chestnut, cork, and pine forests, and has specimens imported from Portugal's possessions, such as palm, camphor, acacia, and fir trees, but chiefly the Lusitanian cypress, imported from Mexico. Magnolia and lavender, as well as orange and lemon trees, are included among the four hundred types grown here.

Another of Bussaco's attractions is the Manoeline architecture built with soft white limestone. The region is spotted with old monasteries, chapels, and hermitages hidden among the vast timber tracts on whose border is "Iron Ridge," the scene of Massena's defeat by Wellington. A famous hostelry is the Palace hotel, originally built near the old Carmelite monastery for the use of royalty.

Portugal's shopping, like that of many North African countries, is conducted in the streets. Colorfully garbed women sit on stools, with their wares about them. Fish are retailed by men

Homer Smith photo, Chicago
HARBOR AND SKYLINE OF LISBON, CAPITAL OF PORTUGAL

[18]   UNIVERSITY OF KNOWLEDGE

Black Star photo

"TORRE DE BELEM," NEAR LISBON
Like a battleship of stone looms this sixteenth-century tower at the mouth of the Tagus River.

with iron trays on their heads; donkeys bear cans of oil, kerosene, gasoline, and vinegar, and even wood is peddled in the streets. The warm southern part of the country produces tropical and semitropical fruits such as oranges, lemons, nuts, and figs.

LANGUID LISBON

At the mouth of the Tagus River is Lisbon, a city of six hundred thousand people, and Portugal's capital. Between purple mountains and a variegated waterfront the houses of Portugal's largest city cluster along the sloping, hilly streets, a strange mixture of the old and the new. The newer section is proud of the modern buildings and parks along its great main avenue, the Praça do Commercio; in the older sections are narrow streets, lined with blue and brown houses. One seldom sees a wagon; burdens are carried on people's heads and occasionally on heavily laden donkeys. Peddlers fill the streets with their cries.

PORTUGAL [19]

On one edge of the city stands the Sé Patriarchal, a rugged old cathedral built in the reign of Portugal's first king, Dom Alonzo Henriquez. At the other end of the city is the noble old São Vicente, a gigantic Renaissance church, which is the royal burial place. In the Royal Museum of Coaches one finds over a score of magnificently appointed royal carriages.

The watch tower of St. Vincent's is located at the mouth of the Tagus, and from it many explorers have begun their voyages. The fortress, with its ten-foot-thick walls, was once surrounded by water; now it lies among sandbars. In Lisbon's great bull ring, which seats ten thousand people, are held Portugal's elaborate and colorful bullfights. The Avenida, a wide boulevard of Lisbon, leads to a comical little cogwheel train which ascends the slope to the Moorish fortress of St. George overlooking the entire landscape of city and countryside.

PART OF COURT IN NATIONAL MUSEUM
OF COACHES, LISBON
Showing a berlin, a type of carriage of the seventeenth century.
This museum houses one of the finest collections
of coaches in the world.

FAMOUS OLD CASTLE AT CINTRA, PORTUGAL
Originally built by the Moors.

Courtesy
J. Bradford Pengelly

OPORTO, THE CITY OF WINE

From a high railroad bridge over the Douro can be seen the imposing panorama of Oporto, Portugal's second largest city, and its neighboring seaside resort, Granja. In the crowded streets of the city are two-wheeled ox carts, porters with gigantic burdens on their heads, and a few horses pulling light wagons and carts.

The civic center of the town is the Praça de Riviera, a little waterfront plaza. The chief thoroughfare is the Rua das Flores, with its peddlers of gold and silver trinkets. The massive granite buildings of the town are located on the slopes away from the waterfront. The somber cathedral is the dominating structure and is of unusual interest, for, unlike other cathedrals, it contains the barest necessities and no brilliant embellishments.

No traveler should miss the *Romarias*, the great national holiday pilgrimages to the religious centers of the nation, where elaborate ceremonies are combined with singing and dancing in the streets.

PORTUGAL [21]

VACATION SPOT OF KINGS

A short ride by rail from the bustle of old Lisbon is the summer home of royalty, Cintra, unimportant for commercial achievements, but rich in history. The palace is a queer mixture of northern and Moorish architecture. Adorned with geometric patterns, the great dining hall and the Hall of the Sirens are typically Moorish, as is the House of the Moorish Baths, with its gushing fountains. In the other section of the palace is the Swan Room, so named for a gift of swans brought by the Duke of Burgundy when he asked the king for the hand of his daughter, Isabella. Two palaces, the old Moorish castle and the Palace of the Pena, crown the highest points of the entire mountain range.

DETAIL OF ENTRANCE TO CASTLE AT CINTRA

Courtesy
J. Bradford Pengelly

Courtesy The Art Institute of Chicago

CATHEDRAL OF BURGOS
General Franco, Revolutionary leader, used this cathedral as headquarters at times during 1936 and 1937.

SPAIN

Courtesy The Art Institute of Chicago

COURT OF MYRTLES AND TOWER OF COMARES, THE ALHAMBRA

SPAIN has for centuries offered rich returns to those who have visited it in search of romance. This is the land of Carmen, the Moors, and the Inquisition, of Don Quixote, bullfights, and the bolero. Few of the early landmarks of western civilization have more thrilling connotations than the Pillars of Hercules, the Rock of Gibraltar. The very place names of Iberia are pregnant with associations—Aragon, Seville, Valencia, Castile, Barcelona, and Granada. In shape, as Strabo first pointed out, the Iberian peninsula resembles a stretched-out bullskin. The Spanish call it *la piel de un toro extendida*. It was called the end of the earth in ancient times. During the Middle Ages it was the point of departure for the New World. Continental Spain occupies an area of 190,000 square miles and is bound on the north by the Bay of Biscay and France, on the east and southeast by the Mediterranean Sea, and the southwest and west by the Atlantic Ocean and Portugal. Included under the flag of Spain are the Balearic Islands in the Mediterranean, the Canary Islands near Africa, and territorial possessions in Africa.

Paul's Photos, Chicago

WINDMILLS OF SPAIN
On Spanish plains, such as in the province of Ciudad Real, many windmills of this type can be seen.

The interior of Spain is a large plateau, called the *meseta;* it includes approximately half of Spain and averages twenty-five hundred feet in altitude. On the eastern side, the plateau breaks sharply toward the sea in craggy cliffs. In the Pyrenees, in the northeast, is Pic de Néthou, which towers more than eleven thousand feet. From the *meseta* flow five large rivers: the Ebro, the Douro, the Tagus, the Guadiana, and the Guadalquivir. The Ebro in the northeastern part of Spain drains Aragon and Catalonia on its way to the Mediterranean. The Douro drains the land where the cities of Burgos, Valladolid, and Salamanca have flourished for centuries, and empties into the Atlantic Ocean at Oporto, Portugal. The Tagus rises in the *meseta* near Segovia, flows through Madrid and Toledo, and joins the Atlantic at Lisbon, Portugal. The Guadiana, like an exception to a rule, rises in the Mancha, where according to Cervantes Don Quixote fought a windmill. It disappears into the earth for many miles, then reappears, greater in volume, and flowing southward forms a part of the boundary between Spain and Portugal. Most interesting of the Spanish rivers is the Guadalquivir, which drains Andalusia. Its waters pass four famous Spanish cities: Granada, on the Daro (a tributary); Cordova, once the western Mecca of Mohammedanism; Seville, the arena of realism; and, finally, Cadiz, the seaport of Seville, which lies west of the Strait of Gibraltar.

The appearance of Spain varies greatly within very short distances. In the north are forests of oak, chestnut, beech, birch, hazelnut, maple and pine trees. Evergreen oaks, wild olives, and honey mesquites grow near the Mediterranean. Plains in Murcia and Valencia are irrigated; olive trees grow in Cordova and Jaén. There are vast grazing pastures in the Asturias, orange groves in Valencia and Alicante, cornfields in Galicia, vineyards in the Mancha and about Jerez; and here and there, as any traveler in Spain will find, are extensive areas where only cork trees grow.

OLD MAN OF EUROPE

Historians disagree about the earliest periods of Spanish civilization; but the first people known to have inhabited the peninsula after Stone Age times were the Iberians. Direct descendants of the Iberians are the Basques, who now live in the rugged northern sections of Spain. Later, when the Celts entered Spain, the races intermingled and their descendants are known as Celtiberians. Phoenicians visited the peninsula in the twelfth century, B.C., and found the Celtiberians firmly established. Greeks invaded the country and took possession of the northeastern coast near modern Barcelona. Carthage colonized the peninsula extensively in the fourth century, B.C., but Rome put an end to Carthaginian rule at the close of the Punic Wars. Vandals and Visigoths overran the country in the fifth century, A.D.; and in the eighth century the Mohammedan Moors took possession of it.

THE GOLDEN AGE OF SPAIN

The Christian re-conquest lasted for eight hundred years. After the beginning of the Middle Ages the south was still under the domination of the Moors, who expected the Christian energy to die; national loyalty was divided between the cross and the crescent. But more important than battles in the history of Spanish civilization were the two types of living, which still underlie Spanish culture: the northern, which came from contact with the wandering tribes of Europe; and the southern, which came from contact with the Near East. The combination is reflected in the architecture, sculpture, music, science, and law which made Spain the western mistress of medieval Europe.

Black Star photo. By Pierre Verger
BULLFIGHTING IN SEVILLE
Gaily attired toreadors, victors of many an arena battle, are national heroes in Spain.

National unity was the objective of Queen Isabella who, by her marriage to Ferdinand, united the two Castiles. Success followed her efforts; and then came the greater dream of an American empire. The empire, overseas and Continental, came and vanished. Internal strife deposed and recalled many monarchs. Isolation during the World War left Spain free to endeavor to solve her stormy internal problems.

The nation was being strangled in the noose of lingering feudalism, and the tightening cord was held by the overlapping groups of the nobility, the landholders, the wealthy manufacturers, and the clergy. Agriculture was rapidly becoming less significant than manufacture, and with the growth of industrialism and urbanism the people grew restive and then violent. Riots and strikes were common during and following the years of the World War.

In 1923 Primo de Rivera by a quick stroke seized the wheel of government and made himself virtual dictator. However, his personal influence gradually waned, and in 1930 King Alfonso XIII dismissed him and he died two months later. General Berenguer, who followed him, could not stem the tide of rebellion. He resigned in 1931, and in that year elections showed great strength on the part of radical and republican groups. Alfonso's abdication was demanded, and he quickly left the country. Alcalá Zamora was elected president of the Cortes and subsequently of the Spanish Republic.

The new liberal government initiated many reforms, among which were the abolition of the state church, the institution of free and compulsory education under the direction of the state, and the socialization of large estates. Before these reforms could be fully carried through, there was a swing in the direction of the conservative and reactionary groups, with a swift succession of new ministries. There were strikes and riots on the part of leftist groups, resulting in martial law and the dissolution of the Cortes. This sequence of events brought about the union of all leftist groups, with the result that in the elections of February, 1936, they secured a strong representation in the Cortes. They removed President Zamora and elected Manuel Azana to the office of president. The civil war, which began in July, 1936, grew out of a revolt on the part of the reactionaries and the army against this regime. The Rebel forces, led by General Francisco Franco, starting from Morocco and the west, quickly gained control of the western part of the country and finally took over the northwestern provinces after a long and bitter conflict. The Loyalist armies stubbornly defended Madrid and the eastern section of the country.

ANCIENT RUINS

Throughout Spain are to be found ruins of Stone Age structures. Among structures of the New Stone Age, few are comparable to the dolmens in the Caves of Menga, at Malaga. The swamps of the Guadalquivir hide the ruins of an early city as mysterious as any vestiges to be found in Crete or Chaldea. Few

Homer Smith photo, Chicago
RUINS OF THE OLD ROMAN THEATER AT MERIDA

Roman structures in the world can compare with the aqueducts at Segovia and Alcantara. The theater of Agrippa at Merida is one of the largest Roman theaters ever built. The graceful Roman bridge at Salamanca and the perfect amphitheater at Sagunto are notable.

SPANISH DANCES

The attractive and diverse dances of Spain include the *sardana* of Catalonia, the *muñeira* of Galicia, the *jotas* of Aragon, Valencia, and Murcia. Some are danced by groups; others by pairs of dancers; still others, such as the complex Andalusian dances, are danced by individuals. The *jota* of Aragon, modified to local styles, has been accepted by all of the regions. Few nations possess a greater variety of songs than Spain. Many Spanish songs are of Arabian origin, sounding like cries prolonged with tremors of passion; others are full of a sad sentimentality which overcomes the otherwise carefree Spaniard when his fingers touch the strings of a guitar. The musical accompaniment requires a great variety of instruments: in Valencia, the flageolet; in Galicia, the tambourine; in Andalusia, the guitar; in Aragon the bandore; and everywhere, the castanets, which were originally ripe chestnuts.

FOR THE GOURMET

Spaniards speak of the antiquity of the recipes for their edible *combinados,* and insist that they have a rare perfection of seasoning. The national dish is *cocido* (stew); but a Madrileno likes *garbanzos* (chickpeas) in quantity; or potatoes cooked with pork sausage and bacon, well colored with saffron and in summer accompanied by a salad. The Aragonese likes his fried pimientos; the Andalusian, his hash and fruit; while the conservative Castilian prefers meat balls made of dried beef. Each ingredient in these *combinados* must be a product of the right locality in order to reach perfection; for instance, the ham must come from Villalba, Trevélez, or Montachez; the pork sausages from Cantimpalos or Candelario; the potatoes from Monforte or Ariz; the string beans from Ávila; and the chickpeas from Fuentesauco.

WINES AND GOLDEN APPLES

Spanish wines are incredibly varied. The whole world knows the wines of Jerez, Málaga, and Montilla—sherry, Málaga, and amontillado. Not less known to Spaniards themselves are such other wines as Lucanian white wine, the delicious table wines of both the high and the low Rioja, the strong and bitter wines of Aragon, the Catalán Priorate, the clear wine of Valdespeñas, the red and stinging wine of Yepes, and the wines of Galicia.

Oranges, nectarines, tangerines, pomegranates, peaches, grapes, and melons ripen year after year on Spanish trees and vines. The "golden apples of the Hesperides," which ancient Greeks envisioned, were the Andalusian oranges. Wild strawberries, sweet and small, are grown in Aranjuez and Valencia; oxblood cherries and aromatic pears grow best in Ávila; oranges in Murcia and Valencia are the first to ripen; the best black grapes grow in Málaga; and the best white ones grow near Madrid.

Spain's tragic civil war, which began in July, 1936, destroyed much of the ancient glory of Spanish cities and landscapes. Hurtling bombs and artillery fire wrought havoc among many beautiful buildings which were Spain's heritage. What demolition the war zone cities of Bilbao, Oviedo, Guadalajara, Burgos, Toledo, and mighty Madrid suffered is inestimable.

Some reconstruction has been made, as in San Sebastian, Burgos, and Bilbao. But no restoration can ever perfectly replace the

ST. CATALINA BRIDGE AND APPROACH TO THE BUSINESS
SECTION OF SAN SEBASTIAN
This city suffered greatly during the revolution that began in 1936.

ancient splendor or completely heal the scars. The loss cannot be forgotten in Spain; it is mourned by the whole world. But as long as books are read, as long as tales are told, the old memories will not die. In memory there remains the ravished beauty of such treasures as the Prado and the Puerta del Sol of Madrid; the Alhambra of Granada, the Alcazar in Toledo. Through the wreckage their images rise again, serene in the minds of men.

SAN SEBASTIAN

Few areas of the Iberian peninsula offer such sight-seeing possibilities as the land of the Basques, and few areas have been the scene of such bitter conflict and destruction. The Basques are the direct descendants of the original settlers of Spain, the Iberians; and they are justly proud of this lineage.

Perhaps more cosmopolitan than any other city in Spain is San Sebastian, a fashionable seaside resort. Here it was that many of the former rulers of Spain enjoyed their leisure. Taken in battle by the Nationalists, it was largely restored after its burning. Its wide sandy beaches, skirting the bay and spanned by wide promenades, the gay and colorful costumes of vacationists, the smart modernity of the hotels, and the gayly clad fishermen—all combine to implant pleasant memories in the minds of visitors at San Sebastian.

SPAIN'S "LITTLE LONDON"

Located seventy-five miles west of San Sebastian is Bilbao, capital and largest city of the Basques. With a population of some one hundred fifty thousand, situated on the banks of Nervion River, near where it empties into the Bay of Biscay, Bilbao is the second seaport in importance in the country. The city lies in a vast saucer, hemmed in by mountains on all sides. Shelled, bombed, and burned while hostilities raged, "little London," as it has been called, has rebuilt its bridges and buildings and resumed its commercial activity. The fact that it is the center of the iron industry in Spain, and that it has fine shipyards, added to its strategic importance in the war. In addition Bilbao is the shipping center for agricultural products, since the Basques are skilled farmers.

At five o'clock in the morning the city bursts into action, with whistles blowing, locomotives puffing, and the streets crowded with workers clad in their typical long blue blouses, canvas shoes

Homer Smith photo, Chicago

PART OF THE BUSINESS SECTION OF BILBAO
One of the centers of the revolutionary struggle.

with rope soles, and picturesque caps. Bilbao is awake! Interesting facts are brought to our attention on every hand. By night the fishermen make their catch of tiny creatures something like small eels, which are fried in oil and are a great delicacy. Much of the stevedore work, especially the unloading of coal, is done by women, who carry baskets on their heads. Basque cities have houses of low construction, with the omnipresent iron balconies and gratings and tile roofs. Country homes are of stone and many have endured through centuries.

SANTANDER WAKES UP

A little to the west of Bilbao is Santander, with some eighty-five thousand people, situated on the Bay of Biscay. It suffered a decline but recently revived because of the exportation of minerals from the district. It has a thirteenth-century castle and cathedral. Beautiful beaches, similar to those of San Sebastian, skirt its shore, and like Bilbao it is encircled by a rim of hills. Modern boulevards and plazas make the visitor realize that here is one of the awakening cities of Basque-land.

OVIEDO—TREASURE-HOUSE OF ANTIQUES

Another city in northern Spain is Oviedo, whose struggles in the civil war were only a modern counterpart to the battles of its historical background. Here in the eighth century a thriving city

Homer Smith photo, Chicago
SKYLINE OF SANTANDER, IMPORTANT SPANISH PORT
Another center of the struggle between Franco and the Loyalists.

SPAIN

MADRID, CAPITAL CITY OF SPAIN
Picture shows Calle Alcala, most important street, leading from The Paseo.
The city withstood many violent attacks by Franco's forces.

grew up, but it has lost much of its former importance. As in many of the smaller Spanish cities, much interest revolves around its magnificent cathedral. Built in the fourteenth century, it has magnificent stained-glass windows, lovely marble statues, and silver shrines. The Pantheon of Kings, which is here, was a burial place of former rulers and has many urns containing the regal remains.

MADRID, THE MAGNIFICENT

Madrid is the city of change, the center of Spain. What a wealth of images the very name conjures up in the mind of the traveler! Madrid is not really ancient, for as late as the time of Columbus it had only three thousand inhabitants. The city became the royal residential center in the sixteenth century, but it was not until the eighteenth century that it sprang into great importance.

As the greatest focus of fighting in the civil war, Madrid was bombed and shelled. The republican government moved its quarters from the metropolis when it became part of the actual line of fire, in the thick of the fiercest fighting.

Courtesy The Art Institute of Chicago

BAROQUE ARCHITECTURE OF OLD SPAIN
A doorway in Madrid, by Juan Hospicio—a splendid example of this type of architecture.

Wide avenues, beautiful plazas, and modern skyscrapers make Madrid a really modern metropolis. The most unreliable natural feature of the city is its weather; one day it may be extremely chilly, the following day *muy caliente* "very warm." An old rule is that one should not go without wraps until the "fortieth of May." The neatest street in the city is the Prado, lined with modern buildings, shade trees, fountains, and gardens. Travelers with a true appreciation of art have long sought Madrid's outstanding museum, the Museo del Prado, with its treasures wrought by the great masters. Near it are the Botanical Gardens, a lovely haven of trees, flowers, and shrubs. One of the most frequented places in the city is the Puerta del Sol, focus of political debates and demonstrations.

The city's finest park, Buen Retiro, is studded with historical statues and is unusually pleasing, with fountains, driveways, walks, and riding-paths. The museum is here, as well as the Zoölogical Gardens and the Crystal Palace. Just outside the park is the famous Plaza de la Independencia, around which are some of the city's most modern buildings. The largest plaza in Madrid is the Plaza de Oriente, and near it is the royal palace, the show place of all Madrid.

THE MAJESTY OF SPAIN

The royal palace is a grand structure over five hundred feet long, costing originally fifteen million dollars. The center of attraction is the throne room; on its dais the throne is guarded by gilded lions, one on either side. The room is decorated with magnificent mirrors, crystal chandeliers, and a great painting of "The Majesty of Spain," on the ceiling. Among the other famous features of the palace are the state dining room, brilliantly adorned with marble and bronze; the hall of Girardini, with stain-frescoed walls and a ceiling of porcelain; a gigantic staircase; and a marble-columned chapel, in which are many religious relics. Still other features of this edifice are its gigantic library, with its tapestries and marble-fountained gardens.

One of the most historic spots in Madrid is the famous Plaza Mayor, the scene of many executions, bullfights, and tournaments. Here political prisoners and religious martyrs were burned alive at the stake. Nearby is the famous pantheon of Spain, the San Francisco de Grande. This gigantic chapel is the burial place of Spanish heroes. A famous gateway, the Puerta de Toledo, built in honor of King Ferdinand VII, is decorated with carved figures and images.

In the southeastern part of the city is the Calle de Atocha, leading to the Calle de León and Royal Historical Academy, which houses valuable collections of historical relics of Spain. Behind the royal palace is the Plaza de Armas, an armory, which has an interesting collection of ancient armor used by the early Spaniards.

Few buildings in Madrid carry more of the spirit of the Old Spain than does the Naval Museum; for here are seen hundreds of relics collected by Columbus, Balboa, De Soto, Cortés, and many others. Arrows, quivers, skins of animals, scalp locks, and even human arms taken from the savages of the New World, as well as models of boats used by the Spaniards and Indians, a painting of Columbus' *Niña, Pinta,* and *Santa Maria,* a map used by Columbus in his second expedition, and hundreds of other fascinating articles from that era of exploration. The Real Academia de

Bellas Artes gives pleasure to art lovers; here are seen famous paintings by the old Spanish masters. The National Library, founded in 1711, contains nearly a million books, documents, and drawings.

ONE HUNDRED MILES OF CORRIDORS

Thirty miles from Madrid, is the Escorial, a tremendous burial church, somber as an ancient fortress. This church, built by Philip II upon the direction given in his father's will, was finished in 1584 after years of hard labor. It is 675 feet long and 539 feet wide and has fifteen hundred windows. The corridors in the church are said to have a total length of one hundred miles. Every year Spain honors St. Lawrence, in whose honor this structure was raised.

MOORISH TOLEDO

Toledo, famed for fine swords, is one of the most ancient cities in all Spain. It is said that there was a Christian church established here as early as 587 A. D. Toledo is built upon a raised elevation around which flows the Tagus River like the great moat of an old castle. Towers and spires rise from the city and the spirit of old Morocco seems to pervade the whole place. Under the Moors in the eighth century the early cathedral was the chief mosque of the city. After Toledo was captured by the Christians under Alfonso VI, the old building was wrecked; and a giant new cathedral was erected in its place. This tremendous structure, four hundred feet long and nearly two hundred feet wide, is built chiefly of granite and has eight principal entrances. Beautiful old stained-glass windows, a huge altar surmounted by a canopy on jasper columns, and a great bronze archbishop's throne are the main features of interest in this great church. There are three reading desks in the choir, one of them a brazen eagle with outstretched wings. The mosaic of the Virgin and Child, which is over the great altar, was brought from Rome. Around this cathedral are built a number of fine chapels, including the chapel of San Ildefonso and the chapel of the New Kings, which contains many effigies of Spanish royalty. The cloisters, which encompass a fine garden, have excellent frescoes and lead to the chapel of San Blas.

SPAIN [37]

Courtesy The Art Institute of Chicago
HIGH ALTAR IN THE CATHEDRAL OF TOLEDO

The streets in Toledo are narrow. The houses, having but few windows, present an impressive appearance. Most of the dwellings are of stone construction, and many of the exteriors are decorated with paintings and frescoes. Crossing the Alcantara Bridge that spans the Tagus, one comes upon a ruined castle built by Alfonso VI, to protect the city.

Other churches that the traveler might wish to see are the Santo Tome and San Juan de los Reves. The name of Toledo has always been synonymus with steel; and here is a flourishing modern factory, where knives and scissors are manufactured, and fine engraving is produced.

On the highest ground in this city of ancient Spain stands the famous Alcazar, formerly occupied by royalty. The mighty Moorish fortress was the scene of some of the most bitter fighting in the civil war, and its magnificence was devastated to a tragic extent. But its great white walls and peaked towers will always rise intact in the memory of men.

One place that no visitor should fail to see is the El Greco Museum, containing many valuable works of the great painter.

A STROLL THROUGH SARAGOSSA

Saragossa is not only a great religious center, with a population of 155,000, but is an industrious town as well. It was of great importance from its earliest days, because of its ideal situation as a trading center. It was first named Colonia Caesar-Augusta by the Romans, who were aware of its possibilities. The city has two great cathedrals, both well worth the traveler's time. The cathedral of the Virgin del Pilar is said to stand in the place where the Madonna appeared to St. James while he

BANKS OF THE EBRO RIVER NEAR SARAGOSSA

Through this picturesque valley runs the railroad from Madrid to Barcelona.

Homer Smith photo, Chicago

BARCELONA'S BUSY HARBOR
The monument at left is a statue of Christopher Columbus.

was a missionary in Spain. Just as she is said to have stood on a column before the saint, she stands on a pillar before the great church. The colossal structure, four hundred and thirty-six feet long and over two hundred feet wide, may be entered from three sides. The roof is a great dome resting upon four marble pillars. Over one of the altars stands an image of the Virgin, made of dark wood, beautifully clothed and adorned with costly jewels. This statue is believed to have miraculous powers of healing.

The other cathedral is called La Seo and is dedicated to the Lord Jesus. It is on the site where a mosque formerly stood and is richly finished within, and has many statues and historical relics.

Two other buildings worth mentioning are the Audiencia, where great operas were presented, and the Aljaferia Palace, which now serves as the barracks for troops.

BUSTLING BARCELONA

Long a contender with Madrid for pre-eminence among Spanish cities, Barcelona has a population of a million and a reputation as Spain's leading seaport. In this Spanish city play is subordinated to work. With an extensive world trade, Barcelona has adopted a strictly "business before pleasure" attitude. Not that the people of Barcelona do not have their lighter moments, for they do;

but this Spanish city has a truly cosmopolitan atmosphere and has always been one of the leading Mediterranean ports. Its harbor is much larger than that of Marseilles and is almost as large as that of Genoa. Even in the early days, Barcelona ranked on a par with any important Mediterranean port. The Romans under Augustus realized the possibilities of the site and made it a Roman colony. The city, situated on a rolling plain, is fringed, as are most Spanish ports, by mountains with subtropical scenery.

As a visitor leaves the quays and proceeds up the Rambla, the principal thoroughfare, he is drawn to the statue of Christopher Columbus, a tall shaft surmounted by a huge ball, upon which stands the figure of the great explorer. One may mount the shaft and view the panorama of the city. The base of the statue is guarded by eight bronze lions and adorned with reliefs depicting scenes from the life of the discoverer.

Barcelona possesses many fine churches, outstanding among which is the great cathedral, a beautiful example of Spanish Gothic architecture. Three hundred feet in length and a hundred and twenty-two feet wide, this church is not as large as many to be found in Spain; but it has unusually beautiful stained-glass windows, some of which were created in the fifteenth century. It has thirty chapels, and its cloisters, planted with orange and palm trees, are a welcome retreat on a warm summer day.

Barcelona is of unusual importance in textile manufacturing. In addition to great quantities of cotton, woolen, and silk fabrics, Barcelona produces furniture, shoes, cement, cork, and even locomotives. More than one hundred thousand workers are employed in the cotton mills alone, and the silk mills furnish work for more than twelve thousand. Barcelona is surrounded by a country producing grapes, cereals, nuts, and olives. Its sheep, goats, and cattle are also of importance.

VALENCIA

Until the civil war Valencia was a sleepy city, gazing out over the blue Mediterranean, untouched by the commercial rush of its great neighbor, Barcelona. In the Franco drive against Madrid in the fall of 1936, however, the republican government was forced to move its headquarters from Madrid and its transference to Valencia brought the city new life. The peaceful orange groves and cathedrals saw a new activity sweep through the city. But

SPAIN [41]

Black Star photo. By Warner Conitz

NIGHT DANCING IN BARCELONA STREETS
The *Sardana,* national folk dance, is an occasion of merriment and pleasure for old and young.

Black Star photo. By Neofot
A STREET SCENE IN BARCELONA

Paul's Photos, Chicago
THE HARBOR OF VALENCIA

let us look through the haze of battle smoke and the turmoil of strife to the past beauty of Valencia, which lingers in memory.

The great Gothic cathedral was erected in the thirteenth century. Its curious bell tower, El Miguelete, a high octagonal structure, was built a century later. From the top of this tower can be seen the town and the beautiful irrigated countryside. All the area around Valencia is well watered by a network of canals. The signal for the opening and closing of the gates to the canals is given by ringing the El Miguelete bell. In connection with this watering system, there is a water tribunal which sits every Thursday at high noon to mete out punishment to those who have broken the irrigation rules.

Unlike many Spanish cities, Valencia goes to bed early. As evening deepens into dusk, families sit at their doorsteps waiting for the cool of the evening to drive away the day's heat. Even the cafés close early. Only the dance halls remain open late.

Besides the great cathedral and the Patriarca church, there is the Museo Provincial de Pinturas, which is the art center of the city. Housed in a former convent, it possesses some fifteen hundred paintings, many of which are works of old masters. In Valencia is the biggest bull ring in all Spain. Most travelers want to see the magnificent ruins of the Castle of Santa Barbara, perched on a hilltop near the city. In the climb to the top one passes through thickets of cactus and near antique bastions. From the castle the splendid view of the city, the sea, and the surrounding country gives the best obtainable impression of Valencia.

WHERE MOORISH KINGS HELD SWAY

South of Madrid and about forty miles inland from the blue Mediterranean is Granada. To the traveler Granada has meant one thing, the Alhambra. And certain it is, in all Spain, there is nothing to compare with it. For the Alhambra is one of the world's classic structures.

When the Moors were the ruling class of Spain, Granada was its capital city. According to the story, when Mohammed Abu Abdallah was finally driven from here in 1492 by the armies of King Ferdinand, he paused on the summit of the Sierra Nevadas and, taking one last look at the city he had lost forever, burst into tears. But his mother, the old Aisha, a stern woman, reprimanded him, saying, "Weep not like a woman for that which you could not defend as a man."

Courtesy The Art Institute of Chicago

FOUNTAIN IN THE COURT OF THE LIONS, THE ALHAMBRA

THE ALHAMBRA

The Alhambra, though now of the past, still stands in memory as a mighty citadel and palace. It covers an area approximately eight hundred by two hundred yards and is divided into three parts. The lower end, Alcazabe, is the citadel and included the residences of the Granada governors; the Alhambra proper was the palace of the Granada kings; and the Alhambra Alta housed the officials' quarters. A strong wall, surmounted by towers for defense, surrounds the entire structure.

Approaching the famous ruins, the tourist passes through a wooded park, where old elm trees, believed to be planted by the Duke of Wellington, provide a famous haunt for nightingales. Passing through the Gate of Judgment, where in ancient days all seeking an audience were heard, the visitor ascends the hill to the Plaza de los Aljibez, wherein lies a hundred-foot reservoir edged with myrtle. The Alcazaba or old fortress is a complete ruin, of which nothing remains except the old watch tower, where a huge bell, weighing many tons, daily signals the regulation of the irrigation gates.

The exterior of the Alhambra seems unimpressive; but, as usual, the Moors reserved the building's glorious beauty for the interior. Beyond the Court of Myrtles, which is similar to the Plaza de los Aljibez, is the Gallery of the Ambassadors, where formerly the great councils met, and where the decision to surrender Granada was finally reached. It is a beautiful place with a ceiling of white, blue, and gold, embellished by stars, as though imitating the heavens. The massive walls are beautiful; the floor is alabaster; and the arches supporting the roof are of mother-of-pearl, jasper, and porphyry.

Leading from the Court of Myrtles is the famous Court of Lions, small in size but rare in beauty. Here, in the center, stands the historical Fountain of Lions, a fountain supported by white marble lions, denoting strength and courage. On the second day of each year the water flows into this and several smaller fountains, and the people gather to celebrate the fall of Granada. On this date Spanish girls stage a great contest to strike the bell in the watchtower; the winners, according to legend, will win fine husbands within the year.

In the Hall of Abencerrages, the ruler Boabdil is alleged to have invited all his chiefs to dine and then had them beheaded, presumably on account of an affair of the heart between their leader and Boabdil's wife. The floor is of marble; and the roof is a blend of blues, browns, reds, and gold. Brown blotches on the floor are said to be the bloodstains of the beheaded chieftains.

In the Hall of Justice the decoration and ornamentation is more beautiful than that found anywhere else in the building. Delicate coloring, exquisite workmanship, and intricate designs make this a fine example of craftsmanship. Beyond this is the Hall of the Two Sisters, which takes its name from the two white slabs of marble laid into the floor. Its ceiling is made up of nearly five thousand separate, beautifully blended pieces.

Not least among the attractions of the Alhambra preserved in memory are the colorfully garbed gypsies that dance nearby in the cool evenings. Accompanied by castanets and guitars, they typify the old Spain. The dancers, though, are not all lithe, slender girls. Many plump old gypsy matrons join in the gay *cachucha,* as the dance is called.

Another attraction is the magnificent cathedral, said to be the most perfect Renaissance building in Spain. It is the principal landmark of the conquest of the Moors, whose influence is shown in its architectural features. It is surmounted by a huge dome decorated with seven paintings presenting events from the life of the Virgin. In the four-hundred-foot interior are massive pillars supporting the roof. Nearby is a giant burial place of the Catholic monarchs, the famed sepulchre of Isabella and Ferdinand. The traveler might wish, also, to visit the Museo Provincial, a treasure house of fine paintings of the seventeenth and eighteenth centuries.

Industrially, Granada can lay little claim to prominence; its chief activity is fruit raising. Around the city are well watered plains, where great quantities of oranges, figs, and citrons grow.

A NOISY CITY!

Málaga has not many old sights to offer the visitor; but it is an industrious city and ranks next to Barcelona in volume of exports. It has been called the "noisiest city in Spain." Even in the days of the early Phoenicians, Málaga was an important port, for these traders stopped here to barter for salt fish. It was occupied by the Romans and Moors, but few traces of either remain. With a population of one hundred and sixty thousand, Málaga is situated a few miles north of Gibraltar. It has rich agricultural surroundings, and everyone has heard of the famous Málaga grapes and wines. Other leading products are oranges, cotton, figs, sugar cane, melons, and nuts. Industrially active, Málaga has large cotton mills, smelters, tanneries, sugar refineries, and chocolate factories.

Málaga has a great cathedral, four hundred feet long, light and airy, with a huge four-sided domed altar and splendid wood carvings. The ideal time to visit the city is during Easter week, when all the populace takes part in elaborate parades. Processions of brilliantly garbed religious officials and realistic, polychrome images of Christ and our Lady of Sorrows are augmented by impressive pantomimes and dramas of the life and resurrection of Christ. In Málaga, Holy Week is the great event of the year.

MOORS AND FINE LEATHER

The spell that Cordova, a city of more than one hundred thousand people, weaves around the visitor is one of ancient lore rather than of modern progress. Its fame of old for its fine leathers has long since died. Nevertheless, it is a delightful place. The Cordovan architecture is definitely Moorish. Eminent arch-

AN OLD ROMAN BRIDGE AT CORDOVA

aeologists believe that at one time the ancient town extended along the Guadalquivir River for twenty miles. Little excavating has been done, however. History records that the city once had a million people, three hundred mosques, six hundred inns, and nine hundred public baths.

As the traveler approaches the great cathedral down the Paseo del Gran Capitan, he is delighted with the beauty of the promenade. Its wide expanse, bordered by palm and orange trees, is a treat to the eye. The cathedral is one of the few Moorish masterpieces that was left intact when the Moors were driven out. Originally a great mosque, it has been converted into a Christian cathedral. It is an enormous edifice, five hundred and seventy feet in length and four hundred and twenty-five feet wide. About one-third of this area is in the court, the balance being devoted to the magnificent mosque. The entire area is enclosed within a wall surmounted by thirty-five towers. Part of the main gateway to the court has been torn down and has been replaced by a high tower, more in keeping with the accepted cathedral style of architecture.

COURT OF ORANGES

The dominant beauty-spot of the whole massive structure is the Court of Oranges, formerly used for ablution purposes. Here one finds five beautiful fountains set against a background of orange and palm trees. Lofty columns support the great shell-shaped roof of marble. The entrance to the court is a gigantic arch supported by two blue and two green columns. Not least among the features of the structure is the great court surrounding the interior. Here one wanders amid a forest of columns, some twelve hundred in all. Many of these columns were brought from Nîmes, Carthage, and Constantinople.

SEVILLE

Below Cordova on the Guadalquivir River is the flourishing city of Seville. Though located about fifty miles from the sea, Seville, because of the navigability of the Guadalquivir, has a busy waterfront. The climate in winter is not unlike that of Florida in the United States, and the winter landscape is studded with blooming roses and hyacinths.

COLONNADE OF THE HALL OF AMBASSADORS IN THE ALCAZAR AT SEVILLE

Courtesy
The Art Institute
of Chicago

SPAIN

Courtesy The Art Institute of Chicago

GIRALDA TOWER OF THE CATHEDRAL IN SEVILLE

Seville is rich in historical background, for here Christopher Columbus was formally received on his return from the first voyage to America. Much of Seville's early power was lost, but about the middle of the eighteenth century it was restored.

HOLY WEEK PROCESSIONS

As in Málaga, the high light of the year is Holy Week, a time of processions, dramatic presentations, and great religious fervor. Few cathedrals offer the splendid sight-seeing possibilities of the Seville cathedral. It is a mighty edifice, second in size only to St. Peter's in Rome. For a time, the Spaniards used old mosques for churches; then they began to build the structure that now stands, a cathedral requiring almost a hundred years to complete. With walls eight feet thick and a rectangular belfry reaching heavenward for three hundred feet, it is one of the most impressive of Spanish cathedrals. The structure is topped by a female figure symbolizing Faith.

Another place of exceptional interest is the Alcazar, ancient palace of the Moorish Kings. As in the case of few other Moorish structures, it is a masterpiece of massive architecture.

Women of Seville are exceptionally beautiful and wear gorgeous shawls, combs, flowers, and the traditional mantilla. It is sometimes difficult to distinguish the wealthy from the poor because of the rich adornments they all affect.

CADIZ

No other city of Spain can lay claim to such importance in olden days as can the venerable city of Cadiz. For three thousand years, this port has been active in world affairs. Ancient Greek geographers took cognizance of its importance, the Romans under Caesar and Pompey held it in high esteem commercially, and the Carthaginians under Hannibal moored their lordly fleets in its harbor. Established by the Phoenicians in 1150 B. C., it was considered the "jumping off place" of the western world. The Phoenicians lost it about 500 B. C. to the Carthaginians, who held sway until the Romans defeated them in the Second Punic War. Under the regime of Caesar, Cadiz became one of the strongholds of the empire. The Goths conquered the city in the fifth century and held it until the invasion of the Moors about 800 A. D.

PLAZA OF ISABELLA II IN CADIZ

Later it was regained by Spain, and the Moors were expelled. Being an exceedingly rich port, it suffered many attacks by pirates, the most successful attack resulting in the capture of fifty treasure-laden vessels which were taken to England in 1596 by Lord Essex. From then on Cadiz suffered from French invasions, civil wars, and a general decay. Of late, however, Cadiz has regained some of its former importance and carries on an extensive foreign trade. Its most important exports are olive oil, cork, fruit, lead, and wine. With a population of seventy-nine thousand, Cadiz possesses a culture superior to that of the nation as a whole. Its streets are cleaner, its courts much freer from the presence of beggars, and its women more attractive than those in any other place in the country. The weakness of the port is the persistent smuggling of goods to escape the heavy duties imposed. The population is a mixture which includes Negroes, Moors, sailors from every nation, and Spanish soldiery. One of the leading occupations is fishing.

Cadiz is a snow-white city set upon a long narrow promontory, beautiful against the sparkling blue of the sea. Great stone walls from thirty to fifty feet high surround the city. The tourist, upon landing in Cadiz, steps on a broad quay called the Muelle. Proceeding through the city, he is impressed by the narrow and surprisingly clean streets, close-set houses, and the brilliant glare of marble and whitewash. Practically every house of importance in the city has its own watch tower.

There are two cathedrals; the newer one, built in 1722, is a classic structure. The old cathedral, originally built in the thirteenth century, was destroyed by Lord Essex but was later partially rebuilt. A lofty watch tower, the Torre del Vigia, affords a fine view of the entire city. On the Plaza de la Constitucion, a civic center, the visitor may observe the daily life of the city. The Academy of Fine Arts, a magnificent gallery, also attracts the tourist bent on inspecting art treasures.

WATCHDOG OF THE MEDITERRANEAN

Like an ominous squatting bulldog, redoubtable Gibraltar guards the narrow entrance to the Mediterranean. Though it is British territory, it is a part of the Iberian peninsula, extending into the Mediterranean. The fortress is built upon a great rocky plateau more than one thousand feet above the sea. This great bluff measures about two miles north and south and nearly a mile east and west, the total circumference being about seven miles.

Like the other important landmarks in southern Spain, it was first held by the Phoenicians, then by the Romans, the Goths, the Moors, and the Spanish. In 1704 Sir George Rooke, the British admiral, captured the citadel of Gibraltar, and his occupation was ratified by the British government. Spain made a vain attempt to regain it later in the same year. And again during the American Revolution Spain and France made attacks on the fortress, which lasted from 1779 to 1883. A blockade was set up to starve out the defenders under Sir George Elliot, the governor of Gibraltar. But provisions were carried through the blockade to the starving garrison, and Gibraltar was defended until the seige was ended.

Gibraltar is divided into eight fortified sections and is honeycombed with portholes from which the British can pour a disastrous fusillade without endangering themselves. Cannons are so situated as to control every part of the Strait. It is difficult for anyone but an English citizen to visit the fortifications. Usually visitors are shown only the lower part, and cameras and note-

SPAIN

Courtesy The Art Institute of Chicago

Gibraltar, famous fortified point commanding entrance to the Strait of Gibraltar. The village of the same name nestles at the foot of the hill.

taking are strictly forbidden. It is said that about six thousand men are stationed here, and a twenty-million-dollar harbor has been completed.

The government of the fortress and village near by is, of course, strictly military. Gibraltar, though valuable, has cost England the amazing sum of a quarter of a billion dollars to develop and maintain. There are other interests here for the tourist. Among them are the Alameda, or public garden; the cathedral; and the panoramic view, which includes the tips of two continents with the waters of the sea between. The population of the town of Gibraltar is a mixture of Moors, Portuguese, Spaniards, Africans, Jews, and Highland soldiers.

Courtesy Swiss Federal Railways   Photo by A. Pedrett, St. Moritz

THIS JOB CALLS FOR STRENGTH AND SKILL!
Climbers exploring the fantastic glacier realm of the Piz Bernina near St. Moritz, Switzerland.

SWITZERLAND

LUCERNE, SWITZERLAND
Photo by Wehrli, Zurich

This charming city reposes like a precious jewel in a glorious setting of mirror-like lakes and lofty mountains.

THE MOUNTAINS OF SWITZERLAND, majestic as they may seem to the new arrival, have a beneficent quality and seem to shed peace and mercy over all who come within their range. As complement to the masculine grandeur of the towering Alps is the more feminine and gracious beauty of the lakes which lie, serene and lovely, among those mountains. The lakes are content to be secondary to the peaks as attractions to travelers, content to be admired as set in the splendor above them. The people who dwell in this earthly paradise are in keeping with its beauty. Strong, hardy folk who from constant association with grandeur have taken on a certain degree of it themselves, they encourage the tourist to come without becoming in the least degree humble or servile. Any one who knows Switzerland is as impressed by the natives of that land as he is by the scenery. Of various ancestries, they speak German, French, and Italian in different sections of the one nation as well as Romansh, also known as Ladin, an unfamiliar language derived from Latin. But in spite of this lack of unity in national language and back-

Paul's Photos, Chicago
THE FAMOUS KIRSCHGARTEN HOUSE IN BASEL
This building is now the permanent home of the Bank for International Settlements.

ground, the Swiss are a living testimony that international harmony is not merely a dream of idealists, but a real possibility of achievement.

Because of its non-belligerency it offered the League of Nations an opportunity to develop peacefully in a section of Europe not steeped in bitter memories; and Geneva was finally chosen as the seat of the great movement toward international amity.

BASEL, THE NORTHERN GATE TO SWITZERLAND

On entering Switzerland at the extreme northwest corner of its frontiers, the tourist finds the famous old city of Basel, situated on both banks of the Rhine. On the left bank, on two hills which are separated by the gracious valley of the tributary Birs, is Gross-Basel, the old section of the town; while on the other side of the river is the portion of the city known as Klein-Basel, the manufacturing district. Basel has a proud record as one of the oldest towns in the Swiss Confederation. During the Middle Ages Basel was one of the great free towns of the empire, although she did not become a member of the Swiss Cantons until 1501.

Basel offers a panoramic view from the right riverbank, as one looks across the Middle Rhine Bridge. The bridge itself is broad and beautiful, but more impressive is old Gross-Basel rising on the left bank, where, towering above all, is the ancient Minster, the cathedral of the bishops of Basel before the Reformation. The cathedral, which lost its bishop when Protestantism entered the city, dates back to 1019. Most of its present construction belongs to the fourteenth century, when the Minster was almost entirely rebuilt after an earthquake and fire had ruined it.

The cathedral is a stately building of red sandstone, with slender twin towers of graceful design rising from an impressive façade. The modern roof and windows add to the beauty of the imposing edifice. Inside, the rich sculptures make it one of the loveliest cathedrals in Switzerland. Adjoining the choir of the cathedral are extensive cloisters which reach to the terrace behind the Minster, called the Pfalz. From this Pfalz can be obtained a splendid view of the Rhine and the Black Forest. Not far from the cathedral is the house of Johannes Froben, the scholarly printer in whose home the great Erasmus died in 1536.

Having seen the famous old university and fine museums and gardens of which Basel boasts, we go by train past the battlefield of St. Jacob, where in 1444 thirteen hundred Swiss kept twenty-five thousand Frenchmen from penetrating farther into their country.

Paul's Photos, Chicago

CATHEDRAL TOWERS OF BASEL RISING ABOVE THE RHINE

UNIVERSITY OF KNOWLEDGE

Paul's Photos, Chicago

THE FAMED UNIVERSITY OF ZURICH
It was founded in 1832.

SWITZERLAND'S INDUSTRIAL CENTER

After passing through the "Cherry-Land" of Basel, and the canton of Aargau, we reach Zurich, the largest Swiss city with almost a quarter of a million population. In the heart of beautiful undulating country, it is the center of industrialism in northeastern Switzerland. The location of Zurich is remarkably beautiful. Rising on both banks of a clear, pale lake, with the chain of snow-capped Alps in the distant background, the city lies in the vale of the Limmat River. A prosperous town since the early Middle Ages, and tracing her lineage back to prehistoric and Roman times, Zurich has long been one of the leading cities of Switzerland, in intellectual, political, and commercial endeavor. In 1351, after having been in league with the cantons Uri, Schwyz and Unterwalden for over half a century, the canton of Zurich joined the Swiss Confederation. Continuing her lead at the time of the Reformation, she reared and fostered Zwingli, and was the first of all the Swiss cities to take up the Protestant religion.

Dating back to the times of Carl the Great, the old cathedral, with its twin towers, dominates the scene from the river. Situated in the heart of the old part of Zurich, the cathedral is not damaged by the ever increasing modernity of the city as a whole. But of greater interest to most travelers is the Zwingli Museum with its many historical documents. After visiting the University and the famous Federal Polytechnic School, the Swiss National Museum, and the *Kunsthaus*, (or art gallery), one should by all means take the railway to the summit of the Uetliberg, from which spot the city of Zurich is seen to best advantage. Dotting the shores of the lake beyond the main city are many busy little industrial villages and pleasant bathing beaches, while rising above the low mountain groups are the mighty Alps, white and untouched by the men below them.

MONKS AND EMBROIDERY

In traveling through beautiful country on the way to Lake Constance, you reach St. Gallen. Founded as a monastery by Irish monks in the seventh century, St. Gallen is still the home of priceless manuscripts and old books. It was one of the most important religious and cultural centers in the early Middle Ages. Today this city carries on in its great traditions. A large cathedral, an industrial museum, and the University of Commerce are proof of its progressive activities. The town itself lies on a slope and is surrounded by meadows, hills, streams, and orchards. Its most important product is Swiss embroidery, for which it is the headquarters of the entire Confederation.

LAKE CONSTANCE

From St. Gallen the railroad descends steeply to Rorschach, the first port we reach on Lake Constance. Although this lake cannot vie with some of the other Swiss lakes in beauty, its breadth, populous banks, and green hills with the Appenzell chain of the Alps in the distance make it very attractive. The chief city situated at the northwest end of the lake is Constance. From 781 to 1827 this town was an episcopal see. Its beautiful cathedral was built originally in cruciform Romanesque style in 1052, and was remodeled into Gothic style in 1435 and 1680. The tower, surmounted by an open spire, commands an excellent view of the lake and city as well as of the mountains, especially the snow-clad Säntis.

The most interesting building in all Constance is the "Kaufhaus" erected in 1388, with its medieval Guild Hall. It was in this building that the conclave of Cardinals met for the great Council of Constance, 1414-1418, for the reform of the medieval Church and to decide which, if any, of the three contending popes was the true one. As a part of the purging, John Huss was tried and condemned as a heretic. In spite of the safe-conduct he was burned at the stake just outside the city wall on July 6, 1415. Another memento of John Huss is the Dominican monastery, on an island in the lake, in which the famous reformer and precursor of Luther was confined.

LUCERNE—THE "LIGHTHOUSE" ON THE LAKE OF THE FOREST CANTONS

The city of Lucerne enjoys the most beautiful possible location at one end of the vivid blue-green lake which is surrounded by high towering mountains. It is one of the finest holiday spots of the world. The dazzling snow peaks which contrast so strikingly with the brilliant and ever changing color of the water and the slopes of the mountains themselves make Lucerne and the environs a sight never to be forgotten. The city itself is a fascinating combination of a new and old world. The most modern of hotels provide the tourist with every comfort; the *Kursaal*, noted for its music and varied entertainments, gives him a place for play; while the old city, walled and towered, with quaintly roofed wooden bridges, is a joy to those who are interested in the picturesque and the historical. Of the old town, the ancient cathedral, which ranks among the great Gothic churches of the continent, is indisputably one of the finest in the nation; the Spreuer Bridge, the medieval Kapellbrucke adorned with many religious and historical paintings, and the ancient Water Tower containing the municipal archives for centuries, are outstanding old landmarks.

THE LION OF LUCERNE

Surmounting a dark pool of still water on the bare face of a rock near the Glacier Gardens is the Lion of Lucerne, one of the most famous of all sculptures by Thorwaldsen. Erected to the memory of the Swiss Guard which died defending the Tuileries in Paris in 1792, the monument commands attention for its fine representation of resignation, stricken power, and fidelity to a lost cause.

SWITZERLAND [61]

Paul's Photos, Chicago

THE LION OF LUCERNE

Thorwaldsen's masterpiece has a unique setting in a niche hollowed from a steep cliff. The lion is 30 feet in length, and while a spear protrudes from its side, it still guards the Bourbon shield and lily. The monument commemorates the bravery of the Swiss guard at the opening of the French revolution.

First inhabited by prehistoric lake dwellers who built their homes on piles in the lake waters to avoid the wild beasts which filled the forests, Lucerne is now an international resort of the highest sophistication. Offering every sport and every amusement, the city attracts the fashionables of the whole world.

WILLIAM TELL

At the south end of Lake Lucerne is Altdorf, the center of the locality in which William Tell lived. In the town square there is a monument to the famous archer, and everywhere about the old town are mementoes to the hero. Altdorf was the home of the Tell family, and is therefore most intimately connected with the

Paul's Photos, Chicago

SWISS DAIRY WORKERS AND THEIR CATTLE
The *Alpazug,* a scene from the open-air performance of Schiller's *William Tell,* showing the descent of the dairy workers and their cattle from Alpine realms to their homes in the valley.

legend, but he was born in the town of Bürglen at the foot of the Klausen Pass. Throughout the summer of each year presentations of the Schiller drama of *William Tell* are given in Altdorf and Interlaken every Sunday afternoon. The cast at each place is composed of amateur actors, all of whom are natives, and the stage settings are those of nature. The costumes are singularly faithful reproductions of the clothes worn by Tell and his associates, and to increase the verisimilitude they even use real cows in the opening scene.

During the nineteenth century historians proved to their own satisfaction that there was no truth in the legend of William Tell, and that there never was a man who had to shoot an apple from his son's head or die. But the Swiss people loved their William Tell and hated to give him up. More recent investigations have revealed that there is a strong chance that the delightful old legend is true, and that the mistakes in dates and the general improbability which misled the skeptic historians of the last century are not so significant.

THE GRISONS

South of the cantons St. Gallen and Glarus is the largest of the Swiss cantons, the Grisons or Graubünden which occupies the eastern extremity of the country. This canton is quite distinctive in climate, scenery, and its inhabitants. The "Graubündners" are a devout and industrious folk, with a large share of the Swiss independence and self-reliance. One of the interesting spectacles is to see these pious people in their quaint native costumes at their religious processions.

The center of the Grisons Canton is Chur, or Coire, which is the capital and the city from which the rail lines to all points in the canton radiate. The town dates back to early Roman times, has an interesting Swiss-Gothic cathedral, and a Rhaetian Museum well worth visiting. Not far from Chur is Arosa, a resort famed for its pure and dry air, winter sports, as well as its delightful summer recreations.

Davos and Davos Platz, two cities forming one metropolitan group, are on the slope overlooking the lovely Landwasser River. Among the oldest and most famous of the high Alpine health resorts, it is equally famous as a winter sports haven. Boasting of a great ice rink, splendid toboggan and bobsleigh runs, as well as the ski slopes of the Parsenn, Davos is the home of many international sport events each season. Between the city proper and the Platz is the so-called "English Quarter" which, for more than a half century, has been the home of English and American visitors.

ST. MORITZ

The most famous spot in all the Grisons is beyond doubt the fashionable St. Moritz. Best known as a winter sports center, it is also a popular spot in the summer, when smart vacationers from the world over meet there in search of pleasure and cool comfort. The gathering place calls not only the healthy who enjoy athletic exercises, but also those who need more than rest and change. The mineral waters at St. Moritz have been famous for centuries.

The proud tall mountains, glistening white under a brilliant sun and bright blue sky, make a sight never to be forgotten. For it is in winter that the mountains of Switzerland reach their acme of perfection, and it is then that the world congregates there to enjoy the many pleasures which the Swiss have in store for them.

MAN IN FLIGHT

Skiing, joyous test of skill on the winter snows, the most important of all sports in Switzerland during the cold months, is an artistic performance and a magnificent achievement when well done. The most exciting thing to the Alpine visitor is the ski jump during the races. All other amusements and resorts are deserted the day of the contest; local folk and visitors leave everything to crowd about the Leap and to watch with bated breath as skier after skier races over the top of the Leap, soars through the air and comes to rest sometimes over two hundred and fifty feet from where he started.

Skiing is not only a thrilling act of artists put on for the amusement of visitors, but also a sport in which the amateur can participate. Alpine climbing takes on a new significance for those who learn to ski—and the Alpine ski schools teach the rudiments of level skiing in one week. Groups of guests gather with the skis, set out and easily climb up the mountains on their smooth

Paul's Photos, Chicago
CHAMPIONSHIP HOCKEY GAME AT ST. MORITZ
Here visitors from all over the world watch renowned skaters in action.

SWITZERLAND

STEADY, OLD BOY!
A skier commencing his swift downhill glide on the Corviglia slope above St. Moritz.

runners. The whole trip is an excursion through fairyland, for all about is smooth, glistening snow rising to the surrounding peaks. From the mountain top you can get a most exhilarating view of silvery white castles thrusting their beauty into the serene but brilliant blue of the sky.

And then the downhill run! You get a small sample of the emotions which must fill the ski runner as he leaves the leap and starts his aerial journey, but yours, though not so acute nor so intense, has a comforting security which only adds to the pleasure. Smoothly skimming the soft firm whiteness below you, you attain incredible speed with great ease. This run is the climax of every tour, for it is not only exciting, but also restful to muscles which have been fatigued by the long climb upward.

SPORTS ON ICE

But skiing is not the only winter sport offered in the Alps. Splendid rinks give every guest the opportunity of skating, skilled instructors teach the fundamentals to those who have never skated before, and the artists of the profession are on hand to perform. At their exhibitions they do more than skate, just as the great skiers do more than ski. In their dances on the ice they seem to fly, even as do the jumpers. They are grace itself, doing routines which would do the best of ballets credit. Bobsleighing and tobogganing are also encouraged, and thrilling courses have been built for those who have the courage to try them. Even horse racing on snow and ice is popular, though it takes a brave man to enter such a race.

Switzerland is truly a wonderland in winter, with her snow-covered peaks, and her ice-sheathed slopes glistening under a radiant sun whose almost tropical brilliance turns the ice and snow into living light.

In the summer St. Moritz is hardly less lovely. The peaks remain snow covered, but the slopes leading up to the pinnacles turn from white to green, and all about are fresh wild flowers, making the whole scene one of gay splendor and color. And again St. Moritz is the center of the fashionable vacationing world. Instead of ski meets and skating matches, golf and tennis facilities attract the guests, and, between tournaments, give those who enjoy such sports the opportunity of playing on some of the sportiest golf links and best kept tennis courts in the world. In the summer more attention is paid to the social whirl, if possible, than during the winter season, and each night finds the elegant hotels bright with lights and vibrating with music as smartly gowned women and their escorts dance in the heart of luxury and beauty.

Leaving, with regret, St. Moritz, we travel through wild country downhill until the dizzy heights of the Upper Engadine are left behind, and you are again in the world of men.

THE ST. GOTTHARD PASS

Heading on up the upper Rhine Valley to Andermatt, we reach the world-famous St. Gotthard Pass. There are two possibilities for crossing this pass now. One is the railroad which goes through one of the world's longest tunnels, and the other is by the efficient passenger motor service maintained by the Swiss post office.

During the winter months the tunnel is the most popular because of the cold and the danger of traveling mountain roads in ice and snow. The tunnel, which is more than nine miles long, reaches from Göschenen to Airolo and is laid with a double set of rails. It passes more than a thousand feet below Andermatt

SWITZERLAND [67]

Courtesy Swiss Federal Railways
GREAT ST. BERNARD HOSPICE IN SWITZERLAND
Over 1,000 years old, this venerable haven occupies an imposing mountain site
8110 feet above sea level.

and more than six thousand below the Kastelhorn Mountain which rises directly above the center of the tunnel.

The workmen who drilled the tunnel—between twenty-five and thirty-four hundred men were employed daily for nearly eight years—had to bore through schist, gneiss, serpentine, granite, and dolomite. The serpentine was the hardest, and the dolomite the most troublesome to manage because of the amount of water it contained, which made the problem of engineering all the more difficult. Twice, the tremendous pressure of the roof of mountains crushed the tunnel in, and the task was almost given up as impossible, but it was finally discovered that a vault of ten feet of solid masonry would keep the mountains in their proper place. Today, the fast trains make the run through the tunnel in about fifteen minutes! An added improvement is the use of electricity instead of steam for power.

During the summer season many tourists prefer to make the trip over the St. Gotthard Pass by open busses so that they may enjoy the variety of the scenery. The first part of the Pass is the Schöllenen Gorge, which was called by the poet Schiller "The Valley of Horrors." The name was well chosen, for it is a grand but somber defile nearly three miles long, leading, with many windings and hairpin turns, between the huge, forbidding granite rocks which frown down on the foaming, frothing Reuss River. An exciting part of this trip is the crossing of the famous Devil's Bridge, a single granite span over an awful abyss at the bottom of which the Reuss plunges in a roaring waterfall. Nearby there is a large Russian cross carved in the rock to commemorate the fierce battle there in 1799 when the Russians and Austrians under Suraroff drove back the French under Lecourbe.

As the route continues beyond Andermatt to Hospenthal one may see the ruins of a magnificent old baronial castle, so built on the crags of the mountain that it seems a part of nature's work, and not of man's. So in the Middle Ages did men live. Seizing upon the most unapproachable spot in their locality; building out of the native rock; planning their structure according to the designs of God which surrounded them, and which they knew to be well-nigh inaccessible, they built castles impregnable to man. Those which remain are a living testimony, as is this one near Hospenthal, to the fact that time and natural causes brought about the crumbling of the still stern old castles, not attacks by men.

Leaving the old castle to brood over its ruthless past, the road goes on, mounting with many twists and turns to a height of sixty-eight hundred feet. At this peak, in the heart of a bleak and rocky region, are two tiny lakes, often frozen even in midsummer, and the famous Hospice, which is only less renowned than that of the St. Bernard Pass. Passing this high point, you next descend rapidly through the Val Tremola, a rather dismal valley frequently dotted with snowdrifts throughout the summer, and where avalanches are far from rare. To compensate for these none too pleasant characteristics, the south side of the pass is noted for its rich Alpine blooms. Surrounding each snow drift may be seen the famous edelweiss mingled with other more brilliant blossoms. It is impossible to conceive of such a riot of flowers in the heart of this forbidding country, and near to the rocky region of the Valley of Horrors.

ITALIAN SWITZERLAND

Once through the pass the traveler is in an entirely different country. He immediately senses that a different language and different customs must prevail in the southern portion of the

SWITZERLAND [69]

Confederation, for not only does the landscape shed its Alpine character but the vines, flourishing on the slopes of the gentle hillsides, and the campanili, rising above the picturesque villages, betoken an Italian rather than a German atmosphere.

Airolo is the first of the towns you reach which is thus Italian in culture. Lying in the Valle Leventina, it is a popular summer and winter resort especially for Italians who come up through the valley in which Lake Maggiore lies, through Bellinzona, and the Leventina, bringing with them a portion of their culture and habits, which clings to the native inhabitants, and to the landscape. Although the city itself is not one of the most interesting, it is the center from which many delightful excursions may be made. As it is at the end of the St. Gotthard Pass, it naturally attracts those who wish to see that famous pass. Airolo is also the starting place for a trip to Dissentis through heavily wooded sections, and partly in the open where one gets a fine view of the Ticino mountain range. There is also a little shrine atop a mountain which is quaint and appealing in its simplicity, and which is near a rock bearing a very ancient inscription.

Courtesy Swiss Federal Railways   Photo by E. Steinemann
A BIT OF PARADISE ON LAKE MAGGIORE AT LOCARNO

CASTLES IN THE AIR

Proceeding down the Valle Leventina through the towns of Biasca, Claro, and Gorduno—all of which plead with their beauty that you stay longer than you have time—you come to Bellinzona, the capital of the canton Ticino. That city has a strikingly picturesque air because of the three proud old fortresses commanding the view, and which, from their lofty positions seem almost to be castles built in the air. Still well preserved, they carry about them their traditions, and make the past live again. They were once the strongholds of the three governors of Uri, Schwyz, and Unterwalden, alternate rulers of the area which now forms the canton of Ticino.

The best view of the town is from the train just past the neighboring village of Giubiasca. From the slopes of Monte Ceneri, overlooking walnut and chestnut groves of great richness, we see Bellinzona nestling in the valley, snug and happy under the protecting presence of her three magnificent fortresses which seem to refuse to give up their old duty of guardianship. Embellishing the charm of the view of Bellinzona from Monte Ceneri is the background of mountains with a glimpse of the northern end of the Lake Maggiore, the largest of the three lovely "Italian Lakes."

THE NICE OF SWITZERLAND

Continuing, we soon pass the mouth of the wild Val Verzasca, a ravine of many turbulent waterfalls, and then skirt the lakeside for a few miles before arriving at Locarno, which, because of its popularity as a spring, autumn, and winter resort and its mild climate, is known as the Nice of Switzerland. Locarno is one of the oldest towns in the Confederation, dating back to the sixth century B.C. Much of the ancient architecture remains to provide vivid and pleasing contrast with the suave sophistication of the modern hotels and casino.

On alternate Thursdays peasants from all the surrounding districts pour into the towns for the market which is held in the Piazza Grande, a great square which extends almost the entire length of the town from the quay. The multi-colored costumes, the noise, the smells of fresh garden produce, and the whole picture of natural peasant life are peculiarly interesting to the visitors

Paul's Photos, Chicago
LOCARNO, ON LAKE MAGGIORE, IN SOUTHERN SWITZERLAND

who swell the already large crowd as they watch the bargaining and perhaps buy a thing or two.

All along one side of the Piazza Grande are old buildings with antiquated Italian arcades on the ground floor, which give the square an indescribably quaint, old-world flavor. And at the southwest end of the town, visible from the Piazza, rises the ruined old castle of the Dukes of Visconti, once tyrants of Milan.

The finest show place in the neighborhood of Locarno is beyond all doubt the pilgrimage church of Madonna del Sasso. Situated on a wooded rock high above the town, commanding a splendid view of the lake, and completely dominating the scene, it is one of the world's lovely bits of architecture. It was founded in 1480, rebuilt in 1569, and has been kept in remarkably good condition. As interesting as the exterior is, the main features of the church are the "Flight into Egypt" by Bramantino, and the "Entombment" by Ciseri, both fine examples of Renaissance art.

As much as any thing else, Locarno serves as a center from which to make excursions about the very beautiful Lake Maggiore. The upper nine of the thirty-seven miles of the lake are Swiss, and on the shores of these nine miles are many famous resorts, Stresa, Pallanza, Baveno, Cannobio, Brissago, and the Borromean Islands, to mention only a few. The whole region is one riot of glowing color with even the lake varying in tint from pale green to vivid blue. Rising from the colorful water are slopes on which grow fruit orchards of every sort, oranges and lemons, olives, palms, and garden and wild flowers in profusion. And beyond the cypress trees, which reveal the truly Italian character of the landscape as does nothing else, rise Monte Rosa and other snow-topped summits which preserve the Swiss note.

LUGANO AND HER LAKE

Not far from Lake Maggiore is the smallest of the three Italian lakes, that of Lugano. The most important town of the Lugano district is the beautifully situated city of Lugano, the natural center of the lake locality. Although there is some disagreement as to which is the most beautiful of the three lakes, most people are willing to bestow the palm upon this one, as much because of the charm of the city as because of the exquisiteness

Paul's Photos, Chicago
GARDEN OF PRINCE FREDERICK LEOPOLD ON LAKE LUGANO
This southern Switzerland scene shows Monte St. Salvator in the background.

of the lake. The best view is that which the traveler gets first from the Lugano station. Below him, in the green amphitheater formed by the slopes of the mountains Brè and Salvatore, the town spreads out picturesquely along the lake shore. And the lake, a deep, vivid blue, is in another amphitheater formed by steep mountains, whose bold outlines strive to equal the striking beauty of the dominating mountain of the district, Monte Generoso.

The city itself is another of the half-modern, half-medieval cities of this area which so fascinate the traveler. Quaint arcaded streets lead up to twentieth-century hotels, fine old churches look down on bathing beaches, and the old-fashioned *Kursaal*—the amusement sections of Swiss towns for centuries—attracts sophisticates from all over the world with its mingling of old and new pleasure devices. A very successful resort center, Lugano can also attract lovers of art with the marble façade of her Cathedral of San Lorenzo, statues by Vincenzo Vela, and the fresco of the passion in the Church of Santa Maria degli Angioli which was done by Bernardino Luini.

Leaving Lugano, gay with Mediterranean flowers, behind, we will again head north, with the Bernese Oberland as your objective. Having already taken the route through the St. Gotthard Pass, you will probably go across the Valle D'Antigorio, that tip of Italy which juts into Switzerland. At Iselle, you take the train through the Simplon tunnel, which is even more famous than that of St. Gotthard. It is twelve and a half miles long, and is double, the two tunnels being connected by tranverse galleries.

At the northern end of the Simplon tunnel is the quaint and interesting old town of Brigue or Brieg. Although the town is small, it has always been very important as the starting place to the pass which has been used since the Roman legions went into Gaul through the mountains.

GOING AGAINST THE RHONE

Leaving Brigue, we have our choice of going to Interlaken through Gletsch, which is up the Rhone valley, or through Visp, Kandersteg, and Spiez. Either route is lovely, but the train service is likely to be better through Gletsch, and the Rhone is a beautiful river. Just out of Brigue, we reach the Morel station where there is a splendid view of the Great Aletsch Glacier, and beyond it the beautiful Aletsch Forest which is a national reservation.

Shortly after passing by the forest you come to Fiesch, where, if you have time, you will stop over to take a trip up the Eggishorn, a mountain 9,626 feet high, from the top of which there is a truly remarkable view. On the northern side of the base of this mountain is the famous Lake Märjelen, which has been formed by blocks of ice which detach themselves from the Great Aletsch Glacier and melt into the lake. The rest of the trip is a restful journey through many tiny villages of dark brown chalets and whitewashed chapels.

In the basin of the valley from which the mighty Rhone Glacier has receded lies Gletsch, a small town which is a center for those who wish to enjoy the scenery. It is awe-inspiring to see the great glacier, white and foreboding, wedged in between mighty peaks which seem to be sentinels watching its every move, ready to act at the slightest indication that the glacier is about to break loose and wreak the destruction which it seems to threaten constantly.

THE GRIMSEL PASS

Heading north from Gletsch, you go over the Grimsel Pass, which takes you through Grimsel Hospice, Handeck, Guttannen, Innertkirchen to Meiringen, the chief town of the Hasli Valley. Unfortunately, there is very little left of Meiringen which is of interest because of disastrous floods and fires during the last century, but one or two ancient chalets and some church excavations are worth notice. Aside from these, one's attention is drawn to the very fine wood-carving which is done here.

Lying between the lakes of Thun and Brienz at the head of the Lütschinen valley is Interlaken, one of the internationally famous resorts of Switzerland. Skilfully combining the tone of a fashionable center with the true rustic character of the environment, Interlaken is one of the delightful places in Europe.

The social center of the town is the *Kursaal* Casino, a luxuriously decorated amusement palace in the heart of a beautiful garden. The establishment can boast not only a large concert hall, theater, and gaming room, but also an American bar. Every week, balls, symphony concerts, operettas, and fireworks displays are offered for the entertainment of the hosts of people from all over the world who throng to the town. The especial attraction of the *Kursaal* is the series of open air performances of the Schiller drama, *Wilhelm Tell,* which are given during the summer.

SWITZERLAND

Paul's Photos, Chicago
ALPINE DWELLER WITH HIS CHILDREN, HIS GOAT
—AND HIS ALPHORN

Local markets and quaint Swiss shops are rich in skilfully done samples of Swiss handiwork. Interlaken is a shopping center for homespun linen and handmade embroideries. It is also a source of many of the finely carved wooden figures and ivory bric-a-brac which come out of Switzerland, not to mention the exquisite potteries of the Oberland.

THE JUNGFRAU

But the most important feature of Interlaken is the nearness to the Jungfrau, one of Switzerland's most beautiful mountains. Seen from Interlaken, it is a breath-taking sight. Towering above the green, forest-covered hills which are between the city and the mountain, the Jungfrau lifts her whiteness into the blue sky above —proudly, serenely, and imperiously. It is obvious that the mountain is conscious of her beauty, knows that her jagged slopes and uneven crest make an unparalleled spectacle. The sunlight tints the whiteness of the snow to gold at times, and makes the whole seem to be a molten mass of precious metal. At other times it is rather an exquisite fabrication of the purest crystal. Always it is a rare and compelling wonder. But many people are not content merely to view this mountain, and every year thousands make the trip from Interlaken to the peak and risk their lives in climbing it.

BYRON'S "MANFRED"

Not far from Interlaken is the historical ruin which from 1232 was the seat of the noble family of Unspunnen. It was from the tragic history of two of the barons of this family that Lord Byron got the idea of writing his dramatic poem *Manfred*. It is true that the poem centers around Mont Blanc, but the country is much the same, and one can easily believe that the events he related took place in the forbidding old castle, which still retains a part of its former glory in spite of its decrepitude. In the early part of the last century famous shepherd festivals which attracted the nobility of all Europe were held at Unspunnen. Madam Vigée-Lebrun, who painted most of the famous portraits of the unfortunate Marie Antoinette, did a large painting of the festival scene as she saw it, which is now hanging in the Bern Museum of Fine Arts.

After seeing these and other sights around Interlaken, you head north toward Bern, the capital of the Federation of Swiss Cantons. A massive old town of exceptional loveliness which impresses itself immediately upon the new arrival, Bern is so situated as to appear to be a picture in a frame of unsurpassed beauty. In the center of a high, undulating plateau, it looks up to the shimmering mountains which fringe that tableland. The city itself is composed of dignified old streets lined with the characteristic arcades, which run in long parallel lines from east to west, intersected by quaint old gateways which breathe forth the mystery and romance of another age. Enhancing these fascinating old streets are fine churches, monuments and medieval fountains, all surmounted by statues of saints and great men of the city. Further embellishing the streets is the glow of inviting color which comes from the shops in the arcade. High swinging bridges connect the old Bern with the new and modern city which lies across the deep river valley.

SWITZERLAND [77]

Paul's Photos, Chicago

THE TOWERING JUNGFRAU
The visitor at Interlaken will not readily escape the challenge of this mighty peak above the Bernese Oberland

SWISS FEDERAL PALACE AT BERN, THE CAPITAL

THE OLD BERN

In old Bern, one of the most interesting spectacles is the Minster, the lacy, ornamented spire of which rears itself gracefully above the sky line. Another is the famous clock tower in the center of the town. And not to be forgotten is the long row of federal palaces which is dominated by the Parliament Building whose dome vies with the cathedral spire for attention. But most interesting is the Bear Pit which lies at the foot of the Nydeck Bridge. For centuries this pit has harbored several bears which are well tended and cherished by the citizens, for they are the heraldic emblem of the city.

The new Bern, though not as interesting historically and not as picturesque as the old part of the city, is certainly not to be ignored. The city is rich in museums, in libraries, and in schools. Most important of these schools is the university, which is surrounded by numerous institutes. For those who seek amusement there is an artificial ice rink, a bathing pool with machine-made waves, and the never to be forgotten *Kursaal,* which to many seems the best in all Switzerland. There is also the Rose Garden, from which may be obtained the best view of the old city.

From Bern splendid train service takes you to the Lake of Neuchâtel. It was in the little town of Yverdon at the southernmost tip of this lake that Pestalozzi, a pioneer of educational methods, turned the castle into a school and perfected his system which has achieved world-wide renown, and has had such a significant influence upon education everywhere.

LAUSANNE

Heading south again, you are soon in the city of Lausanne on the north shore of Lake Geneva. Just before the train reaches the city you get a lovely view of the sky line, medieval and beautiful, over the serene blue of the lake which is backed by a wall of snow-capped mountains. The whole picture is so impressive that it hardly seems real until you see that the white specks on the lake are tiny sailboats whose rapid progress across the water means life and not artistic skill.

Lausanne's history goes back to Roman times when there was a Celtic town of Lousonna on the shores of Lake Geneva. Although there are some interesting and archaeologically important remains of this old town, most of it was destroyed by the Alemanni, who rebuilt the town according to their own wishes in the fifth century. From the end of the sixth century Lausanne was the see of the Burgundian bishopric of Avenches. In 1434 it became an imperial town under the jurisdiction of the bishops and counts of Savoy until 1536 when, under the influence of the Reformation, it broke away from the old rule and fell under the influence of Bern. In the nineteenth century it became the capital of the Vaud Canton and as an independent city was incorporated into the Swiss Confederation.

VOLTAIRE'S REFUGE

Since the eighteenth century Lausanne has been the rendezvous of brilliant society, but that society never has been so sparkling as it was in the middle of the eighteenth century when Voltaire, staying at Mon Repos, gathered around him the greatest wits of the Old Regime. The popularity he gave to Lausanne caused emperors and other royalty to flock there. Gibbon lived in

APPLE BLOSSOMS AND CATHEDRAL SPIRES AT LAUSANNE

Paul's Photos, Chicago

Lausanne for ten years, and in 1787 finished his *History of the Decline and Fall of the Roman Empire* in this haven, of which he said, "All the pleasures of society and of sound philosophy have found their way to this part of Switzerland, where the climate is the mildest, and abundance reigns. Its inhabitants know well how to unite the politeness of Athens with the simplicity of Sparta."

Lausanne continued its tradition of attractiveness and in the next century received, among other celebrities, Madame de Staël—who had the distinction of being the only person Napoleon ever feared—Napoleon himself, as well as both his wives, and the poet Byron, who wrote his *Prisoner of Chillon* at the Anchor inn. Dickens wrote *Dombey and Son* in Lausanne, and today the city is still the social and intellectual center it was when these great men and women found it so delightful.

The well preserved remains of its past are what give the town of Lausanne its air of illustrious originality. On the top of the hill is the Château Sainte-Marie, a true fortress in perfect condition, which, flanked by its four turrets, was in the fifteenth and sixteenth centuries the residence of the bishops of Lausanne. After the militant bishops had been replaced by governors from Bern the fortress became their dwelling-place. Now it is the seat of the Vaud Canton government.

"A TIARA CROWNING THE TOWN"

As Victor Hugo said, the spire of the ancient cathedral, noble and impressive, rises from the very heart of the town like "a tiara crowning the town." The cathedral, which is reached by a covered wooden staircase, is the nearest perfect example of Gothic architecture in Switzerland. Built in the early half of the thirteenth century before Gothic had become too ornate, it boasts a rose window almost thirty feet in diameter which is one of the most ancient as well as largest of its kind. Interesting tombs, statuary, and paintings add to the splendor and attractiveness of this gem of a Gothic cathedral.

The Place de la Palud, ornamented by the Fountain of Justice, dates from 1726 and, in keeping with its surroundings, has preserved its antique tone. Immediately in front of it is the Town Hall, whose pent roofs and graceful bell tower were built in 1675. In contrast to the elegance of the stained-glass windows of this building—which are said to be the work of the famous painters on glass, Hans Funck and Henry François—is the fruit and vegetable market held bi-weekly on the Place de la Palud. This market is a very old and picturesque Lausanne institution whose origin no one knows, but with which no citizen would part.

"THE OLD ORDER CHANGETH"

But Lausanne is not all history. Many of the lovely old buildings have had to give way before the advance of modern city planning and architecture. The Rue de Bourg, once the fashionable residence street of old Lausanne is now the chief commercial street in the city, and all the seventeenth- and eighteenth-century mansions have disappeared; in their place have risen completely modern office buildings. And when the Swiss go modern they do so thoroughly. Many of the new buildings are designed by modernist architects whose work most of us rarely see except in movies and magazines. The Hospital Nestlé is a case in point, while the Radio House is an even more striking example.

Because of its many fine schools and educational facilities, as well as because of its fine climate and amusement possibilities, Lausanne has been called the "City of Young People," and the title is well deserved. No matter at what time of the year you go to Lausanne you will find bright young faces outnumbering the old by two to one. And these young people not only add to the charm of the city, they keep it vigorous and vital in spite of its great age and the natural tendency to rest on its laurels.

One could go on for hours describing the parks such as that of Mon Repos, in the center of which is the building where Voltaire was once a guest. The sunny bay and harbor of Ouchy with its lakeside promenade and rare trees deserves a page to itself, as do the athletic facilities which Lausanne offers her guests and citizens. Lausanne is also a medical center of importance as well as the home of much that is fine in modern art, but we can not tarry too long, for we must hurry to the Matterhorn.

"THE PRISONER OF CHILLON"

Following the course of the lake, you soon reach the eastern end and the village of Territet, near which is the old Castle of Chillon. Jutting out into Lake Geneva is the tiny peninsula on which the castle was built. Practically impregnable against the onslaughts of medieval troops of knights and archers, the fortress has proved as impregnable against time as well and today stands almost exactly as it was in the Middle Ages. The best view of the castle as a whole is obtained by a backward glance as the train leaves the spot.

The castle and its dungeon have been made immortal by Byron's *Sonnet on Chillon* and the *Prisoner of Chillon,* in both of which he discussed the sufferings of François de Bonivard, an exponent of Swiss liberty imprisoned in the gruesome old keep by the Duke of Savoy in the sixteenth century. The prison was a corridor in the castle, down the center of which seven groined Gothic pillars, each with a ring and chain attached, stood guard over the unfortunate victim, and which today are eloquent testimony of the misery of that patriot.

Considerably south and east of Chillon the Matterhorn rises on the boundary between Switzerland and Italy. Probably no mountain has ever so captured the world's fancy as has this monument to God's architectual skill. The best view is from the other

SWITZERLAND

THE HISTORIC CASTLE OF CHILLON ON LAKE LEMAN

"Lake Leman lies by Chillon's walls;
A thousand feet in depth below
Its massy waters meet and flow;
Thus much the fathom-line is sent
From Chillon's snow-white battlement."
—Byron: *Prisoner of Chillon.*

side of the lake, from which spot, on a clear day, you see not one but two Matterhorns. Rugged and imperious, the proud old mountain thrusts its jagged crest high into the clear blue of the Swiss sky and seems to dare any mere human to attempt to climb it. Many have done so. A few of those have lived to gloat, but many have not lived to regret their folly in taking the dare. Rising from deep snow, much of the mountain is actually too steep to hold the blanket of soft whiteness with which heaven tries to tone down the severity of the peak's outline.

THE GREAT ST. BERNARD

Not far from the overpowering Matterhorn is the Great St. Bernard Pass, famed throughout the Middle Ages and down to the present for the monks of St. Bernard who maintain a hospice there and who with their heroic dogs save many lives every year.

Paul's Photos, Chicago

MIGHTY PYRAMID NOT MADE BY HANDS
The Matterhorn, towering high above Zermatt.

Living there all the year 'round, in one of the coldest habitable spots in the world, risking their lives daily to hunt people lost in the snow, the ten to fifteen Augustinian canons have an efficiency life of about fifteen years, after which they have to retire to more beneficial climates where, broken in health and useless, they live on as monuments to their own self-sacrifice. The pass itself is beautiful and historically interesting. The Romans are recorded to have used it in 105 B.C., and since that time the names of Constantine, the Lombards, Charlemagne, and Napoleon have been connected with it in one way or another. Made wealthy during the Middle Ages by the beneficence of monarchs and nobles who realized the worthiness of the cause, the Hospice of St. Bernard now experiences days of want, because many persons who accept the free hospitality have not the gratitude or decency to put money into the almsbox which supports the monks and pays the upkeep of the accommodations with which they are so generous.

After you have left the Great St. Bernard—we trust you left a gift at least equal to the amount you cost the kind canons —you again head for Lake Geneva, this time making for the southern tip and the city of Geneva. Delightful as are the other cities of Switzerland, no one city has had a greater influence on the world at large than this city has had. The birthplace of Rousseau, the home of Calvin, the birthplace of the Red Cross, and the seat of the League of Nations, it has frequently been thought of as the most important city of the modern world.

CAESAR'S GALLIC WARS

Geneva's first appearance in history was appropriately made in one of the world's most famous books, Caesar's *Commentaries on the Gallic Wars*, in the year 58 B. C. Following the collapse of the Roman Empire, Geneva became the capital of the kingdom of Burgundy, after which it fell under the influence of the House of Savoy. In the sixteenth century it began making attempts to break away from what had long been an odious domination, and with the outbreak of the Reformation, which it zealously espoused, her attempts were successful. With the Reformation she accepted the rule of Calvin who established a rigid and tyrannical theocracy, the effects of which she still bears. Torn by internal dissension after this theocracy passed away, Geneva finally, in 1814, joined the Swiss Confederation, of which she has been a part ever since.

Paul's Photos, Chicago
GENEVA'S MARVELOUS HARBOR
Rousseau's Island is seen on the right, and in the background looms lofty Mont Blanc.

The skill of the Genevese at watch making, for which they have been famous since the sixteenth century, has never been contested. Giving attention to attractive design, these artisans seldom sacrifice accuracy to appearance, so that their watches are famed the world over. This mechanical skill carries into allied fields and gives the city fame as the center for mathematical instuments, musical boxes, and jewelry also.

One of Geneva's proudest possessions is the monument to the Reformation, a modern monument which faces the University and is backed by the picturesque old town walls. Paying especial tribute to Calvin, Geneva's own leader in the Reformation, the monument also commemorates Luther, Knox, and other great Protestants. It is a striking artistic entity consisting of a white wall before which are three statues in a group, on either side of which, at more distant intervals, stand other statues on pedestals of their own. The whole reflects the strong influence which the Reformation, and especially Calvin, had on the history and character of the city.

LA SALLE DE LA REFORMATION

Near the lake, just off the Quai des Eaux-Vives is another memento of the Reformation, La Salle de la Réformation in which is the Calvinium. This Calvinium is dedicated to the memory of John Calvin, and is full of memorials and possessions of his. But one cannot single out any one spot as the place which revives the memory of that great and stern disciplinarian. The whole city is a memorial to him. There is a tablet at Number Eleven Rue Calvin which marks the site of the house in which he lived. Under the pulpit in the cathedral is a chair in which he is supposed to have sat. Nowhere, and at no time, is one allowed to forget that Geneva was the home of the great leader.

Crowning the highest point in the old part of the city is the Cathedral de St. Pierre, a Romanesque building of which the oldest part dates from the tenth century, although it was added to throughout the Middle Ages and on into the present. There are several monuments to great French Calvinists in the Cathedral, one of them to Henry, Duke de Rohan, a great military leader of the Protestants against Richelieu, and another to Agrippa d'Aubigné, the historian of French Protestants and confidant of Henry IV of France, who died in Geneva an exile in 1630.

NEW PALACE OF THE LEAGUE OF NATIONS AT GENEVA

Not far from the cathedral is the Town Hall, a magnificent Renaissance building of the sixteenth century. Its most striking feature is that it is entered by a ramp which, instead of ascending to the main floor, mounts to the third.

Not far away is Number Forty Grande Rue, the home of Rousseau's grandfather, where the turbulent philosopher of the eighteenth century was born. The real home of Rousseau was at Number Twenty-seven Rue Rousseau, where he spent his boyhood. Geneva has tried hard to make recompense for the harsh way she treated her great son by preserving what mementos of him still exist, and by erecting the Jean Jacques Rousseau Museum wherein are displayed statues, prints and engravings, and portraits which preserve the memory of the author of the *Social Contract*.

THE LEAGUE OF NATIONS

On the Quai President Wilson, so named in honor of the founder of the League of Nations, is the temporary headquarters of the League. Just beyond is the Parc Mon Repos near which, in the Rue de Lausanne, is the Perle du Lac, a fine public park in which is the Palace of the League of Nations. The Palace is an imposing building which stretches for some distance along the lake front where it enjoys an attractive view, and also where its beauty is enhanced by the loveliness of Lake Geneva.

In the same park as the Palace of the League is the International Labor Office, another impressive building devoted to international amity. There is also the Ariana Museum. The ground floor of this museum is devoted to rare examples of pottery, porcelain and earthenware. Some beautiful Roman, Greek and Etruscan remains are on display and are worth visiting. On the floor above are some splendid paintings of the old masters: Michelangelo, Raphael, Van Dyck, and others. There is also a remarkable collection of old silver plate, jewels, carved ivories, and Gobelin tapestries, as well as sculptures and rare old manuscripts. In the lower part of the park is a Botanical Garden, and the Delessert Herbarium which many consider the best in the world.

Geneva, the symbol of international amity, is in all respects fitting to be the home of the League of Nations, the most important attempt so far at achieving that amity. With a glorious past which still clings to her old buildings, known for centuries as the haven of those whose desire for liberty and for progressive thought has made them unwanted in their homes, she is today as modern as any city in the world. Broad streets and modern hygienic standards, coupled with pure and bracing air, make her a delightful place to live in as well as to visit—a rare tribute to any city. Her manufactures and the intelligence of her citizenry aid her to maintain the place she has won for herself in the past and increase her general attractiveness. On the whole, she is well fitted for her role of leader in peace and progress.

ITALY

ON THE GRAND CANAL IN VENICE
Tourist-laden gondolas pass one of the famous reproductions of the Lion of St. Mark.

ITALY has always been a magnet for travelers. It offers something alluring, satisfying, and definitely interesting to every type of person and to people in every walk of life. It is not reserved for the few but is for the many, and it generously shares with all its great esthetic inheritances and natural splendors. No other country lays such a wealth of art, such an array of breath-taking beauty, or so many charming and picturesque by-paths at the feet of its guests.

Italy's history covers twenty-seven varied and dramatic centuries. The span extends from early Etruscan times and later to the founding of Rome, traditionally by Romulus and Remus, the lost babies suckled by the wolf, to the present spectacular and efficient regime of the Corporative State. During these centuries, Italy has seen the greatest heights of glory and power, when, under the earlier Emperors her possessions completely surrounded the Mediterranean and included Britain and what is now France, Spain, and part of Germany. These resplendent years, during which she absorbed all the culture of the East, were followed by centuries of darkest desolation when the barbarian hordes swept down from the north and left only wanton destruction

THE ROMAN EMPIRE IN THE DAYS OF TRAJAN,
EMPEROR 98-117 A.D.

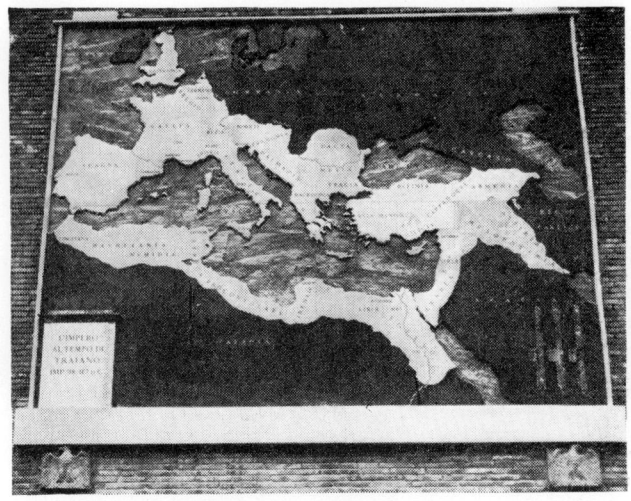

Courtesy Italian Tourist Information Office, N. Y.

and waste in their path. After eight hundred years a new line burst through the ashes left by the barbarians and the Renaissance was born to make Italy once more the center of art and learning of the world.

In 1848 a leader stepped forth, and Carlo Alberto, King of Sardinia, great-grandfather of the present King Emanuele III, made the first statute to unite the kingdom before abdicating in favor of his son, Vittorio Emanuele II. The latter, with the force of arms, the aid of that fiery red-shirted patriot Giuseppe Garibaldi, Giuseppe Mazzini, and the able statecraft of Camillo Cavour, completed the formation of the United Kingdom of Italy.

Again in 1915 there was desperate war. It shook the foundations of the country, drained it of its man power and material resources and left the inevitable and chaotic aftermath; but today Italy is undergoing a reorganization led by Benito Mussolini.

The result of all this is a fascinating and unique land, where we find remains of the highest Greek culture, the tell-tale signs of Moorish invasions, the finest examples of Byzantine art, the most complete visual story of pagan life in the world, the black charred footsteps of the Huns and Goths, and the golden glories of the Renaissance. Hence Italy is not only a natural paradise, but a vast storehouse of unrivaled artistic treasures which have been systematically and painstakingly preserved and offered to all with a warmth of hospitality and a smile of welcome not found in any other country.

NAPLES

Naples, originally an old Greek city taking the name Neapolis (new city) as opposed to the older Greek city of Partenope adjoining it, covers the crescent hillside that half encircles an iridescent bay. At one tip rises Vesuvius with its constant plume of steam, floating serenely across the turquoise sky, and farther out the mauve form of Capri rises from the opalescent sea.

The grim old Castello Nuovo, that stands at the entrance to the embarkation mole, was the home of the kings and viceroys of Naples. Its elaborate doorway is the triumphal arch of Alphonse of Aragon, built to commemorate his victory over this southern kingdom in 1442.

From it, Via Partenope skirts the sea to the *Fontana della Santa Lucia* at the corner of the Marina and Via Caracciolo. The Castel dell'Ovo, now a military prison, stands there on a rocky

Courtesy Italian Tourist Information Office, Chicago
THE PIAZZA PLEBISCITO IN NAPLES

foundation connected with the mainland by a ledge just wide enough for a bridge-like street. Clinging about its base like barnacles are those characteristic Neapolitan cafés. Plates of oysters, fresh from the nearby water, hold down the red- and blue-checkered cloths against the fresh sea breeze, and strolling musicians wander amongst the tables.

A broad boulevard, the Via Caracciolo, follows the bay to Posilipo on the other point of the crescent. It passes the Aquarium, with its collection of semi-tropical fish from the Bay of Naples, and farther on the Piedigrotto and Virgil's Tomb. It is not the panorama alone that is so lovely, for enchanting vistas appear before the eye at every turn.

The Royal Palace, San Carlo Theater, the Cathedral, and San Francisco da Paolo are in the center of the city and from the Piazza Plebiscito a tram goes to the National Museum. This former barracks contains the famed collections unearthed from the buried cities of Pompeii and Herculaneum.

Fifteen miles away, these pagan cities lay sensuously at the foot of Vesuvius, unmindful of its many warnings until that fatal day in 79 A.D., when the great eruption consigned them to oblivion for 1800 years. The hot ashes and steam, which destroyed Pompeii, corroded and oxidized its statues and other works of bronze. In contrast, those taken from nearby Herculaneum are in perfect condition. This patrician city was smothered by cold ashes followed by torrential rains, which combined with the ash, encased the city in a plastic mass that became solid rock from thirty to eighty feet deep. In consequence, excavating there has been a much slower and more difficult task than at Pompeii, where the deposit was loose and only half as deep. For these same reasons, the finds at Herculaneum are in almost perfect condition, entirely unaffected by ravages of time.

After more than a century of careful and scientific excavating, these two cities have been restored exactly as they were at the moment of their almost instantaneous burial about 1900 years ago. The very bread to have been eaten that day was found in the ovens. Charred olives, nuts, and cereal in jars were found in the kitchens, and glass bottles, vases, jewelry, and even toys in other rooms. The magnificent statues, bronze lamps, and marble chairs and fountains came from the peristyles and atriums, that were the gardens and reception rooms of the family. The floors of these rooms were of the most intricate mosaics and the walls were beautifully frescoed.

ITALY [93]

Courtesy Italian Tourist Information Office, Chicago

RUINS OF A ROMAN BATH AT POMPEII

A funicular railway (cable car) crawls up the steep slope of Vesuvius to accommodate those who wish to see not only a phenomenon of nature, but the actual source of the impersonal giant that engulfed whole cities, perfectly preserving their records and civilization for posterity. In the crater, molten, glowing rock writhes and curls, while flames, smoke and lava shoot skyward from the thundering cone.

The auto strada (tool road) from Naples passes Herculaneum and Pompeii and connects with the Amalfi Drive. This world-famed ribbon of road loops around the mountainsides above the Mediterranean where the water churns itself from deepest blue to purest white against the jagged rocks.

Amalfi, which in the eleventh century rivaled Genoa and Pisa as a sea power, is now a hanging garden at the mouth of a deep ravine. The black and white marble cathedral stands at the head of an impressive flight of steps leading up from the piazza. The cloister at the left of the portico is small but unusually charming

Courtesy Italian Tourist Information Office, Chicago
THE MOTOR HIGHWAY "AQUALI POMPEII" ENTERING NAPLES

—with Saracenic pointed arches and spandrels ornamented by broad interlaced bands of stones that follow the line of the openings.

A new "Grotto Smeraldo" (Emerald), entered directly from the highway is fantastically beautiful. The diffracted light forms a luminous pool in the cavern where stalactites and stalagmites build fairy castles and miniature cities on every side.

Courtesy Italian Tourist Information Office, Chicago
GENERAL VIEW OF CAPRI

From Amalfi the road swings back to Naples through Sorrento, another city that was commercially important during the Middle Ages. It now lies sleepily in luxuriant groves of orange and lemon trees on a cliff which drops precipitously into the bay. Its beauty and mild climate make it a popular winter resort for English people. Boats from Naples touch at this village-like town enroute to the island of Capri, the favorite residence of Augustus and Tiberius.

The subject of song and poetry for centuries, Capri still allures and enthralls artists and laymen alike. San Michele, the gilded Madonna in the hermit's cell on the mountainside, and the glistening white domes of Ana Capri overrun with roses, each adds its potent charm to Capri's fascination. The enchantment of this island, dotted with pink and white houses is that of a summer cloud, intangible and evanescent.

ROME

The new electric train makes the trip from Naples to the Eternal City in about two hours. From the station one steps almost at once into the fifteenth-century Piazza Esedra, centered by an immense fountain, which plays its delicate spray day and night as all Italian fountains do. The water for this, the last gift of the popes in their plan to beautify the city, comes through the Aqua Marcia which was built in 144 B.C.

At the right of the square are the Baths of Diocletian now the National Museum or Museo delle Terme. It houses the finest collection of plastic art from the standpoint of excellence, outside the Vatican, including the fifth-century Greek, "Venus of Cyrene," the "Kneeling Niobe," and a headless statue of Juno found on the Palatine Hill.

The Piazza Venezia may be considered the heart of both ancient and modern Rome, for it is surrounded by the evidences of Rome's Imperial glory and in it is the Palazzo Venezia where Il Duce has his office and skilfully guides the nation's difficult course.

The gigantic monument of glistening white marble with golden statues was built to honor Vittorio Emanuele II, and to commemorate the founding of the United Kingdom of Italy. Next to St. Peters it is the most dominating structure in Italy.

ROME: THE PIAZZA VENEZIA, WITH MONUMENT TO
VITTORIO EMANUELE II

At the head of the stairs on the *Altare della Patria* lies Italy's Unknown Soldier with a never ceasing guard of honor.

To the right of the monument is the Campidoglio or Capitoline Square, the center of pagan and early Christian life. It was built on the smallest of the seven hills of Rome and was originally entered directly from the Forum lying back of it.

When Michelangelo was commissioned by Pope Paul III to rehabilitate the square, he reversed its direction and built a sweeping entrance called the Cordonato. Michelangelo also designed the three handsome palaces around the square. He built those at the right and left, but unfortunately his design was abandoned by the man who did the one across the back with the exception of the double steps leading to the main doorway. In the center of the Campidoglio is the equestrian statue of Marcus Aurelius, one of the rare metal antique works of art in existence. It formerly stood before St. John Lateran, the church built by Constantine the Great, the first Christian emperor. From this, the Christians, to whom Rome had been abandoned when Constantine moved the capital to Byzantium, inferred that it was Constantine himself, which accounts for its conservation.

These early Christians, in their religious zeal, ruthlessly pillaged and destroyed everything pagan. The colosseum, temples, and forums were veritable quarries for the builders. They used the columns and marble in the new Christian churches, and destroyed almost everything else, even burning great quantities of marble to obtain lime. They further added to the oblivion of the Roman Forum by making it the city dump until it was completely lost to view. It then became a horse market and eventually cheap shops and tenements covered it.

From a small terrace between the Palazzo Senatori and the Palazzo Conservatori the Roman Forum spreads out in an uninterrupted panoramic view. This Forum was a marsh land drained by Tarquinian the Proud in 579 B.C. to form a market place for the people living on the surrounding hills. It was gradually used as a general meeting place until it became the center of Roman political life and one of the famous historic spots in the world. The laws promulgated there during the first to third centuries have been the basis of the law of the modern western world.

Courtesy Italian Tourist Information Office, Chicago
CAMPIDOGLIO PALACE IN ROME (DESIGNED BY MICHELANGELO)

Across the Via dell'Impero, which connects the Piazza Venezia and the Colosseum, is Trajan's Forum with its marble column wound with scenes depicting his victories. These carved pictures have been a great source of information to writers and historians because of their infinite detail and splendid state of preservation. The statue of Trajan, which originally topped it, was replaced by one of St. Peter in 1585 at the instigation of Pope Sixtus V.

The Colosseum, at the other end of the Via dell'Impero, was built in the garden of the Golden House of Nero. A miniature lake which occupied this space was drained by Vespasian after Nero's death, and the construction of the great amphitheater was immediately begun. It was built of travertine on the outside, concrete covered with marble on the inside, and the cornice at the top held bronze sailyards which supported awnings of golden silk. Lavish and unspeakably cruel spectacles, often lasting from morning until night, were staged in the arena to delight the bloodthirsty populace. These included the death and torture of hundreds of Christian martyrs. The Colosseum, too, was stripped of all usable material after Constantine left Rome. Even the bronze cramps were removed leaving the disfiguring holes in the arcaded walls.

One of the finest of the antique monuments stands beside the Colosseum, connecting the Sacred Way, which traversed the Forum, with the Via dei Trionfi, which leads past the Baths of Caracalla and on to the Catacombs in the Via Appia Antica. It is the triumphal arch of Constantine, built in 312 A.D., to celebrate his victory over Maxentius at Saxa Rubra.

One of the most attractive, as well as beautiful, features of Rome is its *Piazze* (Squares). They run the gamut from the majestic elegance of *Piazza San Pietro* to the picturesque Piazza Mattei that surrounds a fountain so perfect in design that some authorities attribute it to Raphael. It is the *Fontana delle Tartarughe*, named for the four turtles that boyish figures playfully give a hand over the edge of the basin.

The gayest and most colorful is the Piazza da Spagna where handsome baroque steps, leading from the square, divide into two sweeping curved flights which meet again at the base of the *Trinità*. Banks of moist, fragrant flowers fill the lowest steps. Their brilliant reds, pinks, yellows, and blues pierce the shade and rival the gaudy colors of the umbrellas placed protectingly

ITALY

Courtesy Italian Tourist Information Office, Chicago

FAMOUS ARCH OF CONSTANTINE THE GREAT IN ROME

Courtesy Italian Tourist Information Office, Chicago
ST. PETER'S CATHEDRAL, ROME

over them. The mellow glowing walls of the rose and apricot palaces inclose and fill the square with an aureole of warmth, and many intriguing shops, now occupying their first floors, satisfy the collector's every desire.

Rome's churches are innumerable. St. Peter's is a church not alone of Rome, but of the world. It is the largest of all Christian basilicas and was a hundred twenty years in the building. Rich in art and a work of art itself, it is the mausoleum of St. Peter, who lies beneath the high altar, and of the popes who are buried in magnificent tombs throughout the church. The steps of St. Peter and the square with Bernini's colossal and encircling colonnade, are the only part of the Vatican City open to the public and are, in consequence, subject to Italian police control.

The Vatican City is the result of the Lateran Treaty signed by Mussolini and the Pope in 1929. By it a new domain was created—a sovereign state—completely under the control of the Pope and his administrators. It lies just back of St. Peter's and includes the Vatican Palace and Museum, the Governor's Palace, a railway station, and several less important buildings. The public entrance to the apartments of the Pope is at the right of the church through a wing of the colonnade. There the Swiss guards and gendarmes stand, dressed in the elaborate and colorful uniforms that add so much to the pageantry of the Papal Court.

The major part of the Vatican Palace has become the world's greatest museum. Many of its most priceless and unique works of art are those which are a part of the palace itself. Amongst these are the Sistine Chapel, the Borgia Apartments, the Raphael Rooms, the Library, Capella Paolina, and the Loggetta of Raphael. In the court of the Belvedere are the "Apollo Belvedere," "Laocoön," "Hermes," "Perseus," and a "Daughter of Niobe," and several rooms contain innumerable original Greek and Roman statues and fragments. In the picture gallery is an extensive collection of primitives and Renaissance masterpieces.

The modern grandeur of Rome is best exemplified by the colossal, ultra-modern university buildings that centralize an organization which had been scattered throughout the city.

Photo ENIT, Rome

THE VATICAN CITY: DOME OF ST. PETER'S

PLAN OF THE VATICAN CITY

1. St. Ann Street
2. Pellegrino Street
3. Belvedere Street
4. Printing House Street
5. Post Office Street
6. Pius X Street
7. Ascent to the Gardens
8. Garden Avenue
9. Ascent to the Zecca
10. Government Street
11. Bastion Street
12. Perugino Street
13. Arcade of Pier Luigi of Palestrina
14. Mosaic Street
15. Observatory Street
16. Guglielmo Marconi Street
18. Zitella Boulevard

A. St. Peter Square
B. St. Egidius Square
C. Heating Plant
D. Zecca Place
E. Government Place
F. Station Square
G. St. Stephen-of-the-Abyssinians Court
H. St. Martha Square
I. Braschi Court
L. Sacristy Court
M. First-Roman-Martyrs Court
a. Olmo Court
b. Triangle of the Gateway
c. Holy Office Court
d. St. Damasus Court
e. Marshal Court
f. Pappagalli Court
g. Borgia Court
h. Court of the Guards
i. Belvedere Court
l. Library Court
m. Pinetree Court
n. Corazze Court
o. Triangle Court

ITALY

GROUP OF STAT-
UARY IN THE
FORUM OF
MUSSOLINI

Courtesy Italian Tourist
Information Office,
Chicago

The Foro Mussolini is part of the university group, but its use is not limited to its students. All of the younger generation of Rome, both boys and girls, receive the finest physical training, and enjoy the facilities of this great physical academy. The stadium, its top mounted with gigantic statues, accommodates twenty thousand people, has an immense swimming pool adjacent, and buildings for indoor sports and gymnasium work in inclement weather.

Everything possible is being done to improve and care for the health of the youth of Italy, and the Institute Carlo Forlanini plays an important part in this vast work. It is a great tubercular hospital, the last word in equipment, scientific knowledge and care.

Another achievement of the Fascist régime is the draining of the Pontine Marshes and subsequent establishment and development of two splendid agricultural sections, where the uninhabitable, malaria-infested swamps had been.

Littoria and Sabaudia are thriving rural communities. The architecture is modernistic in style and the buildings modern in equipment. Each community has its Palazzo Comunale, fine post and telegraph office, church and schools, in addition to the farm and town houses, that were built by the central government in Rome.

Each city of Italy is unique, each completely individualistic, each has its own particular charms, reasons for fame and even a characteristic type of architecture. Some are simple and picturesque, some almost mystic, while others are palatial and dignified; but Rome alone is awe-inspiring and majestic in its stately grandeur.

FLORENCE

In Florence the Renaissance was born. Here it was cradled and fostered by the Medici, the greatest of all Florentine families; and it was Anna Maria Ludovica, its last surviving member, who gathered from its palaces throughout Italy the galaxy of art that made this city the art center of the world. Her noble spirit and farsightedness were shown in the remarkable wording of her will, for though this bequest was never to be removed from Florence, it was not bequeathed to the Florentines alone, but for "the benefit of the public of all nations."

San Lorenzo is the church of the Medici and they lie in its lapis lazuli and turquoise Chapel of the Princes, and in the adjacent Sacristy, where surmounting the tombs of Lorenzo the Magnificent and his brother, Guliano, are those famed statues of Michelangelo, "Morn and Evening" and "Day and Night."

The nearby Palazzo Riccardi was the first home of this family and the scene of their most illustrious years. Its gorgeous salons surround the jewel-like chapel, decorated by Benozzo Gozzoli, who depicted the "Visit of the Magi" on its walls, making each important character a Medici portrait.

From the Piazzale Michelangelo, above the Viale dei Colli, the pale-rose dome of the Cathedral, Giotto's Campanile, the grey castellated tower of the Palazzo Vecchio, and the pointed spire of La Badia cut through the patchwork of tiled roofs about them. In the foreground the ancient Ponte Vecchio, its sides stained and heavy with clustered goldsmith work, the catenary arches of the sixteenth-century Ponte Santa Trinità, and the Ponte Carraria span the vagrant yellow river Arno whose meanderings divide the city.

On one side of the river beyond the Piazza San Felice, where Elizabeth and Robert Browning lived, is the Pitti Palace, the last home of the Medici. On the other, connected with it by a corridor which forms the upper story of the Ponte Vecchio (Old

Courtesy Italian Tourist Information Office, Chicago
LOGGIA DELLA SIGNORIA IN FLORENCE

Bridge), is the Uffizi Palace, the government office during the time of Duke Cosimo I. These two buildings now house the greatest collections of art in the world, the result of the unceasing labor, generosity, and excellent judgment of the Medici during the three hundred years of power, and the keen vision and benevolence of Anna Maria.

The Palazzo Vecchio became the second home of the Medici when Cosimo I took his bride there for greater safety. At the same time, he placed his personal guard of Swiss lancers in the Loggia opposite the entrances to the Uffizi. The Loggia dei Lanzi now forms a handsome background for several excellent groups of statuary. Here Cellini's "Perseus" stands, holding aloft the dripping head of Medusa, and in his youthful calmness, gazes at her lifeless body beneath his foot.

In the square before the "Old Palace," Savonarola was burned at the stake after having changed the tenor of Florentine life by his preaching and writings.

Michelangelo, Machiavelli, Galileo, Rossini, and many other illustrious men are buried in Santa Croce, the oldest and most beautiful of the Mendicant churches. Giotto frescoed two of its chapels after painting for forty years in the churches from Assisi to Padua; and in a third hangs Donatello's wooden crucifix that was so criticized by Brunelleschi.

Florence, "La Città dei Fiori" (the city of flowers), appeals to the intellect and to the heart. To think of Florence is to think of Del Sarto, Fra Angelico, Botticelli, Raphael, Michelangelo, and the Medici, for their names are synonymous with this true city of the fifteenth century, this city that is the repository of the finest and most prolific expressions of the Renaissance.

HILL TOWNS

Between Rome and Florence in the hills of Umbria are those old and fascinating cities known as the "Hill Towns." There are eight in all, but Orvieto, Assisi, Perugia, and Siena, which is over the border in Tuscany, are the most interesting.

Assisi was the home of St. Francis and his presence seems still to invade its steep, twisted streets. Pots of flowers and vines hang everywhere on the weather-beaten walls of the houses and each door bears a colorful tile with the message: "Pax et Bonum" ("Peace and Good Will").

The church of St. Francis triumphs in beauty that reaches the sublime. The walls and ceiling of groined vaulting sparkle and shine through the half-light and deep shadows of the Lower Church. Professor Mather says, "It is the most beautifully pictured Gothic ceiling in the world." In the Upper Church, gold stars on a cerulean ground, framed by arabesque bands of rose, crimson, green, and yellow fill the vaults above Giotto's frescoes in the nave, and Cimabue's majestic, blackened ones, in the transepts.

Nowhere is the spirit of Christianity so deeply felt as in this magnificent yet simple church, built over the body of the saint whose life was one of gentle self-sacrifice, and whose teachings included the love of birds, animals, and flowers.

Perugia, named for "Augustus Perusia," who rebuilt it after it was burned to the ground in 40 B.C., is within sight of Assisi. A university town, rather than the home of a saint, it has a charm naturally quite different though equally appealing. The buildings are historic and artistically and architecturally fine, and there is much of real worth to be found in them.

ITALY

GENERAL VIEW OF A SECTION OF SIENA

Courtesy Italian Tourist Information Office, Chicago

The Guelph lion and the Perugian griffin seen everywhere and symbolic of the city, are copied from those over the main doorway of the Palazzo Comunale. These, the originals, bear chains and commemorate an important victory over the Senesi in 1358.

SIENA

"Siena opens her heart still wider to thee" is carved in Latin over the Camollia gate and it gives the key to the spirit of this medieval city that has retained so many of its old customs, manners, and traditions. Truly a "hill town," it has abrupt and winding ways leading to picturesque corners at every turn: from its summit can be seen the fertile fields below and in the distance the lavender grape-laden hills of Chianti.

The cathedral of glistening white marble with courses of black and touches of palest pink has a façade by Giovanni Pisano that is the finest Italian Gothic. The interior is extremely beautiful, of black and white marble surmounted by a ceiling of richest polychrome and heavy, gold-leafed carvings. The *graffito pavimento* (inlaid floor depicting Biblical characters) of rose, black, and white marble is so rare and exquisite that it is uncovered only six weeks of the year. The largest of the Niccolo Pisano pulpits occupies the central space in the nave.

In the adjacent Cathedral Museum, Duccio's "Majestà" commands the attention and tribute of all, even in this land so rich in great altarpieces.

Simone Martini's enchanting general, on his lozenge-caparisoned charger, decorates a wall in the Palazzo Pubblico, and in another room are the first allegorical frescoes representing the "Good Government of Siena" and the "Results of Good Government," by Lorenzetti.

No city of Italy has more personal and appealing charms or more gracious and hospitable people.

PISA

Situated similarly on the Arno and about an hour's ride from Florence is Pisa, probably better known for its Leaning Tower than for its inherent beauty and interesting background.

Pisa was originally a seaport and the Pisans a crusading people, who waged war constantly and successfully against the Saracens and naïvely guarded their port at night by stretching a huge chain across it.

The Cathedral was built just a hundred years before that at Siena to commemorate their greatest victory over the Moors at Palermo. The unusual façade consists of a rather plain lower story with four colonnades, one above the other, decorating the upper part.

The Baptistry opposite was built in 1153. It is a round, domed building of marble with elaborate Gothic touches which were added in the fourteenth century. It contains also a pulpit by Niccola Pisano, smaller than that at Siena, and hexagonal instead of octagonal.

The Campo Santo is the Pantheon of Pisa, and tradition says that fifty boatloads of earth were brought from the Holy Land to make the burial ground on which it is built. The cloistered walls are magnificently frescoed and the colonnade is a marble filigree.

Courtesy Italian Tourist Information Office, Chicago
PISA, SHOWING THE BAPTISTRY, CATHEDRAL, AND FAMOUS LEANING TOWER

ITALY

Courtesy Italian Tourist Information Office, Chicago
THE TOMB OF DANTE IN RAVENNA

The Leaning Tower, or Campanile, too well known to dwell upon, has been considered for centuries one of the Seven Wonders of the World.

These buildings are grouped together in the Piazza del Duomo and form an imposing and significant ecclesiastical conservatory.

RAVENNA

Ravenna, on the Adriatic, is the Byzantium of Italy. It was originally a lagoon city like Venice and the seat of the Imperial Court during the first part of the fifth century. No other city in the world offers so many and such remarkable examples of fifth-century art, commonly called Byzantine. Many of the mosaics, although restorations, are still marvels of workmanship and color. Those in the Mausoleum of Galla Placida, erected in 440 and restored in 1898 in the fifth-century style, are of the rarest and most beautiful blue.

Dante, one of the world's greatest poets, is buried here, where he found a peaceful refuge after his exile from his native city, Florence.

VENICE

Venice, made the "Bride of the Adriatic" each year in an elaborate ceremony, is the most charming and glamorous city of Italy. Her close contact with the resplendence of the Orient, supported by her almost fabulous wealth, made Venice a city of unrivaled elegance and ostentatious brilliance. Every canal is lined with soft-colored palaces of warm pinks and creams. Their lacy Gothic windows embroider the marble façades, and Byzantine wrought-iron grilles cover the garden casements and doorways.

The Piazza San Marco, illuminated by the blazing glory of St. Mark's golden mosaics, is the center of Venetian life today as it has always been. Countless little tables and chairs accommodate the carefree people who gather here for aperitifs before luncheon, tea in the afternoon, and for coffee after dinner, and to listen to the concerts given three times a week.

In the Piazzetta, the marble palace of the Doges recalls the radiant days of the fourteenth and fifteenth centuries, when the glory of Venice was at its zenith. It is a combination of Eastern motifs and the finest Gothic, and in sharp contrast to the Byzantine-Romanesque basilica standing beside it. The principal entrance to the courtyard is the Porta della Carta (Door of Paper), so named because edicts and official notices were posted on two Hellenistic pillars just in front of it. The Scala dei Giganti, with the colossal figures of Mars and Neptune at the top, connects with the second-floor arcade and is the official entrance to the Palace.

Venice cannot be thought of without remembering that Titian lived and died in this lagoon city, that he did most of his work here, continuing with increasing ability, enthusiasm and spirit until his ninety-ninth year. In the Accademia delle Belle Arti (Academy of Fine Arts) are many of his masterpieces, as well as those of Bellini, Tintoretto, and Veronese.

Graceful gondolas leave the Grand Canal, gliding under miniature arched bridges, that appear almost like porcelain in their

VENICE: THE WORLD-FAMOUS BRIDGE OF SIGHS WHICH CONNECTS THE PALACE OF THE DOGES WITH THE PRISON

fineness, to the Rialto where flat-bottomed boats of fruits, flowers, and vegetables make gaudy, festive pictures as they tie up to the narrow sidewalks. From this scene of rural abundance, these most entrancing of all small boats slip noiselessly on through the labyrinth of palace-lined canals.

St. Marks, the Palace of the Doges, avenues of silvery water in the moonlight between walls of Gothic palaces, singing gondoliers, exquisite and fragile glass, the lace and rich brocades, are a few of the things which rightly give to Venice its fitting title, "The Gem of the Adriatic."

VERONA

Romantic figures of literature and opera add to the interest of many Italian cities and towns, and perhaps the best known and loved of all these are Romeo and Juliet.

Not far from the center of Verona and the big open market

Courtesy The Art Institute of Chicago

VERONA, SHOWING STEPS FROM THE COURT OF THE PALACE

is a narrow medieval house with a second-story window opening onto an ancient balcony directly above the street. It is not difficult to see the lovely, childish figure of the daughter of the Capulets, standing there, almost breathless with love while the youthful Romeo poured out his heart from the pavement below. Another of Shakespeare's plays, one of his earliest, is *Two Gentlemen of Verona*. Dante found his first refuge here after his banishment from Florence, and Petrarch and Giotto both stayed several times in the Palazzo dei Signori.

A group of imposing and temple-like sarcophagi across from the Palazzo della Ragione (Court of Law) house the interred Scaligeri, the family which ruled Verona for generations; and one of the three great amphitheaters of Italy is plainly visible from the station. This one is in much better condition than either that at Rome or Pola.

To wander about the streets, without the spur and lash of a set program, is the best way to understand and appreciate this poetic old city, situated almost on Lake Garda in the heart of a fruit-growing and wine-making district.

CORTINA

Around the toy-like village of Cortina d'Ampezzo, the Dolomite mountains blaze against the clear blue sky as they catch the fire of the setting sun. Furry masses of pines in the foothills shade off into meadows, brilliant with wild flowers, that are like Aubusson carpets. The forget-me-nots make great patches of turquoise against the deep blue of gentians, and swirls of pink and rose columbine are bordered with pale yellow anemones and lavender bells. Over these same stretches, later in the year, the vivid clothes of the skiers make clear silhouettes against the glistening sweeps of snow.

A half hour's ride from Cortina at Pieve di Cadore is a Swiss chalet, brown and weather-beaten, that stands in an aura of glimmering light. Inside are a few pieces of rough furniture before a broad hearth and a stone-hooded fireplace. This was the birthplace and early home of Titian; and it was the mountains around Cadore that he painted as the view seen through the window in his masterpiece, the "Presentation of the Virgin."

CORTINA D'AMPEZZO
Majestic mountains and pastoral land combine to make the setting of this town one of beauty and charm.

BERGAMO

The ancient city, Bergamo Alta, is situated high on the hill with its picturesque old buildings separated by narrow, crooked streets. This delightful spot was the home of many famous men including the artist Palma Vecchio, Colleoni, the great *condottiere*, and the famous composer Donizetti.

Probably the finest equestrian statue ever made is that of Colleoni by Verrocchio. It stands beside the church of SS. Giovanni and Paolo in Venice. The tomb of this dramatic figure and his daughter is here in the chapel of Santa Maria Maggiore. The chapel in general may be over-elaborate, but the figure of the young woman is exquisite and there are some excellent frescoes by Tiepolo in the ceiling. It may have been the inspiration of Colleoni that prompted Bergamaschi to join Garibaldi's famous "1000."

The train from Milan arrives at the station in the lower town and the funicular railway connects this newer section with the old on the hilltop.

MILAN

The history of Milan is colorful. After having been the seat of the Imperial Court of Constantine, it was completely destroyed by Frederick Barbarossa in 1162. It was soon rebuilt and in 1277 the Visconti dominated Milan and a large part of northern Italy. In 1450, the *Condottiere* Sforza seized control and established the court which became even more brilliant under his successors until the marriage of Bianca Sforza to Emperor Maximilian I ushered in diplomatic difficulties and war with various countries of Europe.

The Cathedral was begun in 1386, but perhaps because it was so close to these northern countries, some French and German architects were employed to collaborate with the Italian. The result was constant friction that so impeded its progress that the church was not completed until 1500. Whatever unpleasant working and social conditions came from this combination may well be forgotten, for the flower that resulted from their infused ideas is magnificent. The only Norman-Gothic building in Italy, it is elaborately fragile, being completely covered with fine-spun turrets, statues, and delicate carvings. The interior in contrast is monumental, harmonious, and symphonic in its perfection of design. Many authorities consider the Cathedral of Milan the finest example of church architecture ever constructed.

Leonardo da Vinci's "Last Supper" is on the wall of the refectory of the small, fifteenth-century church, Santa Maria delle Grazie. The tragedy is, that da Vinci painted this masterpiece in *tempera* (pigments mixed with water and eggs), which is quickly affected and ruined by dampness; so only a shadow of this famous picture is visible today.

Milan is the leading commercial city of Italy, a real metropolis that is humming with the activities of business, modern building, and scientific production.

THE LAKES

In the Lake District, the Alps are set with sparkling emeralds of water in wreaths of magnolias and camelias. Lake Maggiore, one of the largest of these natural jewels, is sublime in its beauty. Each of its islands has a limpid double in the translucent water, and the changing blue and violet of the distant snow-crested mountains are repeated along the shores.

BELLAGIO STREET, COMO, IN BLOSSOM TIME

Isola Bella, in particular, is like part of a painted landscape. It is a pyramid of ten terraces narrowing toward the top. Each is richly decorated with statues, urns, and flowers, with a few accenting notes of dark, spear-like cypress. The island was originally a barren, rocky pinnacle until Count Borromeo had the points leveled off and soil brought from the mainland to fill the crevices and later the terraces. He named the island Isola Isabella for his mother.

LAGO DI COMO

An hour from Milan on the way to Lucerne is Lago di Como (Lake Como). Again more dream-like than earthly, it is a rare combination of sophistication and simplicity. Abrupt foothills, lightly tinted with pink and white villas that fade away into the chestnut and walnut trees back of them, closely encircle the lake. There is a peculiar luminous quality to the air in Como that adds to its romanticism and veils it in an unreal light.

The town of Como, the center of the silk industry, is delightful, with shops everywhere filled with lustrous swirls that overflow into the windows in silken rainbows.

The Cathedral is more than worthy of note. Its unusual doorway is a perfect example of the High Renaissance. The excessive profuseness of detail is its essential characteristic and difference from the style generally used in and about Florence.

GENOA

Genoa, a popular embarkation port, is today Italy's largest maritime center and has been an important harbor since 1248.

Galeazzo Alissi with his palaces, especially adapted to the sloping sites and winding streets, characterized and put his stamp on Genoa's architectural style.

Columbus was born in this seacoast town. An extensive collection of his personal belongings and articles pertaining to his world-changing voyages, are in the Palazzo Bianco at No. 13 Via Garibaldi.

Courtesy Italian Tourist Information Office, Chicago

SANTA MARGHERITA LIGURE
A general view of the city showing beautiful white villas on the mountainside.

Genoa is an ancient commercial port that has held and developed its supremacy through the centuries. It is an interesting combination of the old and the new, of the artistic and the commercial that is unusual in Italy.

Extending both north and south from the city is the Riviera, that semi-tropical shore where San Remo, Santa Margherita, Portofino, and Rapallo lure people from every part of the world. Their beauty is captivating; they are havens for the fatigued traveler and a joy to the winter vacationist.

SICILY

Fortunately almost all liners make Sicily a regular port of call. It is the island at the toe of the boot that was settled by the Greeks a thousand years before Christ. Along its rugged coast a snowy froth edges the cobalt water, and on the hills remains of ancient temples stand silhouetted against the cloudless sky. In the villages clustered on the shores, diminutive donkeys, in tinkling red harnesses and with feathered pompons standing up between their ears, rattle gaily painted carts over the cobbled streets.

The island was the battle ground of the Greeks, the Carthaginians, the Normans, Romans, French, and Spaniards; and traces of all of them can be seen in the dark faces and proud, self-important mannerisms of the Sicilians of today. They are gay and persistently youthful and they love and hate with equal intensity and violence. The people are almost fanatic in their enthusiasm and child-like beliefs. At no place in Italy is a festa loved so much or converted into such a beautiful and dramatic spectacle. Undoubtedly Sicily is at its best on holidays.

The island's history is told best, briefly, by this paragraph from one of F. Marion Crawford's historical works:

> "Three epochs stand out from the chaos of myth, legend, and history; the development of farming by the Sicilians, about 1200 B.C., the introduction of commerce with the Phoenicians after that time, and the gradual growth of a higher civilization under the Greeks, from the time of their landing in the eighth century before the Christian Era, until the Carthaginian wars with Rome, and the subsequent wreck of Greek art and thought under the atrocious governorship of Verres, between 71 and 73 B.C., during which,

TAORMINA, WINTER RESORT IN THE PROVINCE OF MESSINA, EASTERN SICILY

with the connivance of his father, the senator, he pillaged all Sicily at his will. The Roman rule became in the fourth century, the rule of Constantinople, and next in history, when the Goths had ruled for a time, the Arabs began to take Sicily in the year 827 A.D., the Normans came after them, completing their conquest of the island in 1091, and through them the German imperial house of Hohenstaufen, reigning from the fifth year before the preaching of the first crusade, until the downfall of the Ghibellines in 1268. Then the French, under Charles of Anjou, during the years that ended in the Sicilian Vespers, in 1282, after which the Sicilians chose for their king Peter of Aragon, and because both he and Charles of Anjou continued afterwards to call themselves kings of Sicily, the two kingdoms of Sicily and Naples became known from that time as the *two Sicilies,* and were still so called under Ferdinand the Catholic, after Naples was annexed to Aragon, and both became Spanish monarchies. In 1700 began the Spanish succession, after which Victor Amadeus of Savoy was King of Sicily for a time, until Sicily and Naples were again united under Charles the Third of

Courtesy American Museum of Natural History, N. Y.

VOLCANO ON THE ISLAND OF LIPARI, ITALY, IN ERUPTION IN 1888

the House of Bourbon. Last of all, in 1860, the two Sicilies were united to the modern kingdom of Italy. 'There is no part of Europe which has been dominated by a greater number of different races, and none where each has left such deep traces of its domination. The Goths and Vandals are the only people who ever held the south for a time and left no sign of their presence; but their holdings were short, and their occupation was followed by a disappearance so sudden that their brief rule never earned the designation of a kingdom.' "

The story of the Greeks in Sicily is best told by the history of Syracuse. The colony was founded in 734 B.C., and it dominated the island for 1000 years. In 289 B.C., when the last strong ruler died, Syracuse fell and Sicily became disunited. The fact that fewer remains of her greatness are left than of almost any other ancient city shows that her destruction was deliberate and continuous. A few columns of the sixth-century Doric Temple of Jupiter are the only ruins in the city now standing intact.

The story of the rule of later years is told by Palermo. This Saracen stronghold was captured after ten years of fighting by the Normans who first arrived on the island about 1000 A.D. One hundred and fifty years later the island had been completely conquered and William II, the son of William the Bad, and the wise and capable Margaret of Navarre, sat on the throne. He ruled the island well but lived in the manner of the Moslem kings surrounded by extravagant luxury, Moorish handmaidens and concubines. This anomaly, strangely enough, produced its counterpart "in those Christian churches of Palermo which were the florescence of the Arabo-Norman culture."

Of these the Cathedral and the Palatine are in Palermo and the Benedictine monastery and Duomo of Monreale are about four miles outside the city on the hilltop.

Monreale contains Byzantine mosaics that are marvels of workmanship and design, further embellished by a setting of exquisite Arabic detail. The cloister of Saracenic arches has columns in pairs, some of carved stone, others set with gold and colored mosaics; and in one shadowy corner stands a lovely Moorish fountain. This church of gold, marble, and porphyry, built by a twenty-year-old Norman king, is one of the most beautiful churches in the Western World.

The Palatine Chapel was built by the grandfather of this boyish ruler and looks like a heavily jeweled casket. It, too, is something definitely of the East, replete with Eastern beauty.

The Cathedral in the city has suffered from several disconnected restorations resulting in a confused architectural picture especially distasteful after having seen Monreale.

In contrast, the little entrance court of the Museo Nazionale is a delight, with its humanistic and typically Italian fountain, and roses climbing everywhere.

In Sicily there is a blending of the East and West, the North and South. This island may well be the last stop and final view of a land of such varied interests, remarkable possessions, and glorious beauty; of a land whose soul is poured out from every opera stage, whose art is studied by all people, whose civilization combined with Christianity was the greatest of all world influences.

THE MEDITERRANEAN ISLANDS

THE VALLEY STRETCHING AWAY FROM THE PALACE AT PHAESTUS

GIBRALTAR

As befits the world's most impregnable fortress, Gibraltar from a distance is one of the most imposing of sights. Gray and rugged, it has all the appearance of a veteran of many wars. Once you are ashore, however, the natural aspect of "The Rock" is less martial; yet honey-combed with subterranean passages, at the mouth of each of which is a battery of deadly guns, the mighty Rock of Ages is completely in command of the Straits of Gibraltar.

Among the many stories connected with The Rock, there is one about Queen Isabella of Spain. When her forces were trying to take the fortress from the Moors, the queen sat down nearby and declared that she would not leave till the Spanish flag flew over the citadel. Had the lady kept her word with the intended meaning, she would probably have died there; but the Moorish governor proved himself the knight, eager to save a fair lady in distress, and politely hoisted the Spanish banner for a brief moment so that she might move.

The town of Gibraltar, which with the garrison has about twenty thousand inhabitants, is a crown colony of Great Britain. The Straits of Gibraltar divide Spain from Morocco and join the Mediterranean Sea with the Atlantic Ocean.

CATHEDRAL OF PALMA DE MALLORCA, BALEARIC ISLANDS

Paul's Photos, Chicago

THE BALEARICS

Just off the Spanish coast, to the east, lie the Balearic Islands, which belong to Spain. They are thoroughly delightful places to visit, because of their warm, dry climate and the golden sunshine that fills one with a delicious languor. Majorca, the largest island, is very beautiful. Its low hills are covered with semi-tropical vegetation. Citrus fruits are plentiful; and vines produce the fine grapes for wine. Olive and cypress trees are found everywhere; and billowing fields of golden wheat are lovely to gaze upon. Added to such natural beauty, there is much of historic interest. Splendid old castles surmount hills or rise from the edge of the water. In the castles, in museums, and in shops are examples of Spanish and Moorish armor.

CORSICA

Lying just north of Sardinia is Corsica, famed as the birthplace of Napoleon. The island belongs to France; but the language spoken here is Italian. With warm coast towns and mountains which are often very cold, Corsica offers whatever type of climate the traveler may like. It is a safer place now that the stilettos are not so frequently used as formerly. Although banditry of the romantic sort has nearly died out, there is still an air of bravado, which calls to mind Corsican stories of the past. Corsicans are very courteous hosts to their guests, and one does not leave their island without regret.

SARDINIA

Mountainous, windy, and subject to violent rainfalls in the autumn is Sardinia, a land never called gentle. Situated west of Italy and south of Corsica, it is one of the most attractive of all the Mediterranean islands. Most interesting are the varied native costumes. Each locality has its own type; but all are colorful, gay, and graceful. Bright red is a favorite color, and nothing could be more becoming to the beautiful, dark-skinned women of the island. The numerous native dialects vary so much in the different sections, that the people who speak different branches of the local tongue have to use Italian to make themselves understood by one another. Ancient remains bear witness to the fact that Sardinia often passed from one conqueror to another before it finally came into the present possession of Italy.

BIRTHPLACE OF NAPOLEON ON THE ISLAND OF CORSICA

LACE SELLERS
ON THE ISLAND
OF MALTA

Paul's Photos, Chicago

MALTA

The British colony of Malta is made up of the islands of Comino, Gozo, and Malta. They are situated in the Mediterranean about sixty miles south of Sicily. A rich vegetation, which continues the year round, has given the Maltese a certain right to speak of their home as the "flower of the world." In 1814 the islands were annexed by Britain upon the request of the Maltese. The British have made of Malta a fortress almost as impregnable as that of Gibraltar. Malta is the ancient seat of the famous Knights of Malta. In the course of its history it fell in turn into the hands of the Phoenicians, Carthaginians, Greeks, Romans, Saracens, and French. Roman villas and tombs vie with early Christian catacombs and crypts in attracting the attention of travelers. In many old buildings there are rich carvings, precious metal works, paintings, and tapestries.

CRETE

Crete, as befits her place in classical antiquity, belongs to Greece. Although full of archaeological treasures left by the Minoans, and later by the Greeks and Romans, the outward aspect of the island is rather Italian. Fortifications of the Venetian type are everywhere in evidence, and one cannot forget for a minute that the island once belonged to Venice. Crete was in turn lost by the Venetians to the Turks who conquered the island in 1665 after a twenty-year siege, and held it until 1913, when they were forced to give it up at the end of the Balkan War. Candia, the see of the archbishop of Crete, has many old fortifications; as has Canea, the seat of the government.

Sailing north from Crete, we travel directly into the Aegean Sea, which lies between Greece and Turkey. These waters are dotted with more than two hundred little islands, which form the group known as the Cyclades. Of these the largest are Paros, Andros, Naxos, Melos, and Thera or Santorin. One cannot pass these enchanting isles without recalling how the "glory that was Greece" has been immortalized for posterity in the many master-

Courtesy J. Bradford Pengelly

KNOSSUS, VIEWED FROM THE PALACE

RUINS OF XU
BASILICA AT
CORTYNA, NEAR
PHAESTOS

pieces wrought in marble from Paros; how the incomparable "Venus" was found at Melos in 1820; and how Thera and many of her sister isles have preserved Greek and Roman treasures through the centuries.

RHODES

Rhodes is the principal island of the group known as the Dodecanese, which belong to Italy. Its chief city, bearing also the name of the island, is surrounded by walls and towers and is guarded by a moated castle, all of them in unimpaired perfection. The medieval appearance of the city was implanted by the long rule of the Knights of St. John of Jerusalem, later known as the Knights of Rhodes and finally as the Knights of Malta, who gained control during the Middle Ages. Excavations made here have brought to light much valuable information for enthusiasts of Greek and Roman antiquity.

THE MEDITERRANEAN ISLANDS   [129]

CYPRUS

A third British possession in the Mediterranean, Cyprus, lies at the far eastern end of the Mediterranean Sea, about fifty miles west from the coast of Syria. As early as 1100 B.C. it was settled on by the Phoenicians; and it was successively owned by the Greeks, Assyrians, Persians, Egyptians, and Romans. In the sixteenth century it fell to Turkey; and in 1878 to Great Britain, by whom it was formally annexed as a dependency in 1914. Among the relics of the Middle Ages which may still be seen on the island is the Virgin Castle, which stands today in almost perfect condition. And for students of ancient history it offers many stimulating subjects for study.

CORFU

The largest island and the richest one in the southern Adriatic Sea is Corfu, which has been a possession coveted by many people for many centuries. It has had many different rulers, but at present it is a part of the kingdom of Greece. The island is called

Courtesy J. Bradford Pengelly
GREAT COLUMNS AT ENTRANCE TO THE HARBOR OF RHODES
These are said to mark the spots where the feet of the great Colossus stood

Courtesy J. Bradford Pengelly
INCLINE SAN TORIN

LINDO ON THE ISLAND OF RHODES
This was a famous center in Roman days.

by the Greeks "Kerkyra." Corfu is about thirty-eight miles long and varies in width from three to twenty miles, having an area of about 275 square miles. It is very hilly, with one mountain that rises to a height of three thousand feet. The scenery of Corfu is

PALACE OF ACHILLEION, CORFU
Winter home of former Kaiser Wilhelm II.

CAVERN OF LOIZOS, ISLAND OF ITHICA

exceedingly beautiful, combining as it does the rugged and pastoral. There are interesting historical incidents connected with the island. It is commonly associated with the Phaeacia of Homer's *Odyssey*. The Venetians have left in great walls, fortifications, and buildings many traces of their occupancy which lasted from 1386 to 1797. The British ruled Corfu from 1815 to 1864 when, through the influence of Gladstone, a lover of things Greek, it was restored to Greece. The capital of the island is Corfu, which is an attractive city combining ancient and modern elements. It is a progressive town of thirty-three thousand people. Corfu is famous for the great palace known as Achilleion which was for many years the winter home of Kaiser Wilhelm II.

ITHACA

Ithaca is a small but famous island near the mouth of the Adriatic Sea, a short distance south of Corfu. It is celebrated because in Homer's *Odyssey* it is described as the home of Odysseus. Certain excavations on the island confirm the references made by Homer. It is only a small island but an exceedingly beautiful one. The little town of Vathy nestles around the bottom of a small, enchanting bay, which is one of the finest places in the world for a stimulating swim.

Courtesy The Art Institute of Chicago

TURKISH COBBLERS AT THE ENTRANCE TO THEIR SHOP

TURKEY

Paul's Photos, Chicago

TEA IN TURKEY
Natives trying out home-produced tea in place of the usual Turkish coffee.

ANCIENT RUINS and carefully preserved mosques, crumbling fortifications and streamlined buildings, veiled women and women in modern dress, primitive farming and modern factories—such are the combinations of the old and the new found in Turkey today. The energy of the Turkish people is making their country a modern state, even in the midst of reminders of their past. The story of Turkey has its beginning in mythology. Through the Bosporus, which separates European and Asiatic Turkey, Jason sailed in search of the Golden Fleece; and farther west, across the Dardanelles, Leander swam to see his beloved Hero.

History records early events that occurred around the ancient city on the Bosporus—Byzantium—which was founded by the Greeks. Here many wars were fought. On one occasion Philip of Macedonia made an unsuccessful attempt to attack the city. The moon broke through the clouds and revealed his approach to the people of Byzantium. In gratitude they took the crescent moon and scimeter as an emblem, which was much later adopted by the Moslem conquerors.

A FAMILY CARRIAGE IN TURKEY
Complete freedom from blowouts, skids, and speed cops!

When the Roman Empire extended to the East, Constantine chose Byzantium as his capital because of its strategic situation, and the name of the city was changed to Constantinople. Constantine built fortifications which made the city impregnable and served as a protection to all his Byzantine Empire. He built splendid edifices, established schools, and made Constantinople a great trade center. The next four centuries brought repeated struggles with enemies. In 800, the Byzantine Empire renounced all connection with Rome and continued to grow in the East until the eleventh century. About 1200 the Crusaders captured the land and pillaged Constantinople. They took back to Western Europe some of the rare art treasures, which Constantine had brought to beautify his city. In 1453 the Ottoman Turks captured Constantinople. Their power and glory continued to grow until it reached its height under the great Suleiman in the sixteenth century.

Decline set in, and, aside from a few conscientious rulers who tried to rule well, Turkish history was the story of corrupt sultans interested only in luxurious living, with intrigue and bloody wars brightened only by such flares as the eighteenth-century craze for tulips. During the nineteenth century, the Balkan States freed themselves. In 1907 the Young Turks deposed the sultan and established a new constitutional monarchy, but because of their inexperience they made little improvement. Turkey limped along and finally met defeat in the World War.

Then the brilliant Mustafa Kemal Pasha, more familiarly known as *Ataturk* (chief Turk), organized a revolt in Asia Minor, set up a government at Angora, drove the Greeks out of Asia Minor, and recovered Constantinople. In 1923 Turkey became a republic. Turkish vocabulary was substituted for Arabic, and the name of Constantinople was changed to Istanbul, Angora was changed to Ankara, and Smyrna to Izmir. All people were required to take surnames. Ataturk (father of the Turks) undertook a series of sweeping reforms to modernize his country, and Turkey faced West.

THE LAY OF THE LAND

The country is as rugged as its history has been turbulent. Turkey now occupies the peninsula of Asia Minor (about 285,000 square miles) and about 9,000 square miles of Balkan territory. Most of Asiatic Turkey is a huge tableland, which toward the east rises into rough mountainous country. On the other three sides it drops to wooded foothills, from which valleys extend on the north, west, and south to the seas and to flat plains in the southeast. European Turkey is a continuation of these foothills and valleys. The northern coast and Istanbul have sharply contrasting seasons, with a rather cold winter and a moist, hot summer. The western and southern coasts have a typically mild, pleasant Mediterranean climate, while the rest of the country suffers dry, hot summers and has only light snows in the winter.

A CITY OF PARTS

Approaching Turkey from western Europe, the traveler will find it convenient to visit Istanbul first. His steamer sails up the Sea of Marmara past Princes Islands, favorite summer resorts for the people of Istanbul. Moving into the Bosporus, a narrow passage which divides Istanbul, the traveler gets his first view of the city. On the shore to the right is Scutari, the Asiatic part of the city; while on the left, or west shore, is the European section. The latter in turn is divided into two parts by the curved inlet of the Bosporus called the Golden Horn. The nearest is the old Turkish section of Stambul. North, across the Golden Horn, is the commercial area, known as Galata, and above it on a hill is the European section called Pera. The steamer anchors in the Bosporus, and

Paul's Photos, Chicago
THE GOLDEN HORN OF CONSTANTINOPLE (ISTANBUL)
This body of water presents a particularly beautiful view during the sunset hour.

the traveler proceeds by tender to the city. Along the European shore is the Dolmabagché, the magnificent palace of the sultans, now open to the public. Above it on the hill is the Yildiz Kiosk, a smaller palace, used by the last sultans but now leased by the practical government to Europeans as a hotel.

NORTH OF THE HORN

It is convenient to inspect first the modern section. Here there is one very old structure—the Tower of Galata, built during the fourteenth century. Its foundations date back eight hundred years earlier. The steep, difficult climb up to it is rewarded by a view of the whole city stretched out below, with its innumerable domes and minarets, the Golden Horn gleaming in the sunlight, the blue waters of the Bosporus, and the Sea of Marmara, dotted with boats of all sizes. During the religious festivals, three circles of lights are hung around the balcony of each minaret; and from this tower the entire city appears to be a mass of twinkling lights.

From here one may drive on up to Pera, past the many foreign churches and schools, and those embassies which have not moved to Ankara. Among these many foreign buildings stands the structure which formerly housed the "whirling dervishes." In years past these men could be seen throughout the city, working them-

RAMPARTS OF THE CASTLE OF KUM-KALESI, IN THE DARDANELLES

selves up into a fury of devotion. Today their rites, like many practices of old Turkey, are prohibited by the government.

CONTRASTING COSTUMES

Having come down the hill, the traveler may cross the Galata bridge over the Golden Horn to Stambul. Across the bridge stream automobiles, street cars, and pedestrians. The attire of the people reflects the modernization program. Some are dressed in the smartest western European fashions. Many poorer men who cannot afford good clothes wear curious combinations of old trousers, badly fitting jackets, worn shirts, and battered hats. No longer does one see the colorful fez; because it was symbolic of the old order in Turkey, its use is now prohibited. Yet those people still faithful to Islam find hat brims inconvenient, since in praying they must touch the ground with their foreheads; so they wear either little brimless caps or sport caps with visors which can be turned back. Many of the poorer women still wear the old-fashioned black cotton *charshaf*, a sort of robe which covers them entirely and with its graceful folds conceals their ill-fitting, motley western dresses. One may even see peasant women from the country still veiling their faces, in spite of Ataturk's liberating order that permits them to go unveiled.

[138]

PART OF RESIDENTIAL SECTION OF ISTANBUL
From the center of this largest city and seaport of Turkey rises the noted Souleymanie Mosque.

STAMBUL'S MOST FAMOUS STRUCTURE

Having crossed the bridge, the traveler is in old Stambul. To the left, not far from the bridge, is the magnificent mosque of Santa Sophia completed by Justinian in 538 A.D. This is the third Santa Sophia constructed on the same site, the first two having been burned. Six years "of the labor of men and of angels," says the popular tradition, were required to build it. It is surrounded by many smaller-domed buildings. Its full glory is apparent after one has entered the vast church and stands under the great dome, which is one hundred and eighty feet high. On a pillar can be seen the bloody handprint of the Moslem conqueror who rode into the church in 1453, had the altar removed, and built minarets to transform the church into a Moslem temple. In various parts of the church are priceless mosaics depicting Christian scenes. Though many Moslems wished to destroy them, their ruler ordered them to be preserved and only plastered over. Parts of the mosaics showed through, however, and the present Turkish government has had the plaster removed. The mosque has been converted into a museum, in spite of the violent protest of the Moslems.

TURKEY

Nearby is the site of the Hippodrome, which was a vast amphitheater used primarily as a racecourse, but also for great public events. The amphitheater has crumbled away, and today only the remains of three monuments are to be seen.

MANY MOSQUES

At one side and partly covering the site of the Hippodrome is the Mosque of Ahmed I, famous because it is the only one with six minarets. At the time it was built, the Mosque at Mecca had six minarets, and the Moslems regarded Ahmed's structure as a sacrilegious imitation; so he added a seventh minaret at Mecca, and everyone was content. Though it is impossible to see all the mosques, one should not fail to see the mosque of Suleiman the Magnificent, on another hill of the city. Its dome is even larger than that of Santa Sophia, and it is believed by some to be the most beautiful and imposing of all Turkish mosques.

So stand the mosques throughout the city; and five times each day, as in centuries past, muezzins send out the call to prayer:

God is Great (5 times).
I testify that there is no God but God (twice).
Come to prayer.
Come to salvation.
God is Great; there is no other God but God.

Courtesy J. Bradford Pengelly
THE LITTLE AYA SOPHIA IN CONSTANTINOPLE, BUILT IN 444 A.D.

But even in this the hand of modern Turkish administration is seen; for the call is now given in Turkish instead of ancient Arabic, and it is heeded by the older generation only. Moslem religion is no longer compulsory, and the modern young people have rejected the faith of their fathers.

RICH TREASURES AND MEMORIES OF THE PAST

In contrast we may turn to the most romantic and colorful place of all—the old seraglio, palace of the sultan, situated on the cypress-covered point of the peninsula which separates the Bosporus and the Golden Horn. Crossing a square past an exquisite fountain, the traveler enters the main gate. To the right a road leads to the Imperial Ottoman Museum, which houses a treasured collection of bronzes, marble sculptures, tombs, and ancient Greek tablets. Privileged visitors may cross the court through a gate and go into the treasury. Through this gate in bygone days the sultan's enemies passed to be executed. The treasury contains fabulous jewels—the Persian throne of beaten gold, ornamented with emeralds and rubies; a golden tankard set with over three thousand diamonds; an emerald the size of a

Homer Smith photo, Chicago
SANTA SOPHIA AND SITE OF THE ANCIENT HIPPODROME
Santa Sophia in Constantinople, now a museum, was once a Turkish mosque, and before that a Christian church, built by the Emperor Justinian in 532-537.

TURKEY [141]

Paul's Photos, Chicago
GATES TO THE PALACE OF THE FORMER SULTANS
The palace faces east and borders the Bosporus for about one-third of a mile. As many as 700 persons lived there at one time.

hand; and figures of all the sultans who reigned from 1451 to 1839, each in his imperial robes and jewels.

Another cypress-lined road leads to the palaces of the harem—scene of romance, revelry, tragedy, and bloodshed. Here, too, only a privileged few may enter and view the quarters of the women and the throne room, which, decorated with beautiful arabesques, contains the magnificent golden throne.

SHOP AND SEE

Another feature which no one is willing to miss is the Grand Bazaar. Walking through the narrow, winding streets, many of which are covered by roofs, one may enjoy bargaining for rich silks, exquisite tables inlaid with mother-of-pearl, richly colored rugs and shawls, fine porcelain and brass ware, ivory and sandalwood ornaments, exotic perfumes, and fabulous jewels.

On a hill along the Bosporus, though not in the city itself, is the famous Robert College, founded by the Americans in 1863. Here nearly all the leaders of the Balkan nationalities were trained before the war; but since Ataturk's ascendancy, the school is educating the Turks themselves. Below Robert College is Roumeli Hissar, a massive castle built by Mohammed in preparation for the attack on Constantinople.

Paul's Photos, Chicago
NATIVE WOMEN OF TURKEY IN THE MARKET PLACE

One should drive out to the wall along the northwestern part of the city. Built from the Golden Horn to the Sea of Marmara, and in some places over one hundred feet high and two hundred feet thick, it protected Constantinople from the barbarians and Turks alike. At the central gate near a grove of cypresses the Turks entered, in 1453, because the defenders inside were too weak to resist. Only three times in sixteen centuries was it penetrated. From the wall can be seen other reminders of Turkey's past: the shell-scarred brown hills, where the Bulgarians crushed the Turks during the Balkan Wars.

BASILICA CISTERN

Other examples of defensive architecture are found in the underground cisterns built to supply the city with water in time of war. One, the great Basilica Cistern, may be entered through the courtyard of a Turkish house. It is three hundred and thirty-six feet long and one hundred and eighty-two feet wide. Its roof is supported by three hundred and thirty-six Corinthian columns, which are thirty-nine feet high and give it the atmosphere of a cathedral.

Despite its glories, Istanbul is rather sad. The practical, progressive measures of the present government have eliminated much of its glamour and mystery. When the new government was set up in Ankara, the center of Turkish affairs shifted there, and the population and prosperity of Istanbul declined. It is only natural that the traveler's interest should turn toward Anatolia, or Asiatic Turkey.

TO FLY?

Turkey has a new airline from Istanbul to Ankara, passing over Yaliva, a modern mineral-spring resort encouraged by Ataturk. It is located at the foot of Mount Olympus, which has recently become a center of winter sports. In this area also is the town of Bursa, center of the most passionately faithful Moslems. Ataturk subdued the inhabitants by choosing the town for the first reading of the Koran and the call to prayer in Turkish instead of Arabic. Many travelers prefer to travel by railroad rather than by airline, on the track built by the Germans as part of the Berlin to Bagdad project.

The first city of importance to be reached is Eskishehir, located in a wide valley surrounded by low hills. Trench lines and wrecked buildings remind us of the campaign in 1922 against the Greeks. This city keenly felt the loss of the shrewd Greek business men who constituted the main commercial class, but it is working to develop its own leaders. In this flat, mud-colored town, through which a muddy river flows, are such modern large-scale enterprises as an electric bakery and a huge sugar factory owned by the state. Here and there is a natural airdrome with a station of the air force and an aviation school. Near the city are a model farm and experimental station operated by the Ministry of Agriculture.

Most picturesque of all its activities, however, is the meerschaum industry. Here, in one of the few places in the world where meerschaum is found, it has been mined for nearly four hundred years. The industry has dropped off somewhat since the war, but one can still visit workshops where men sit on cushions, sorting and polishing the lumps of meerschaum. In the streets can be bought meerschaum cigarette holders and pipes, carved boxes, and novelties in the shape of roses or daisies.

CITY OF IZMIR

Continuing southwest by train, we reach the fascinating city of Izmir, formerly called Smyrna. As the train nears it, the rocky, mountainous country begins to give way to more fertile land, for Izmir is in the heart of the most productive part of Turkey. The largest city in Asia Minor, it ranks second only to Istanbul in the Turkish Republic.

Dating back to Greek times, when it was the center of the fame of Homer, it was an early stronghold of Christianity, until its capture by the Turks around 1400. Recently it was important as the scene of the war of the Turks against Greece. Here in 1922 the Turkish army crushed the Greeks and avenged the Greek massacre of the Turks thirteen years before. Three days later a disastrous fire broke out in the Armenian quarter, and for a week the sky and the harbor glowed red as the fire spread to the French and Greek sections, destroying one third of the city.

Today evidence of the tragedy can still be seen. Wreckage has been cleared, and some sections have been rebuilt; but there are still great, dusty open spaces, where hundreds of homes and business establishments once stood. So these scars are overshadowed by the beauties of the city. Leaving a street car at the waterfront, one looks out beyond the wooden barges and steamships to the bay, whose waters are a peculiar blue, reflecting the blue of the sky, almost lovelier than any blue ever seen. Turning to face the city, one sees along the curving shore a line of white buildings, the only ones in this section which survived the

Paul's Photos, Chicago

VIEW OF THE CITY OF IZMIR
The many pointed minarets crowning the city's mosques give the city a truly Mohammedan aspect.

fire. Behind, the city extends, spreading up the hill among cypress trees. Beyond, towering green and purple mountains provide a majestic background for the city.

FOREIGN FAIR GROUNDS

The traveler is abruptly brought back to earth by the realization that one of the white buildings is a motion picture theater, built, however, in harmony with the Turkish architecture of its surroundings. Even many of the modern business and apartment buildings, which have replaced the ones destroyed by the fire, have Turkish details around doors and windows. Some distance back from the waterfront is a large five-sided, wooden-fenced area, on which stand numerous large buildings. At the short side is a large gate, surmounted by high, square, white columns. This is the Izmir International Fair Grounds. The traveler fortunate enough to be here in September will enjoy visiting it, mingling with crowds of up-to-date city people and oddly dressed back-country folk, seeing the exhibits which proudly display Turkey's industrial and agricultural progress and the products of other nations as well.

In front of the Fair gate is the public square, nearly circular in shape, with trees, flower beds, grass plots, and benches. In the center, accessible by four broad walks at right angles leading in from each side is a huge statue of Kemal Pasha, the *Ghazi*, or Conqueror, as he is respectfully known. This statue is only one of hundreds to be seen throughout the country, a significant fact to one who would understand Turkey. The Koran, as does the Bible, forbids the making of an idol in the form of an image of God. Man is made in the image of God, therefore the making of statues or portraits of man was not permitted while Islam was the official religion. Since the grip of religion has been released such reproductions are permitted, and the *Ghazi* permits statues of himself because he feels that it helps to develop national unity and patriotism.

There are many other evidences of progress. Many playgrounds have been built throughout the city. One, as the natives proudly point out, has been converted from a graveyard. The city boasts a large library of books in the Turkish language. Both in the city and surrounding villages, we may visit progressive schools where, by books, posters, and exhibits, the children are instructed, and instilled with enthusiasm for their country.

INDUSTRY

Those interested in tobacco will enjoy visiting a tobacco factory, where piles of tobacco leaves are sorted, humidified and dried, and are then shipped to America for manufacture. In the city also is a depot where the raisins, for which this region is famous, are prepared for market. There are several cotton mills, where the hot, damp rooms are brightened by sprays of flowers placed near the looms.

Far more unpleasant is the tannery, where men are paid a relatively high wage, since they must endure a horrible odor, stand knee-deep in yellow water, and wash buffalo hides, which they run through huge rollers, or put in the metal boxes where they are left at least six months.

In contrast to these industrial scenes is the old Turkish quarter and the bazaars which survive or replace the ones destroyed by the great fire. Here a walk through the narrow, cobblestone streets reveals cool cobble houses, mosques, and white houses, whose overhanging bay windows protrude through acacia and wistaria trees. Occasionally one encounters a little square with a beautifully carved old fountain and luxuriant old trees. Tightly crammed in the bazaars are copper and enamelware, many kinds of rich, famous Smyrna rugs, pungent licorice, heaps of fruit, and bags of nuts. Attracted by the displays of fruits and sweets in the restaurant windows, one may overcome his astonishment at the array of fried sheep's heads and go in to eat typical Turkish food —soup of *yoghurt,* (a sour liquid made from milk, perhaps with green herbs and rice in it), stuffed vine-leaves, a green salad, or perhaps a green vegetable, or ladies' fingers, cocks' combs served with Madeira sauce, and rose-petal jam tarts. The simpler staple foods include eggs, bread, cheese, and figs; the latter are an important part of the diet of peasants, who attribute their long life to these foods.

SCENES IN THE COUNTRY

A pleasant drive may be made through the countryside, over modern paved roads, through villages whose white houses, schools, fences, and public buildings are spotlessly clean. The roads are lined with fields of grain, groves of olives, vineyards, and orchards of pears, peaches, pomegranates, quinces, and the figs for which Izmir is noted. Peasants work cheerfully in the fields, and

PEASANT HOME IN AN OLD TURKISH VILLAGE

at harvest time load the fruits in tubs and carry them into town in carts or on donkeys. Here dwell many of the Turks who have been brought from the Balkan countries.

Few evidences remain of the past history of Izmir because of the devastating earthquakes which have at least four times rocked the city. Floods, fires, and wars have done their part to reduce the city to dust. Outside the city, however, there still stands the Caravan Bridge, built over a hundred years before the birth of Christ, as part of a Roman highway. In this region also is Diana's Bath, a beautiful clear spring, which fills the city reservoir for the water supply. There remain also the ruins of several aqueducts, the oldest of which was built by the Romans in the third century B.C. to bring water from a source fifteen miles from the city. By another road from the city one passes the site of the theater, once a mighty structure seating twenty thousand people. Today there remain in the natural bowl only parts of the proscenium, or background of the stage, and the vaulted stone entrance into the orchestra.

MOUNT PAGUS

Above it on Mount Pagus are the great stadium, outlined in the sky, and, most notable of all, the ruins of the fortification, called the Castle. It is a conglomeration of Greek, Byzantine, and Turkish architecture, for the three empires successively used it over a period of two thousand years.

The trip up Mount Pagus is well repaid by the view itself. Around and below is a magnificent panorama: the rich green and gold of the orchards and fields; the city and the thirty-four-mile bay to the south; to the east the valley of the River Meles, rich in Homeric legend, the aqueducts, and Bridge of Caravans; to the north the lofty mountains, including Mount Olympus.

THE RUINS OF EPHESUS

Returning to the city, one may then make by train the fifty-mile trip to Ephesus. The aqueduct, along the drive from the station, is silhouetted against the sky, its high pillars still joined in some places to form huge arches. Within the city one finds here a pile of marble, there a crumbling wall, elsewhere red granite columns, a cluster of stones, or a single tall column, reflected in the tranquil waters nearby. These are the only remains of the glorious pagan temples, Christian churches, markets, and halls which made ancient Ephesus a city of great beauty. The ruins of the proscenium and before it the broken semicircle seats of stone, behind which juts a high hill, are all that remain of the theater, where once twenty-five thousand passionate people heard Demetrius, the silversmith, cry "Great is Diana of the Ephesians," condemning the new Christian religion, whose rise would end his profitable sale of silver images of Diana's temple. Even the colossal and handsome temple itself, one of the Seven Wonders of the World, whose imposing beauty awed the ancients, is today only a battered foundation sprinkled with heaps of marble. All these ruins are impressive yet mournful reminders of the glory of the past.

TURKEY [149]

THROUGH THE MOUNTAINS TO THE SOUTHEAST

Leaving the western coast, the traveler may next choose to turn to the southeastern section of Turkey. From the rich farming country he comes to plateaus and rugged mountains. Occasionally a little mud village is glimpsed, but for the most part are seen rocky, yellow peaks rising and falling sharply, sometimes dotted with scrubby, shrunken trees or underbrush and often completely barren. It is a relief to come suddenly from the Taurus mountains down into the valley with its principal city, Adana.

Down the mountains rush the rivers Seyhan and Ceyhan, carrying soil to the rich valley through which they quietly flow to the sea. So fertile is the valley that two crops can be grown in a season. Early in the summer it is a sea of green crops and yellow grain, to be succeeded later by the white fields of cotton. The fields and gardens are enhanced by innumerable bushes and trees: jasmine, oak, flowering oleanders and acacias, date, pomegranate, plane, and many kinds of fruit trees.

The city of Adana is the fourth largest in Turkey, with a population of about 73,000. Like most Turkish cities, it consists of an old section and a new one with ultra-modern apartment buildings, pylons in the modern manner, and paved streets. Most of the houses have flat roofs, on which the occupants set beds at

Paul's Photos, Chicago

RUINS OF THE AGORA (CENTRAL SQUARE) IN EPHESUS
Ruins of the once thriving city that was headquarters for the Apostles Paul and John.

night, for the climate is extremely hot. It is a very busy city, the center of the cotton industry, with many factories. Some of the equipment is fairly modern, and efforts are constantly made to improve methods of manufacture and of cotton-growing as well; while the labor conditions, already fair, are being improved.

During harvest time the scene is further enlivened by the crowds of agricultural laborers who come into the city from surrounding provinces, work for the farmers whose crops are too great to harvest without aid, and then leave the city once more. There is still room for improvement in the lot of both agricultural and industrial workers, but they are much better off now than a few years ago. The government is systematically and successfully fighting malaria; and the interested traveler may visit the stations where the people come for physical examination, as well as for advice in their business and family affairs.

TARSUS

Having seen the city and duly admired its greatest pride, the government packing-house, where all cattle must be slaughtered, the traveler may desire to turn to a smaller industrial section. Twenty-five miles west is Tarsus, which was a seaport until the deposits carried down by the rivers pushed the sea back several miles. It was a center of ancient commerce and culture, the scene of a victory of Alexander the Great, and the birthplace of Saint Paul. The modern city, however, shows little evidence of past glory, and its cotton mills attract only an economist or would-be expert desirous of studying industrial conditions.

THE FRUIT BOWL

More attractive to most people is Malatia, a city northeast of Adana. Once more the train climbs and winds through steep, rocky mountains of red and yellow and arrives in a beautiful valley.

The city is thirty-five miles west of the Euphrates River. The entire broad valley is watered by the river and its many tributary streams. Snow falls abundantly upon the tops of the surrounding mountains and, melting in the spring, assures sufficient moisture.

It is a perfect setting for agriculture; and one finds fields of wheat, corn, and melons, and vineyards loaded with tempting clusters of grapes. In vast orchards, the green leaves are mingled

TURKEY [151]

Paul's Photos, Chicago

TURKISH FISHERMEN'S HUTS

with the blue, red, and gold of plums and apricots, and later with apples, pears, cherries, mulberries, figs, and nuts. Even in the old section of the town of Malatia piles of stone and crumbling minarets, sadly reminding the observer of happier days, are interspersed with green bushes, acacia and mulberry trees, and flaming poppies, grown for opium production. Here, as in Adana, one encounters progressive schools and a branch of the Ministry of Agriculture, which advocates modern methods of production and by experiment seeks improved varieties of fruits. With all due respect to the prophets of progress, however, one feels that he will remember not the technical advancement, but the sheer beauty, color, fertility, and wealth of the smiling valley.

UP INTO THE PLATEAU

Northwest of Malatia is the old town of Sivas. A railway is being constructed between the two towns; but until it is finished one must travel by bus. Many travelers may prefer to return to Adana and then go north by rail, rather than undergo the rough motor trip. In any case, a visit to Sivas is worth the effort, for it is a typical and important upland city, of about thirty-five thousand. To reach it one must travel through long stretches of plateau, where the dry, stony ground grows only scant brown and gray grass, bushes, and stunted, scrubby oaks. The countryside is occasionally broken by flocks of sheep, or by a village of flat-roofed huts made of mud bricks or slabs. The people in these regions practically obtain their livelihood from their sheep, using the meat and milk for food and the wool and hides for clothing and other needs.

Around Sivas is a fertile grain area, watered by the Kizil Irmak (Red River), the largest of Asia Minor's streams and, like most of them, not navigable. The city is dotted with beautiful poplars and willows, while the parkway between the two broad lanes of the main road is planted with flourishing young trees. There are, as in other cities, signs of modern activity. The railway station is a plain structure such as one may see in many American towns. Many of the buildings are modern structures, with a suggestion of Turkish architecture only in the brightly colored decorations around doors and windows.

Most of the buildings are constructed with sun-dried, white-washed brick on a wood framework, with the second floor overhanging, and topped by a red-tile room. Some are surrounded by beautiful gardens, shaded by pine trees. In the old town, picturesque bullock carts thread their way through the bazaars, where one may purchase the customary Turkish wares. There is a separate market for each important product; thus, wood, grain, livestock, and the various handwork are sold in different places. Added to the customers and pedestrians are street vendors of fruits, sweets, and drinks.

Not in use, but exquisitely beautiful, is the old mosque of the Seljuks, for this city was a center of the old Seljuk empire. It has the lacy ornamentation of curved lines, caligraphy, and flowers, which constitute Moslem art because of the prohibition of representing human faces or bodies. Distinctive are the blue tiles set into the minaret, of an exquisite hue and durability which cannot be reproduced, for the secret has been lost.

IN THE MOUNTAINS

Northeast of Sivas is an area which can be visited only by special permission, because it is a military zone. The railway is still under construction, and one must travel by bus through dry, yellow mountain-country and tableland, looking down more than five thousand feet into the valley through which winds the Euphrates River. For about nine months of the year it is winter here, with low temperatures. During the short hot summer, one will see vast fields of wheat, for parts of the upland are so fertile that two crops can be raised in a season. In the valley below, the climate is so mild that olives and grapes grow abundantly.

In the vicinity of Erzingan, the first town of importance to be reached, the mulberry trees of the new silk industry have replaced the swampy rice fields which were drained by the government in the interest of good health. In the town itself, which is similar to Sivas in appearance, the majority of its twenty thousand people are Armenians; but in view of the present intense nationalism, they all claim to be pure Turks.

Continuing eastward past the town of Ilica, which is noted locally for its mineral springs, the road next leads to another Armenian town of Erzurum, about the same size as Sivas. It has a similar Seljuk mosque, unfortunately in a bad state of decay. There is a combination of modern buildings (such as the military hospital) and older houses constructed of volcanic stones and mud, with beamed roofs to resist the force of frequent earthquakes. The three circles of earthworks around the city indicate its military nature. Formerly it was also a commercial center, with thousands of camels bringing produce. Since the war it has declined; but the new road running through it, which is to link the Black Sea port of Trebizond with distant Persia, is expected to revive it.

Farther on is Kars, an important frontier town and cattle market as well. Situated near the Russian border, it has many Russian citizens, whose national costumes add color to the street scenes. These people are well received, for their nation has supplied Turkey with much practical and technical aid, though the political tenets of communism are rejected by the Turks.

From Kars the road turns northwest toward the sea, through the rather small, plain town of Ardahan; through more rocky, snow-capped mountains, where live the fierce Kurds, whose resistance has forced the government to deal severely with them; then into wooded country, where the green of the rich foliage affords a pleasing sight to the eye; and finally down to the Black Sea port of Hopa. From here one may take a steamer westward to Samsun; or one may come up to Samsun from Sivas by train and take a short boat trip along the coast.

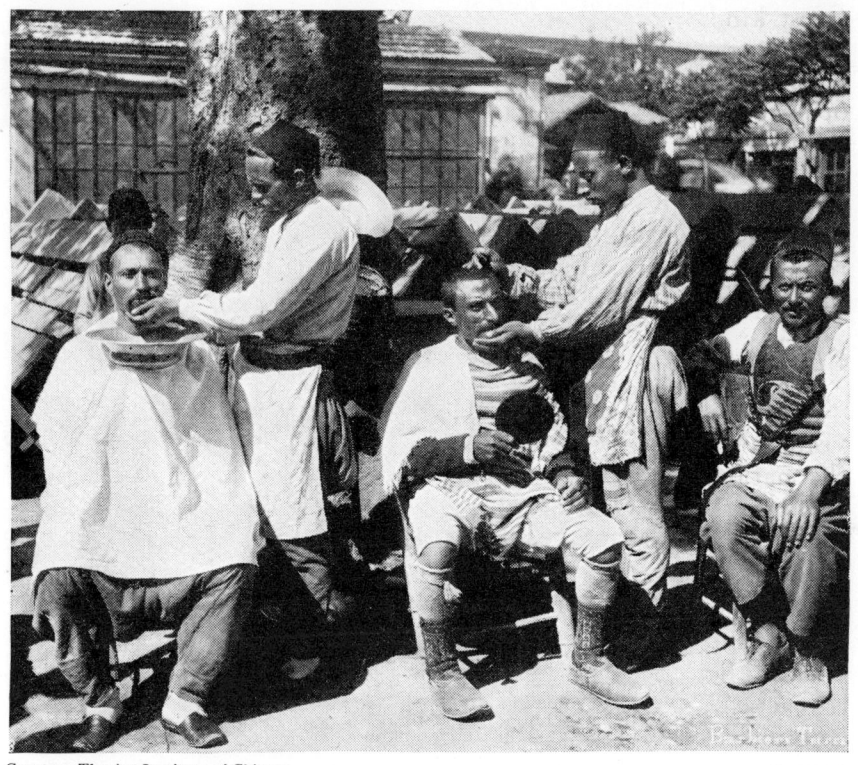

Courtesy The Art Institute of Chicago
"A LITTLE TONIC, SIR?"
Turkish street barbers plying their trade.

THE NORTHERN COAST

In either case, the trip is enjoyable if the Black Sea is not in the midst of one of its fierce storms. All along the Black Sea coast are densely wooded hills of pine and oak, against whose dark rich green, the pink and white houses and mosques of an occasional town stand out invitingly. Occasionally, narrow strips of cultivated land are seen along the shore. The towns, with a few boats in the blue waters of the harbor, are almost all alike in their calm, undisturbed appearance. Zonguldak, a town west of Samsun, the center of the coal area, is an exception; for its cranes and loading devices give it a more industrial appearance. East of Samsun, are the towns of Giresun and Trebizond, around which is the hazelnut area. Thousands of trees produce tons of hazel nuts of the finest kind. Samsun itself is the most important Black Sea port. The center of the tobacco industry of the north, it possesses a government-owned factory which is old but well equipped and operated chiefly by women, who profit by woman's emancipated position under the new regime.

A drive around the city reveals modern five-story apartment houses, large warehouses, and wide-paved streets; but there remain also charming cobblestone streets, with white houses surrounded by beautiful gardens of carnations, roses, and honeysuckle.

CENTER OF TURKEY

It is impossible to linger here longer, for there is still to be visited Ankara, capital of Turkey and center of the new life of the nation. On the train trip to the capital one may stop at Kayseri, the site of a new textile plant. In the midst of a dusty plain rise not only modern factory buildings, but the necessary residences and public halls as well. Here the workers are trained in early youth, free of the prejudices of their elders, to work efficiently and lead in the progress of their country.

Another train ride through the dry plateau, and at last Ankara is reached. It rises out of virtually desert country, a tribute to its builders, who drained the swamps, brought water from a lake, constructed buildings, laid out parks, and planted trees. There is, of course, an old city, with a crumbling fort, old Roman temple, old mosque, bazaars, and narrow streets; and the new city was erected just below the old town. Along its wide, tree-lined streets are large government buildings, apartment houses, and residences. Those which have the arched doors and windows, balconies, columns, little towers, and decorations, were built while there was yet a feeling that there should be a Turkish note to modern architecture. A glorious example of this type is the Ethnographical Museum, particularly its portico with exquisite columns and graceful, slightly pointed arches. But many of the latest buildings are completely modern in every detail.

Ankara is a busy city, with much building construction going on, and its buildings are studied and copied by architects for other cities. An important education program goes on here in the Halk Evi (People's House). A community center is sponsored in every important Turkish town, as well as in the capital, by Ataturk's

National Republican Party. Here organized recreation, athletics, and education are provided for all people. There is an important professional school, where girls learn dressmaking and millinery, following the latest Parisian styles; while young men at the agricultural school, the hospital staff schools, and similar institutions have the latest technical training in various fields. Everywhere signs are printed in the European alphabet, which Ataturk has introduced.

Most important of all in Ankara are the headquarters of Ataturk, the moving spirit of all Turkish activity. Recalling the progressive movements he has seen in all sections of the country, the traveler feels that all have drawn their inspiration from this city. On the other hand, when he remembers the vast stretches of poor, mountainous country populated by backward people, he wonders how long it will be before the advanced methods taught at Ankara will spread through the country. Yet he feels sure that the spirit of the Turkish people, which has transformed many towns from crumbling masses of decay to busy, prosperous, colorful cities, will not rest until its work is completed.

Paul's Photos, Chicago

A MODERN HOTEL IN ANKARA

PALESTINE

A STREET IN JERUSALEM
Men of many nations have trod the streets of this famed old Holy Land city.

PALESTINE, the home of the ancient Israelites, is bounded on the north by Syria, on the southwest by Egypt, on the west by the Mediterranean, on the east by the Jordan River and the Dead Sea. It is about two hundred and forty miles long and varies in width from thirty to forty-five miles, with an area of 10,100 square miles. It has a population of more than one million.

A maritime plain runs along the Mediterranean shore; and the mountain region, paralleling the plain, forms the second natural division of Palestine. The mountains of this region are mainly chalk formations. Caves abound in many parts of Palestine. The best known are the chalk caves at Beit Jibrin, the cave of the Twins in the land associated with the stories of Samson, the Cave of Elijah on Mount Carmel, Kharetum near Bethlehem, and the famous salt cave in Mount Sodom. The Dead Sea valley is unique in its position on the earth's lowest surface, lying three hundred and ninety-four meters below the level of the Mediterranean Sea. Throughout Palestine there are tells, or mounds, beneath which are buried ancient cities. In Tel el Hesy eleven consecutive cities have been unearthed. More than a dozen other such sites have been excavated.

The coastal zone of Palestine has a sub-tropical climate; the mountains have a milder, continental climate; the region of the Jordan Valley and Dead Sea is tropical. Thus the coastal plain is best for the growing of citrus fruits. Mountainsides are terraced to allow agriculture. In the plain of Sharon wheat and barley are grown; and tropical fruits and vegetables flourish in the Jordan Valley.

THE MEETING PLACE OF CULTURES

Palestine's location on the caravan route between Egypt and Syria made it a bone of contention in ancient times. It was seldom free except during the time of the kingdom of the Israelites. It was the meeting place of all the cultures of the Mediterranean world. After possession by the Jews, it was held by the Byzantine Empire, the Moslems, the Seljuk Turks, the Crusaders, the Mongols, and from 1516 to 1918 by the Turks. During the World War it was conquered by Lord Allenby for the allies and was allotted to Great Britain as a mandate by the League of Nations.

The population of Palestine may be divided into three religious groups: Jewish, Christian, and Moslem. Large groups have come in from the Mediterranean countries, and the Jewish immigration has greatly increased. Palestine, with the recent immigration, may become the industrial center of the Near East.

JERUSALEM: THE HOLY CITY

Jerusalem, the capital of Palestine, stands on two rocky hills, Mount Zion and Mount Moriah, 2,500 feet above sea-level. It is a sacred city to Jews, Christians, and Mohammedans. It is quadrangular and is surrounded by a sixteenth-century wall with eleven gates. Only six of these gates are open. David and Damascus are the two main thoroughfares. Within the walls there are four sections: Christian, Mohammedan, Armenian, and Jewish.

The story of Jerusalem is one of warfare. David captured the city and made it the capital of his kingdom. The city had a glorious era under Solomon, who built the great Temple of Solomon on Mount Moriah and fortified the city. A series of invasions by Egyptians, Arabians, and Babylonians left it in ruins. Centuries

Black Star photo By Fritz Henle

ENTRANCE TO THE PLACE OF THE TEMPLE, JERUSALEM

THE DAMASCUS GATE
Called the handsomest of all the entrances to the city of Jerusalem, the Damascus Gate is comparatively modern, having been built by a Mohammedan caliph about 300 years ago on foundations of unknown age.

later Herod erected beautiful buildings and reconstructed the temple and fortifications. Events of Christ's life in Herod's reign were to make Jerusalem the Holy City of the Christian world. Sanctified by the onetime presence of holy men, it is visited by pilgrims, tourists, and students. A beautiful view of Jerusalem and the surrounding countryside may be had from Mount Olivet. One can look down upon the little town of Bethlehem, with its Church of the Nativity, the pool of Bethesda, the Mount of Offence, the Hill of Evil Council, the mountains of Moab, the river Jordan, and the Dead Sea.

Bethlehem, the birthplace of Jesus Christ and of King David and the Ephratah of the history of Jacob, is now a small village of white-stone houses, six miles south of Jerusalem. The population, about three thousand, is wholly Christian: Latin, Greek, and Armenian. The Convent of the Nativity is a large, square building, built by the Empress Helena in 327 A. D., destroyed by the Moslems in 1236, and restored by the Crusaders.

Within the convent is the Church of the Nativity, which is built on the site where Christ was born in a manger. When repairs and additions were needed on the church, they were made in the style of the time the work was done; thus, those repairs of the sixteenth century were by the Greeks, while others made in the nineteenth were by the Latins. When the Moslems conquered the country, they sealed all of the doors and allowed the Christians to cut only one small hole in the walls, in order that the hundreds of thousands of pilgrims who yearly pass through this portal would have to stoop and bow low and thus appear to show the proper reverence. There are tombs of saints and holy men inside this church. Originally the church belonged entirely to the Greek Orthodox Church; but the Roman Catholic, the Armenian or Gregorian, the Coptic, and the Abyssinian all have succeeded in gaining entrance and setting up altars and shrines. The nave, which is by far the finest part of the building, belongs to the Armenians, and is supported by forty-eight Corinthian columns of solid granite. At the crossing of the transept a long passage descends to the Grotto of the Nativity, a crypt where it is said Christ was born. From the grotto there is access to the tombs of Eusebius of Cremona (died 422), Paula (died 404) and Jerome (died 420), and to the cell (now a chapel) where St. Jerome made his translation of the Scriptures.

In Jerusalem the Church of the Holy Sepulcher was built at the place where it is claimed that Christ was crucified. It is a religious museum and contains a number of relics accepted as

Paul's Photos, Chicago

THE MOUNT OF OLIVES AND JUDEAN HILLS

INTERIOR OF THE CHURCH OF THE HOLY SEPULCHER, JERUSALEM

sacred. Inside the church is the Stone of Unction, where Christ was placed to be annointed for burial. Closeby is the shrine known as the Chapel of the Parted Raiment, where the Roman soldiers threw dice for His clothes. The Chapel has been recognized as the property of the Armenians for six hundred years. The most impressive architectural feature of the church is the Chapel of the Holy Sepulcher. Many pilgrims kiss the marble slab under which they believe Jesus is buried.

ANOTHER VERSION

Outside of Jerusalem proper there is a hill which is called the Protestant Calvary, the New Calvary, the True Calvary, or Gordon's Calvary. This is where all but the older sects believe Christ was crucified. It is the only important elevation near the north walls. It is known amongst the Jews as the Place of Stoning. Nearby is a cavern known as the Garden Tomb, which is believed to be the actual place where Christ was buried. Nearby is the Latin Garden of Gethsemane, while in another part of the city is the Greek version of the same place.

THE DOME OF THE ROCK

The most holy place in Jerusalem for the Mohammedans is the Mosque of Omar, also called the Dome of the Rock. The graceful dome of the building rests on an octagonal base which is covered with decorations carved into the rich green marble. The Rock, which is sheltered by this mosque, is said to be the place where Mohammed offered his last prayers before he went to heaven and is said to be marked with his footprints. The Rock, fifty-seven feet long and forty-three feet wide, is surrounded by a high railing, and no one is allowed to go inside this railing.

The floor of the Dome of the Rock is made of beautiful tiles which also serve as the ceiling of the great cavern below. There is a story that through one of these tiles Mohammed drove a certain number of nails, which work themselves through the tile and fall into the cavern below; and when all have gone through, then the end of the world will be at hand. As there are only three of the nails left, one is cautioned to walk quietly and give some money for the preservation of the temple in order to postpone the catastrophe that is awaiting all.

The ground on which the Dome of the Rock is built is known as the Temple Area and is the imposing spot from which one may view all of Jerusalem and much of the surrounding country. This is the place where Solomon built his temple, some of the walls of which are still standing. Inasmuch as it is revered by Jews, Christians, and Moslems alike and through the centuries has belonged to all of these religious groups at one time or another, it, in a sense, can be considered as "the holiest place in the world." Certainly the Jews consider it so.

At one end of the Temple Area is the Mosque of El Aksa, the principal mosque of Jerusalem. This one-time Christian church is the largest individual structure in the city. Although the exterior is bare, the interior is attractively decorated and contains some ancient marble columns which are said to have come from the temple of Herod. Below the mosque are huge caverns cut in the solid rock, which are known as the stables. They were probably originally used as granaries for the great temple of Solomon

Black Star photo   By Fritz Henle
THE WALL OF TEARS IN JERUSALEM

erected there. At the time that Solomon built the temple on Mount Moriah he also fortified the city with high, thick walls, parts of which are still standing at the southwest corner of Jerusalem. They are dear to the hearts of the Jews and are known as the Wailing Wall. Here the Jews come to wail and to pray for the return of the temple, Jerusalem, and Palestine to their people.

One cannot set foot within the country and not feel close to the days described in the Bible. Whether Christ was crucified on precisely this spot, or born in that exact spot, at least it is certain that those events happened fairly close at hand. And it is possible to picture in the mind the same country overrun by Persian, Assyrian, and Egyptian conquerors; adopted later as the home of the Jews after they escaped from Egypt; conquered in turn by Greeks, Romans, Byzantines, and Arabs; the scene of noble and heroic struggles between the crusaders and their Moslem enemies; ruled by the terrible Turks for four centuries; and finally redelivered into Christian hands in 1917 by the British soldiers of General Allenby. Even today it is the site of struggles among Christians, Jews, and Moslems.

Although Jerusalem is really cosmopolitan in character its outward aspects are those of a small town. The houses are exactly as they were in the Middle Ages; especially in the crowded parts of the city. Out of the houses and through the lanes walk Arabs in bright robes and red fezzes, Jews in dark robes and black derbies, with curls hanging down from their heads, and Christians variously dressed. They patronize stores which are little holes in the walls and open bazaars in which the goods are made by hand before their eyes. They go down the very street through which Christ may have walked when He carried His cross, past

Black Star photo By Oscar Marcus
JERUSALEM UNIVERSITY ON MOUNT SCOPUS

THE VALLEY OF JEHOSHAPHAT NEAR JERUSALEM
The site of the Garden of Gethsemene is supposed to be within its confines.

the house where Pontius Pilate lived, and around the quarry from which came the stones for Solomon's temple.

Outside the walls, but still within Jerusalem or its suburbs, are such institutions as the English, German, Italian, and Jewish hospitals; the Jewish, Syrian, Arabic, and Christian orphanages; the Jewish, Moslem, Catholic, Armenian, Coptic, Protestant, and Abyssinian cemeteries; the Greek colony; the German colony; the Russian compound; the Scottish hospice; and the Franciscan, Benedictine, Greek, and Russian monasteries. Each sect seems to be represented by at least one edifice. There are various foreign schools for research, an archaeological museum, and a Hebrew university. The population, approximately a hundred thousand, is increasing. A teachers' training school for men and also one for women have been established.

OVER THE HILLS TO JERICHO

The way to Jericho, a city of the Canaanites, is exactly the same road by which Christ went down from Jerusalem to Jericho. It leads past Gethsemane; over the Mount of Olives to Bethany, the home of Martha and Mary and the supposed site of Lazarus' tomb and the house of Simon the Leper; and past the spot where stood the Good Samaritan Inn, and Quarantania, the mountain of the forty days' temptation. On the way is Wadi el-Hod, formerly known as the Apostles' Spring, where the Lord and His apostles drank. From here the road goes down, down; for we are descending to the Dead Sea, which is thirteen hundred feet below sea-level. Here the countryside is of the desert type, bare and rocky, with no signs of human habitation, except the few Greek monasteries perching on the tops of isolated mountains or clinging to the sides of steep bluffs.

When the Jews returned from their captivity, they wanted Jericho, once their city, for their own. As it was surrounded by high walls and they had no machines of war with which to destroy them, they resorted to another plan. According to the Old Testament, they merely walked around the walls, in silence, seven times and then gave seven tremendous blasts on their trumpets, and lo! the walls were as a heap of dirt. And that is the condition in which we find ancient Jericho today, just a high mound. Excavations conducted in recent years have brought to light remains of the Canaanite city, as well as remains of later cities built above them. However, the new city of Jericho is modern and attractive and has possibilities as a winter resort.

THE RIVER JORDAN

Beyond Jericho is probably the most famous river in Christendom, the Jordan. It is not an especially beautiful stream, but it is the river in which Christ was baptized by John the Baptist. Parts of the valley are fertile, due to the overflow during the rainy season. Papyrus, rice, and cereals are produced in this region. Every year thousands of pilgrims of the Greek Orthodox faith come from afar to be baptized in the famous waters, a privilege highly regarded since the days of Constantine the Great. The Jordan is formed by the junction of two other streams and carries heavy deposits from its banks. The river's sources are in northern Syria and it runs south for some two hundred miles to empty its muddy load into the Dead Sea.

A LONELY SPOT ON THE RIVER JORDAN

BELOW SEA-LEVEL

The Dead Sea is very aptly named. The strong odor is detected long before the sea itself is in sight. As a matter of fact, it is not a sea but a fairly large lake, forty-seven miles long and three to nine miles wide. However, it is a very unusual lake because it has a surface level thirteen hundred feet below the level of the Mediterranean, while the deepest point of its bottom is thirteen hundred and ten feet below its surface, or twenty-six hundred and ten feet below sea-level. Its second peculiar feature is that its water contains about twenty-five per cent of solid substances in solution, the greatest part of which is salt. The Greek Orthodox Monastery of St. John the Baptist is a point of interest in this desolate area.

TO THE NORTH

The pilgrim who wishes to visit the north of Palestine will retrace his steps from the Dead Sea, through Jericho and back to Jerusalem. From there he will follow a route to Syria along which the pages of his Bible seem to turn before him. Bethel, Mount Ephraim, Mount Ebal, Samaria, Nablus (ancient Shechem), the plain of Dothan, the Fountain of Jezreel, the plains of Esdraelon, Nazareth, the Sea of Galilee with its towns of Tiberias and Capernaum—all of these places, familiar in stories from his childhood, will gradually unfold as realities before his

Paul's Photos, Chicago

SPRING OF THE APOSTLES ON THE ROAD TO JERICHO

eyes. His route takes him through a land fairly filled with biblical names, such as: Mount Scopus; Mizpeh, where the watchtower of Benjamin stood; Bethel, where Abram and Lot beheld the plain, and where the younger son of Isaac fled from his brother Esau; Shiloh, where Joshua, Samuel, and Eli lived; and the Well of Jacob, which has been tended these many centuries by the Samaritans.

SAMARIA

Samaria is a division of Palestine, situated north of Judea. This was the country in which ten tribes rebelled, raised their independent state, and formed the kingdom of Israel, in contradistinction to that of Judah, embracing the two tribes of Judah and Benjamin. They established a dynasty of their own, with Jeraboam as their first king. So deadly was the animosity that existed between these two Jewish nations, that, from the time of their severance to the time of captivity of Israel, an almost perpetual state of warfare existed.

The city of Samaria, capital of the kingdom, was situated on a hill, Mount Sameron. This city was founded by Omri, and from that time till its overthrow by the Assyrians it was the residence of all the kings of Israel. It was subsequently restored by Herod, who called it Sebaste. During recent excavations the palace of Omri, foundations of a city gate with a tower on either side, remnants of Ahab's famous ivory palace, a forum, and a senate house were discovered. Ancient tiles bearing Hebrew texts inscribed were also found.

Samaritans, a mixed people, inhabit this region. They consisted partly of the tribes of Ephraim and Manasseh left in Samaria by the King of Assyria, when he carried their brethren away captive; and partly of Assyrian colonists. On the return of the Jews from captivity they declined to associate with the Samaritans, though united with them in religion. The latter attempted to prevent the Jews from building the temple at Jerusalem; and, failing at this, they built a temple on Mount Gerizim exclusively for their own worship. The Samaritans have dwindled to the smallest ethnic group in the world, numbering less than two hundred. They live in Nablus (Shechem) near Mount Gerizim, where once their temple stood. They still observe the paschal

CATTLE OPERATING WATERWHEEL IN PALESTINE

sacrifice. Each year they ascend to Mount Gerizim, where they pitch tents, sacrifice seven lambs (one for each Samaritan family), and remain throughout the Passover festival. Their existence is threatened by dearth of marriageable women, which has led to their lifting the ban on intermarriage with Jews, though not with Moslems. The Samaritans speak and write Aramaic as well as Arabic.

GALILEE

Galilee was a Roman province, comprising all of the northern part of Palestine west of the Jordan. The word Galilee was first applied to a fragment of Naphtali, constituting its northern portion. It was chiefly inhabited by Gentiles. In New Testament times the word had a more extended meaning, and we learn from Josephus that there were an Upper and a Lower Galilee. The Sea (or Lake) of Galilee was called also in the New Testament by the names of Lake of Gennesaret and Sea of Tiberias; and in the Old Testament by the name of Sea of Chinnereth, or Cinnerath. It is a large lake in the north of Palestine, lying 626 feet below

Paul's Photos, Chicago
A STREET IN NAZARETH, DEVOTED TO DYEING CLOTH

sea-level, thirteen miles long, and six miles broad, and 820 feet deep. It occupies the bottom of a great basin and is undoubtedly of volcanic origin. In the time of Jesus the surrounding region was the most densely populated in Galilee; now even its fisheries are almost entirely neglected. The water of the lake is clear and beautifully reflects the varying atmospheric changes.

Ancient Nazareth, the home of Jesus, is in the district of Galilee. It is eleven hundred feet above sea-level and is built partly on the sides of rocky ridges. The first Christian pilgrimage to it was made in the sixth century. The principal building at Nazareth is the Latin Convent, on the supposed scene of the Annunciation; but the Greeks also have erected on another spot a church in commemoration. The traveler is shown also a Latin chapel, affirmed to be built over the workshop of Joseph; the chapel of "the Table of Christ," a vaulted chamber, containing the table at which Jesus and His disciples ate; and the synagogue out of which He was thrust by His townsmen. The Virgin's Well is in the upper part of the town. There is also a Protestant mission and orphanage, Greek and Latin churches, a Scotch and a German hospital, and a Bible depot. The population is well over eight thousand. It is now, as in ancient times, a quiet, rural community. All of Palestine may be seen from the outlook on the hill. The three sacred mountains, Tabor, Hermon, and Carmel may be seen from this hill. Cana, in Galilee, where Jesus performed his first miracle, is a few miles northeast of Nazareth, on a ridge of tableland.

There are other interesting towns in Galilee. Two of them are Tiberias and Magdala. Tiberias, on the eastern coast of the Sea of Galilee, has about ten thousand people, mostly Jews. Here are convents, Jewish synagogues, the Free Church of Scotland mission station, the modern Hotel Tiberias, and hot springs. Magdala has only a few mud huts and some underground ruins. This was the town of Mary Magdalen.

HAIFA

Haifa, once a sleepy village of mud huts, has now grown to be the third most important city in Palestine, with a population of eighty thousand. It has the only good harbor along the eastern Mediterranean coast and serves as a British naval base. There are railroad connections with Damascus and other important points. Haifa is the terminus of the pipe line from Iraq, which carries oil from Kirkuk, north of Bagdad, for six hundred and forty miles across rivers, desert, and mountains. From Haifa the oil is shipped to other parts of the world.

AN ALL-JEWISH CITY

South of Haifa, and on the coast, thirty-three miles northwest of Jerusalem, is the port of Jaffa. Unlike Haifa, it is a city of biblical times and still contains houses which are supposed to have been occupied by biblical characters. It was here that Peter had his vision. The place, which had been destroyed by Vespasian, became a bishop's see, under Constantine. It was the landing

Paul's Photos, Chicago
SABBATH IN TEL-AVIV, PALESTINE
Commercial activity ceases at the sound of the ram's horn.

place of the Crusaders and was taken and retaken by Christians and Moslems. In 1799 Napoleon stormed it and massacred the prisoners of war. In 1832 it was taken by Mohammed Ali and restored to the Turks by British help. It was taken by the British in 1917. The modern Jaffa is a port of entry for pilgrims to Jerusalem, and has a population of about sixty-five thousand. Fruits, chiefly oranges, are exported.

Jaffa is, however, completely overshadowed by the city which lies immediately to the north of it, Tel Aviv, the only wholly Jewish city in the world. Before 1901, the site upon which Tel Aviv now stands was nothing more than waste land covered with sand dunes. But the unceasing vigilance and courage of the Jews

PALESTINE [175]

who wanted a city of their own caused it to grow until by 1910 it had 550 inhabitants; by 1926, 38,000 inhabitants; and by 1935, 130,000 inhabitants, one-third of the entire Jewish population in Palestine.

Many of the Jews who settled here lived originally elsewhere in Palestine; but most of them came from different parts of the world at the call of the Zionist movement. At last the Jews have a home of their own. They have purchased the best land in the country and have become good farmers and laborers. Palestine oranges, raised by the Jews, are famous throughout the world. This agricultural region is now the supply center for new Jewish communities in interior Palestine. Their astounding success, coupled with their ever increasing immigrations to Palestine, and their ability to buy all the fertile land has enraged the slow-moving Arabs, who consider Palestine their country. This accounts for the animosity between these two Semitic peoples.

Paul's Photos, Chicago

A CARAVAN ON THE ROAD TO BETHLEHEM
A camel caravan carrying freight exactly as it was carried in the time of Christ.

[176] UNIVERSITY OF KNOWLEDGE

Black Star photo   By Dr. Martin Hurlimann

RUINS OF ANCIENT BAALBEK, LEBANON, SYRIA

SYRIA

Courtesy The Art Institute of Chicago

MOSQUE OF WALID THE GREAT MOSQUE IN DAMASCUS

AFTER CROSSING the deep blue waters of the Sea of Galilee and the town of Tiberias on its shores, we soon approach the international border into Syria. Although the country does not differ geographically from Palestine, and the people of the two countries look and dress much the same, we immediately notice one particular difference. Palestine is a mandate of Great Britain, and the soldiers are Britishers. Syria, however, is a mandate of France; and the soldiers are an odd mixture of Siamese, Singalese, Arabs, Berbers, and a few Frenchmen, mostly officers. France keeps a large army here by necessity, because the Arabs and the Druses are constantly on the verge of revolt.

FIRE WORSHIPERS

As we enter southern Syria, we are near Jebel Druse, the mountain of the Druses. The Druses are a wild and fanatical Moslem sect who are said to hold many practices connected with ancient religions, such as worshiping fire. The Druse men are tall, strong, and fierce of eye, and have probably started more

[178]

THE EAST GATE OF DAMASCUS
Courtesy The Art Institute of Chicago

massacres and revolts than any other sect of similar size. They hate the French especially. This section of the Syrian countryside is an endless succession of stony wastes and barren mountainsides. Now and again the picture is broken by the appearance of a small Syrian village, its whitewashed houses bearing roofs with pointed domes. As we cross the last range of mountains we come upon Damascus, a city the like of which Palestine cannot boast. There it is—a green gem, flecked with the white of minarets and surrounded by the drab brown of the barren desert. This is the city which was so much like heaven that Mohammed would not let himself remain in it; the city that was famous at the time the Persian hordes were storming the gates of Athens. Many claim it is the oldest city in the world.

But where is the Damascus of old? Where is the great city of the Greeks and the Roman days? Where is the proud city that the Arabs admired so much that they made it the capital of their vast empire? Now the hills surrounding the city fairly bristle with French cannon. Although the French are making efforts to change this city of the East into a small Paris, the city is still predominately eastern. Yet one no longer finds the famous bazaars in which the mighty steel of Damascus used to be sold. Gone are the days when Saladin could cut off a hundred heads with his sword of this famous steel.

Despite all of these changes, however, Damascus is still one of the most fascinating cities of the Near East. It is still the home of the Omayyad Mosque, the tomb of Saladin, and some interesting bazaars. Here also a guide will point out the Street Called Straight, the wall where St. Paul was let down in a basket, and the house of Ananias. Damascus has always been a commercial city. We can see the great khans, the combination hotels, stables, and storehouses, that were used in the past centuries in the trade that passed from east to west through the city. These khans are descendants of the buildings used four or five thousand years ago when Damascus was trading with Central Asia and China and when Egypt was still a young nation. Here pilgrims would stable their camels and spend the night when they were on their way to Mecca to visit the tomb of Mohammed and to kiss the holy Kaaba. Now these venerable buildings, much in need of repair, house modern motor cars.

THE OMAYYAD MOSQUE

The most spectacular sight in Damascus is the Omayyad Mosque, one of the oldest and, outside of Jerusalem and Constantinople, the grandest of all Mohammedan temples. Like the great mosques in Jerusalem and Constantinople, it was once a Christian church. Probably the original structure on this site was a pagan temple. That was replaced by a church dedicated to John the Baptist. Then, when the Moslems took the city and changed the church to a mosque, they kept the same name. It is said that the head of John the Baptist is buried under the central court. When the mosque was restored and beautified, like the Mosque of Mohammed Ali in Cairo, Christian Greek architects were called from Constantinople to do the work. They decorated it with pillars of the rarest marble, adorned the ceiling and walls with semi-precious stones and lavish mosaics, and lighted the whole structure with six hundred golden lamps hung from the dome and the ceiling. It was so wonderful that the people of the Middle Ages believed that genii had helped in the construction. Unfortunately two disastrous fires, one in 1069 and another in 1893, destroyed much of the beauty.

Courtesy The Art Institute of Chicago
TEMPLE OF BACCHUS AT BAALBEK

The Moslems have decorated the walls with Kufic writings, which are all in golf leaf and tell the story of the Koran. Another interesting bit of lettering is over the door of the original church, which now stands near the center of the mosque. The characters are in Greek and in translation read: "Thy Kingdom, O Christ, is an everlasting kingdom and Thy dominion endureth through all generations." Many Christians consider this a prophecy of the time when the mosque will again be a church. Elsewhere in the building dim designs of crosses can be seen through the whitewash with which the Moslems covered them.

Since the fire the most attractive features of the mosque are the four gigantic pillars which hold up the dome; the dome itself, which is one hundred and twenty feet high and a hundred feet in circumference and which has an interior surface highly ornamented with mosaics; and the pulpit, which is built of pure white alabaster.

Just across the street from the Omayyad Mosque is Saladin's tomb, a structure much revered by Moslems. Although the tomb is not remarkable for its size or architecture, it is well known because the Great Saladin, the famous king and conqueror who caused such havoc among the Crusaders, is buried there.

SYRIA

BIZARRE BAZAARS

The bazaars of Damascus are probably the greatest in the Near East. They exceed those of Constantinople and Cairo in both size and variety. After we have wandered among them for ten minutes we begin to wonder whether we shall ever be able to find the way out. Some of the tiny lanes and alleys are circular, some are diagonals, and some run for a short distance only and end in a blank wall. The lanes are lined on each side with small shops and factories. Right before our eyes we can see gold cloth spun, copper trays decorated, fine leather and wood ornamented, and even entire rifles manufactured by hand. As a matter of fact the bazaars are an excellent place to be lost, for one can spend days there just watching the various operations.

Almost every sort of article imaginable can be purchased in the bazaars of Damascus. There are the coppersmiths', the goldsmiths', the tobacconists' and the booksellers' bazaars; the silk bazaar, the cloth bazaar (goods mostly made in Europe and America), the second-hand bazaar for old clothes and antiques,

Courtesy The Art Institute of Chicago
STAMBOULI HOUSE IN DAMASCUS

and the Greek bazaar, where all sorts of copies of antiques are made and sold. If you want a Crusader's sword, a piece of a marble column from the temple of Jupiter, an old Babylonian statuette, or any other relic, these industrious merchants will make it for you within half an hour. In the carpet bazaar they sell small rugs, two by five feet, which are faithful though enlarged reproductions of the American one-dollar bill, complete even to the picture of Washington, the signature of the Treasurer of the United States, and the serial number.

THE SEAT OF BAAL

As the rest of the city is becoming greatly modernized under the French, we leave it and continue to the north until we come upon the ruins of a city which is almost as old as Damascus. This is Baalbek, "the seat of Baal," the ancient Syrian equivalent of Zeus or Jupiter. Tradition connects the names of Cain, Abraham, Nimrod, and Solomon with this city. Solomon is supposed to have strengthened it to compete with Damascus for the trade of the East. Here he built a temple to Baal to please some of his heathen wives.

But it was left to the Romans to build the massive structures which today lie in ruins. When we look at the remains of some of the temples, they bring to memory Poe's reference to " . . . the glory that was Greece and the grandeur that was Rome." In Baalbek everything was built on gigantic and massive lines. There is no beauty here as the Greeks knew beauty, but the tremendous size makes for a grandeur that is overwhelming. For instance, the peristyle of the Great Temple consisted of fifty-six columns that were sixty feet high and seven and one-half feet in diameter. In the nearby Temple of the Sun were forty-six columns over fifty feet high. The inclosing wall of the whole Temple Area is made of huge blocks of stone, the largest ever used in the construction of any known building. Some of these colossal stones measure sixty-four feet long, thirteen feet square and weigh over a thousand tons. That exceeds by far the size of the stones used in the Great Pyramid in Egypt.

There is evidence that the Romans were driven away before they quite finished the temple, for in the nearby quarry there lies the largest single stone ever quarried and removed from its original site. It is more than seventy feet long and fifteen feet

CAPITALS OF THE ACROPOLIS AT BAALBEK
Courtesy The Art Institute of Chicago

square, and weighs fifteen hundred tons. How these ancient people moved it as far as they did and how they intended to erect it is a mystery which has never been solved.

Directly east of Baalbek, bathed by the warm waters of the Mediterranean, is the seaport of Beirut, or Beyrouth. To reach it we cross the Anti-Lebanon mountains and descend into the Lebanon valley. On the mountainside in a few isolated spots are the pitiful remnants of a once great and famous forest, the Cedars of Lebanon, whose wonderful trees were used so much for temple construction and shipbuilding in the olden days. They were so depleted by centuries of cutting that only a few remain; but fortunately these are now protected by a law which the French introduced.

BEIRUT, A CITY OF SCHOOLS

We continue eastward across the valley and then up the Lebanon mountains, from the crest of which we gain a splendid view. In front of us stretch the blue waters of the Mediterranean, sparkling in the sun, while below us, squeezed in between the sea and the mountains, is the city of Beirut. This view of the city is startling because it reveals more steeples than minarets in Beirut. Although the city was famous in the days from Alexander the Great to Augustus Caesar, its present fame rests upon the fact that it is one of the great educational centers in the Near East. To its many schools come Greeks, Arabians, Syrians, Egyptians, Persians, Irakians, Armenians, and Turks; Catholics, Protestants, Gregorians, Jews, Druses, Maronites, and many others. In this city of education, which contains English, French, Italian, Armenian, Jewish, and Mohammedan schools, an American educational institution, the American University of Beirut, has a high standing.

Because Beirut is so Europeanized, it has lost much of the Eastern charm and interest that other cities in Syria and Palestine possess; but only seven miles north of the city is a spot considered by many to be most interesting. Since time immemorial, countless invading armies have swept over Syria and Palestine. A route taken by most of the conquerors was down the small valley of Nahr-el-Kelb, "Dog River," and thence down the coast. As they passed through this small but easily traveled valley, they, in a man-

Courtesy The Art Institute of Chicago

A VIEW OF THE CITY OF BEIRUT

Courtesy The Art Institute of Chicago

POOL OF MAMILLAH IN SYRIA

ner of speaking, left their calling cards, by carving the name of their king and a description of his conquests. After one conqueror had started it, all the rest followed suit; so that one side of the valley is covered with inscriptions of all sorts in all languages. There are the inscriptions of the Babylonians under Nebuchadnezzar, the Assyrians under Tiglath-pileser, the Egyptians under Thothmes III and Rameses II, the Greeks under Alexander the Great, and the Romans under the Caesars. Farther up the valley are the carvings of the Crusaders, the Arabs, and the Turks; of the French under Napoleon III, and finally of the British and French under General Allenby, who conquered this land during the World War. Of course, history did not start with the Babylonians; so to complete the picture there are caves, the walls of which are covered with drawings made by our prehistoric ancestors, the cavemen. Other interesting features are an ancient stone bridge bearing Roman and Arabic inscriptions and an old Roman aqueduct which is still in use.

THE SHIP OF THE DESERT

ARABIA

Paul's Photos, Chicago

MECCA, SHRINE OF THE MOHAMMEDANS
Picture shows the Kaaba, a sanctuary of black stone that has a meteorite for its cornerstone.

THE HISTORY of civilized Arabia covers at least three thousand years. One of its early queens, the Queen of Sheba, is mentioned in the Bible as having visited King Solomon. In the sixth century of the Christian Era the prophet Mohammed was born. He gave Arabia the impulse which started it in its path of conquest. Its warriors soon conquered vast territories, from Persia to Spain. The first centuries after Mohammed's death in 632 were the most glamorous in Arabian history—the days of the colorful capital of Bagdad, of the *Arabian Nights*.

The Arabian empire fell apart and was conquered by the Turks. It was not until the World War that Arabia was permanently freed from Turkish control through the spectacular exploits of Colonel Lawrence. After the war Arabia was divided into several kingdoms, mainly under the protection of Great Britain.

[187]

AN OLD TOWER
OF ARABIA

Paul's Photos, Chicago

ARABIA THE ARID

The million square miles of Arabia are mostly desert. The Syrian Desert makes up all of northern Arabia. The monsoons bring a little rain to the southwestern part of the country. It is a land of dryness, with neither lakes nor rivers and only a few scattered oases. The southwestern portion of the peninsula, mainly Yemen, has been called *Arabia Felix* (fortunate Arabia) because of its temperate climate and slight rainfall. The rest of the country "enjoys" a hot climate which is relieved by the dryness of the air.

The few wild animals of the country are of the desert-loving type, including the gazelle, fox, hare, wolf, hyena, and wild cat. Of the birds the ostrich is the most common. Sand-grouse, pigeons, doves, and quail are also found in most parts. The camel and the horse are the most valuable and useful animals. Arabian camels have only one hump and are considered to be of a superior breed, while the horses are noted for their endurance and speed. The plants of this arid country include the date palm and fig trees. Many fruits, such as grapes, peaches, and apricots, are grown in the oases. Most of the far-famed Arabian coffee is grown in Yemen and Asir.

The seven million inhabitants of the country are, for the most part, of a racial mixture. In some sections of the peninsula a large element of Negro blood is present. In the west there are remnants of a once numerous Jewish tribe. The strange gypsy tribe of Sulub is found in the west. The Beduins are the Arabs who represent the purest Semitic stock.

THE HOLY CITY OF ISLAM

By far the most famous city of Arabia is Mecca, the birthplace of Mohammed. The pilgrimage to Mecca, which the Koran prescribes, makes this city a magnet for Mohammedans of all nations. Pilgrims from Persia, India, the Sudan, Egypt, and other countries give the sacred city a cosmopolitan air.

In the court of the Great Mosque at Mecca is the Kaaba, a small cubical temple, towards which all Mohammedans turn when they pray. In it is found the sacred black stone which was regarded as a god by the early Arabs. The rock, which is supposed to have descended from heaven, is attached to the wall of the Kaaba in such a fashion that the devout pilgrim may kiss it.

The holy city is still without a railroad; but one may reach it by automobile from Medina and Jedda, the other holy cities. Straight across the desert runs a new road from Medina to Ridadh in Nejd, about five hundred miles away. This road and others are used to transport freight, tourists, and those pilgrims who come in motor busses.

Arabia exhibits marked degrees of difference in ways of progress. For example, one may see pilgrims riding in vehicles of the twentieth century to cities that have remained unchanged for a thousand years; and in parts of the country where phonographs are unknown, airplanes are frequently flown.

Paul's Photos, Chicago
SHEIK HAMID, ARAB PRINCE, AND SOME OF HIS RETINUE

THE CHANGING BEDUIN

Not long ago the Beduin rode on a fast horse to hunt game with a loud-cracking but inaccurate rifle. Now many of them hunt the gazelle, ostrich, and other game while they ride in high-powered motorcars of American make, equipped with the most modern long-range rifles.

The picturesque Beduin has changed, since the division of Arabia into many distinct political units has curtailed his freedom of movement. No longer are the periodical migrations of the Beduins frequent sights. In other ways also they have been affected by westernization. One may frequently see camels laden with empty oilcans, which are highly prized in that part of the world. The sons of hard-bitten desert chiefs go to French schools in Syria. The young sheiks living in large cities of Syria and Palestine are often seen wearing the latest London clothes, dancing to the current jazz tunes, attending the latest movies, and frequenting the cabarets. The wandering Beduin is being compelled to turn to half-settled conditions, living like the fellahs, who are peasants whom he scorns.

In the midst of the introduction of strikingly modern institutions and products, relics of a bygone age are still frequent. Through Jedda, the seaport of Mecca, come thousands of travelers for the annual pilgrimage to Mecca and also numbers of slaves who are unlawfully brought into the country. Most of the slaves,

Black Star photo   By Baron von Kummer
SUN-SAILS OVER A CITY STREET IN ASIA MINOR

usually Negroes, are used to perform menial tasks for the Beduins and other tribes. A few of the more beautiful female slaves are destined for the harems of sheiks. In some parts of Arabia slave markets are said to exist despite their illegality.

Arabia is indeed a land of varied sights. Its crowded, filthy streets, with their ear-splitting noises, haggling merchants, and frequent calls to prayer, are much the same as they were in the days of the prophet; camel litters sway through the streets; beggars besiege passersby; lepers whine for alms; heavily clothed women balance water jars on their heads; yet at any moment a passing motorcar or an airplane flying overhead reminds one that Arabia is actively a part of the twentieth century.

Courtesy The Art Institute of Chicago

MINARET NEAR PIR-I-ALAMDAR, IRAN

IRAN

A PERSIAN BAZAAR
An open-air restaurant is doing a good business in rice cooked with raisins and fruits.

PERSIAN GLORY

The early Persians, inhabiting the country that is now officially called Iran, were of the original Aryan stock, whose ancestry is veiled in the shrouds of antiquity. That they were of Indo-European lineage is evident from their language, their customs, and their features. It was under Cyrus the Great in the sixth century, B. C., that the country first became a great nation, conquering Babylonia, Lydia, and Media. Continuing the wars of conquest, Darius I and Xerxes clashed with Greece, only to lose in disastrous battles at Marathon and Plataea, and in a naval encounter at Salamis in 480 B. C. However, ninety years later the Persians, with the aid of Sparta and Greek mercenaries, took advantage of internal disorder in Greece and conquered her. By 338 B.C. Persia, under Artaxerxes Ochus, had overcome all resistance in Asia Minor and rose to the zenith of its power. Alexander the Great of Macedonia seven years later at Arabela defeated the Persian hordes. After the disintegration of Alexander's empire, Persia was torn by internal rebellion and by successive invasions

Courtesy The Art Institute of Chicago
THE MOSQUE OF JUMEH AT VERAMIN

of Genghis Khan and Tamerlane. Then came various wars with Rome, Turkey, England, Russia, and Afghanistan; and, eventually, participation in the World War. In 1925 Mirza Renza Pahlavi became the Shah of Persia.

WOOL FOR THE RUGS

Of Iran's population of ten million, more than two million are nomads, cityless travelers, of mixed races. Zoroastrianism, the early religion, is practiced in some parts of Iran, but Mohammedanism is the most widespread belief. Iran is a mountainous plateau in western Asia, between Afghanistan and India on the east, Arabia and Iraq on the west, and Asiatic Russia on the north. In the north and west are immense forests; in the eastern and central parts are vast burning deserts. The south is arable, and the fruits and flowers grown in this region are widely known for their quality and beauty. The raising of sheep and goats is carried on extensively because of the wool which the Persians use in fashioning their gorgeously colored and patterned shawls and rugs. Most of the rivers are used for irrigation purposes, only the Karum being navigable to any practical extent.

IRAN

THE MOSQUE OF SHEIK LUTF ULLAH NEAR ISFAHAN
Photograph taken from the palace of ali-Kapu.

Courtesy The Art Institute of Chicago

MOSQUES AND MINARETS OF TEHERAN

The capital city of Iran is Teheran. There has been some community life on the site of Teheran since the earliest Persian history. The city is located north of a great nine-hundred-mile desert, and at the foot of the pass which is the entrance to the Elburz Mountains. The city is divided into two parts, the older section to the south and the newer to the north. In the former can be seen survivals of old Persia, with ancient bazaars and narrow, alley-like streets. The newer section is more modern and contains the government buildings, the schools, and the foreign quarters.

Like South American cities, Teheran spreads in all directions from a central plaza, Artillery Square, which is enclosed by barracks and contains war relics and a park. The Imperial Bank of Persia faces the square. The Avenue of Diamonds leads to the royal palace, in which are the throne room, beautiful gardens, courts, the famed Peacock Throne, and various government offices. In the newer section can be found the Masjid-e-Sepah-

AN OLD TOMB IN MESHED

salar mosque with its tiny minaret towering overhead, its walls decorated in true Persian style. The Maidan-i-Mashq, an enormous forty-acre plot of ground in the middle of the city, is used as a parade ground, race-course, football field, and aviation field. The bazaars, however, are the most interesting, thronged with gesticulating Orientals who bargain desperately with the shopkeepers, peanut sellers, ice cream vendors, and traveling performers—all presenting a colorful carnival.

TOWER OF SILENCE

About five miles from Teheran is the village of Shah Abul Azim, with its golden-domed mosque gleaming in the desert sun. Close by, pinnacled on a hill, is the Zoroastrian Tower of Silence, fifty feet wide and about thirty feet high. It is here that the followers of Zoroaster leave the bodies of their dead to be devoured by the vultures. In the summer, when the heat is unbearable, most of the inhabitants who can afford it go to the mountains for relief. From there, with beautiful Mount Demavend in the background, the city appears at its best, enclosed by its wall with twelve turreted gates, the mosques, the gilded domes, and, far beyond, the trackless wastes of the shimmering desert.

THE GLORY THAT WAS ISFAHAN

Under the great Shah Abbas I, Isfahan was the capital city and a glorious one. Now, many of its splendid gardens have become weedy wastes, its beautiful buildings have fallen into cracked ruins, and over all there seems to spread an air of mourning for the past. It still contains one of the most beautiful edifices in the world, Masjid-i-Shah, the royal mosque. Under the afternoon sun, the brilliantly colored bricks gleam with the splendor of diamonds, and the blue dome of the Masjid-i-Lutf Allah, at its side, glows like a sullen sapphire. Entering the lofty gate, Aali Kapu, the sight-seer walks through the gardens which cover a large area with their courts and pavilions, one of which, the Chihil Situn (hall of forty pillars), is the most famous. The bazaars of Isfahan are as colorful and picturesque as any in the world. Under their three miles of canopy throng thousands of noisy gesticulating people. At the open shops customers haggle long and loud with the proprietors. Here the strange bustle seems to belie the city's decline.

But outside the bazaars, in the crooked, smelly purlieus, where Isfahan's six hundred thousand inhabitants reside, only crumbling decay evidences a past glory.

ASHES OF THE PAST

Among Iran's other cities are Tabriz, Meshed, Shiraz, and Kermanshah, where fine woolen shawls are made. Bushire and Resht are important ports on the Persian Gulf and the Caspian Sea, respectively. Sun-drenched, these and other ancient cities bask in drowsy indolence, apparently forgetful of the power and the glory that once was Persia's.

AFGHANISTAN

Paul's Photos, Chicago

ADMINISTRATIVE BUILDING IN DARUL AMAN, AFGHANISTAN

ONE OF THE ANCIENT and most interesting lands of all Asia is Afghanistan. It is bounded on the east by India, south by Baluchistan, west by Iran (modern Persia), and on the north by the U.S.S.R. The total area of Afghanistan extends over 245,000 square miles, and the population is about six millions. Little is recorded of the history of early Afghanistan. It is known, however, that in 1738 Afghanistan was conquered by the Persians under Shah Nadir, and Persian influence steadily decreased. With the hope of putting an end to wars between India and Afghanistan, the British, under Sir John Keane in 1839, deposed a ruler feared for his treachery and replaced the former shah, Shuja. The Afghans rose up and murdered the British envoys in 1841. Cold, starvation, and the assaults of native tribes completely wiped out the British force of twenty-five hundred; but Britain sent a retaliating force of eight thousand men and put down the insurrection. British control was marked by disputes with Russia over frontiers, which were finally settled by commissioners of the two countries at St. Petersburg in 1887. One native ruler after another was deposed or assassinated until Great Britain and the Russian government relinquished all claims to the country. King Amanullah, seated in 1919, insisted on modernizing the country with western methods until the Conservatives rebelled and he was forced to abdicate in 1929. Nadir was forthwith elected and reigned until 1933, when he was assassinated. He was succeeded to the throne by his son, Zahir Kahn, the present shah.

GEOGRAPHY AND CLIMATE

About four-fifths of the entire area is rocky, mountainous, and unproductive. Only the valleys are fertile and well watered. The river Helmund is worthy of mention. For more than four hundred miles it flows in a southeasterly direction and empties into the Hamun swamp. Very little water ever reaches the swamp, however, for most of it is drawn off in canals for irrigation. Temperatures range from extreme cold in the higher regions to intense heat in the lower regions. This country gets most of its moisture from the winter snows and early spring rain. The atmosphere is very dry in this region; the sun shines brilliantly most of the year.

Paul's Photos, Chicago

ROYAL PALACE IN KABUL, CAPITAL OF AFGHANISTAN

A VIEW OF KABUL

INDUSTRY LIMITED

Besides farming, the weaving of oriental rugs is the only important industry. Wheat is the basic food; but barley, peas, beans, rice, and maize also furnish crops of importance. Lumbering, while undeveloped, is possible; for upon the plains are mulberry, tamarisk, acacia, willow, and poplar forests. Most important of the domestic animals are the camel, the dromedary, the horse, the ass, and the mule. The sheep of Afghanistan have exceptionally fine fleeces and their wool is woven into exquisite rugs. Camel's hair and goat's hair are used in weaving cloths and rugs. Wild animals abound, such as bears, tigers, wolves, jackals, hyenas, and foxes. Chief among the exports to India are wool, horses, silk, carpets, and fruits. Cattle are exported to Russian territory.

FOR THE TRAVELER

Afghanistan does not possess theaters, museums, cathedrals, and the many other cultural marks of civilization that tourists usually desire. The traveler in Afghanistan, however, is well rewarded; for the study alone of these hardy people is worthwhile.

Bold and warlike, the Afghans are fond of freedom and are resolute in maintaining it. They are restless and much given to plunder. They are able to withstand great privation. Their language, although distinct from the Persian, contains many Persian words and is written like the Persian with Arabic characters. In religion, as might be expected, they are Mohammedans of the Sunnite sect. Few other races live in Afghanistan, although there is the Hazara (Mongoloid) race, living in the mountains of the northwest; and some Hindkis, an Indian race, reside in the eastern part of the country.

KABUL AND KANDAHAR

Travel is difficult, for there are no railways, no banks, and few highways. Transportation is chiefly by camel. Few modern facilities for comfort are offered. Kabul, with about eight thousand inhabitants, is the principal city and historical center, although its influence has fluctuated from time to time. Other leading cities are Kandahar, Ghazni, and Herat. In general, it may be said that only the traveler thoroughly accustomed to "roughing it" would enjoy himself in Afghanistan. Primitive farm methods, primitive business methods, and undeveloped resources lead the visitor to believe that it will be many years indeed before the marks of western civilization will be evident in this rugged, independent country.

SIAM

Courtesy The Art Institute of Chicago

WAT CHENG, BANGKOK

SITUATED STRATEGICALLY in southeastern Asia, on important trade routes to the Orient, is Siam. Typically tropical, it is rich in natural resources. Its territory includes a large part of the Malay Peninsula, separating the South China Sea from the Bay of Bengal. The west coast of the peninsula is on the direct route between Singapore and the Orient, through the Strait of Malacca. The northern regions are mountainous and densely forested, while the central portion is a broad plain—the great basin of the Menam River and its numerous tributaries.

Bangkok, the capital, near the Gulf of Siam a few miles from the mouth of the Menam River, is a city of about 750,000 people. The old section is built on piles extending out into the Menam River and forms a vivid contrast to the newer section of the city, with its wide streets and fine buildings, centering about the royal palace and gardens.

The entire population of Siam is approximately eleven and a half million, of which about ten and a half million are Siamese. The remainder of its colorful population consists of Chinese, Indians, and Malaysians, and a few Japanese, English, and Americans. The Siamese have broad flat faces and a yellow-brown skin, darker than that of the Chinese but lighter than that of the western Asiatics. The religion of the country is Buddhism.

EDUCATION

Like all other countries within the tropical belt, the inhabitants are not inclined to be ambitious; but as a nation Siam is awakening to educational needs and is developing school systems along modern lines. Elementary education is compulsory, and most schools provide free tuition. The universities stress training in medicine and engineering. Western instructors endeavor to carry through complete courses of instruction, but the Siamese appear to be more interested in athletics than in academic achievements.

INDUSTRY

Nearly eighty-three per cent of the entire population is engaged in agriculture, and rice is the chief product. Livestock of the country includes cattle, horses, ponies, water buffaloes, and elephants. Mining is a prominent industry, although the mineral wealth is mostly in tin. Nevertheless, there are extensive deposits of coal, gold, iron, manganese, antimony, and mercury. Rice, tin, gold, and teakwood form the chief exports. Elephants furnish the motive power in the lumbering of teakwood.

TRANSPORTATION

Highways and railways in Siam are limited to routes connecting leading cities; and a few airlines transport mail, passengers, and freight. These transportation facilities are owned and operated by the government. There is some possibility of the construction of a canal across the Isthmus of Kraw, Britain and Japan vying for the right to make the great cut. Britain would suffer a tremendous commercial and strategic loss should Japan succeed; for Singapore, long the key port of southeastern Asia,

SIAMESE WOMAN
Courtesy Mason Warner

would be cut off from world transportation by the canal. It is interesting to note, however, that Britain already has an airport and fortifications overlooking the site of the proposed canal.

A LIMITED MONARCHY

Although as early as 1511 Siam had commercial relations with the Portuguese, followed later by the Dutch and English, the nation never was subjected to European control. It was an independent absolute monarchy until 1932, when King Prajadhipok was compelled to consent to a constitutional monarchy. In 1935 he abdicated in favor of a nephew, the present King Ananda Mahidol.

TRAVEL

While there are hundreds of interesting temples and fascinating market places, with shrill-voiced peddlers, Siam cannot be considered an ideal country in which to travel. Much of it is unsafe for travelers, as the country abounds in poisonous reptiles, notably the king cobra and Russell's viper. Siam is rapidly progressing, however, and within a few years it will undoubtedly be as safe as it is interesting. At present, Bangkok has the most to offer, architecturally, commercially, and educationally. The temples and statuary of this unique city are different from those found elsewhere. Multi-colored porcelain tile mosaics on walls and the pointed roofs of temples add brilliance and variety to the scene, while the often grotesque but always graceful statues give to Bangkok a truly exclusive character.

FRENCH INDO-CHINA

TEMPLE OF ANGKOR WAT IN CAMBODIA

WORLD TOURISTS go into French Indo-China for only one reason: to view the amazing ruins of Angkor, considered by many to surpass the pyramids of Egypt and China's Great Wall for architectural grandeur.

The traveler desiring to go to Angkor has his choice of two routes. One is from Bangkok, Siam, two hundred miles by railway to Aranya-Pradesa, on the frontier of Cambodia, and from there to Angkor by a hired automobile for one hundred and thirty miles over a road none too good. The other route to Angkor is by ship to the port of Saigon, in Cochin China, on the coast of the South China Sea, and from there by motor bus for more than three hundred miles, passing through the city of Pnom-penh on the way.

[206]

Courtesy The Art Institute of Chicago

CAMBODIAN DANCERS IN THE RUINS OF ANGKOR THOM

The great group of ruins at Angkor contains what remains of twenty-four huge and imposing structures that once were temples, government buildings, royal palaces, reviewing terraces, treasure houses, mausoleums, monasteries and nunneries. Angkor Wat was "the temple of the great city," and Angkor was a great city, for it was the capital of the kingdom of the Khmers, and at one time evidently had a population of more than a million inhabitants.

AN UNSOLVED MYSTERY

The outer walls of the chief temple are two miles long, standing four square, and surrounded by a moat two hundred yards wide. Four great causeways span the moat, and in imagination one can see the great processions of elephants in full panoply, warriors, priests, and dancing girls, that marched in and out of the temple on state occasions. Massive stone towers surmount the four corners of the temple and a central tower rises to a height of more than two hundred feet—all constructed without cement or plaster.

The great government building, the Bayon, was built in 850. This and other ruins are ornamented with carvings and decorations cut in stone that actually required years of labor by hundreds of sculptors. There is a silent splendor, a prevailing awesome spirit, about all of these strange, impressive relics of the past.

Nobody knows what became of the Khmers. The ruins at Angkor are one of the unsolved mysteries of history, for apparently the city was deserted overnight. Archeologists are of the opinion that the buildings were erected in the period between 850 and 1150 A.D.

The valley of the Mekong river is as fertile as was the valley of the Euphrates of old, or the country of the Nile, and is believed to have supported a population of thirty million at one time. And they disappeared—suddenly and completely—leaving only these deserted ruins to record the fact that once they lived, and so for more than five hundred years these colossal and beautiful remains have withstood the elements while fighting the encroachments of the jungle.

Courtesy Mason Warner
IMPOSING RUINS OF TEMPLE AT ANGKOR, INDO-CHINA

Courtesy Mason Warner
TAXI SERVICE AT ANGKOR WAT
The mahout, with his sure-footed elephant, waits for passengers.

THE SIX PROVINCES

French Indo-China, on the southeastern corner of Asia, consists of the colony of Cochin China; the four protectorates of Annam, Cambodia, Tonkin and Laos, and the territory of Kwangcrow, leased from China in 1899. Saigon is the chief port, a hot, humid and dull city in which tourists linger no longer than necessary. Hanoi, in Tonkin, is the capital city.

The six states have a total population of twenty-two million, occupying a combined area of nearly three hundred thousand square miles, an area larger than that of the state of Texas.

THE HAWAIIAN ISLANDS

DIAMOND HEAD, HONOLULU, HAWAII

PARADISE OF THE PACIFIC, the Hawaiian Islands! Twenty brilliant splashes of color on the broad bosom of the sea; twenty mighty volcanic peaks rearing their heads thousands of feet through the deep blue-green of the ocean to rise thousands more in the glorious sunshine of the mid-Pacific; twenty wooded islands strewn with myriads of flowers, fringed with palm trees, bordered with glistening sands, encircled by coral reefs, bathed eternally in the multi-colored surf of dazzling, dancing waters! These are the Hawaiian Islands, far-flung territory of the United States; home of three hundred and fifty thousand happy, hospitable people; objective of world-travelers in search of relaxation and recreation in a setting of unsurpassed beauty.

Called the Sandwich Islands by Captain Cook, when he discovered them in 1778, they were then inhabited by Polynesians under the rule of four warring native kings. Twelve years later Kamehameha I brought all the islands under his strong and beneficent rule and, as their king, established a dynasty that continued in power until 1873. In 1894, following the deposition of Queen Liliuokalani, the islands became a republic, with Sanford B. Dole, son of an American missionary, as president. The long desired annexation by the United States was accomplished by Congress in 1898; and in 1900 Dole was made governor of the territory.

Courtesy Mason Warner   Photo Hawaii Tourist Bureau
IN THE BIRD ISLANDS, MAUI

Missionaries came early to the islands. Christianity was introduced in 1820 and soon became the established religion. Shortly thereafter the great wealth of the islands began to be developed, and the first large pineapple and sugar cane plantations, that are now famed throughout the world, were established. From time to time other peoples of the Pacific came to the islands and blended their culture with that of the Polynesians, in surroundings of beauty, joy, and gaiety.

THE HAWAIIAN ISLANDS [211]

A GRACIOUS WELCOME

Children of the out-of-doors are these laughter-loving native folk. Their charm is as great as that of their peaceful, fascinating homeland. The ready *"Aloha!"* with which they greet all visitors upon arrival at Honolulu means "Welcome!"; and the same greeting given upon their departure means "Fare you well." Their ancient ceremonies add to the glamour of island life: the *luau*, or feast; the *hukilau*, or fishing festival; and, of course, the *hula* dance, typical of the natives' appreciation of life's beauty and rhythm. Hawaii is a musical land. Her songs and her voices both have a mellow, haunting quality. Her language, too, has a simple, flowing rhythm composed with an alphabet of only twelve letters, pleasing to hear and easy to speak.

Diamond Head and Aloha Tower, the great mass of mountain that overshadows the harbor and the famous landmark that welcomes all visitors to Hawaii, first come into view as one approaches Honolulu. Then comes the city, modern, yet romantically different, a city that spreads toward the green, surrounding hills which are massed in dense verdure and speckled with brilliant colors. No sooner has the ship dropped anchor than the visitor is garlanded in *leis*, wreaths of perfumed blossoms, and caught in the spirit of gaiety of this land of sunshine and flowers. One never

Courtesy Chamber of Commerce of Hilo

HAWAIIAN PALACE, KONA, HAWAII

ON WAIKIKI
BEACH,
HONOLULU

Courtesy Mason Warner

forgets the smiling *lei* vendors, flaming shower trees, and luxuriant hedgerows of colorful and unfamiliar bloom; the delightful homes, modern shops, and civic buildings of Honolulu; its markets, bazaars, and oriental temples; its unexcelled hotels, inns, and bungalows. A glorious port of a glamorous land!

ON THE BEACH AT WAIKIKI

To the beach at Waikiki come vacationers from over all the world. For here the "Spurting Water," for which this famous strand is named, provides that greatest of all water sports—riding the breakers on the surf-board. At twenty-five miles an hour they ride, bronzed sons of the sea, balanced atop a slim, graceful surf-board, over the shimmering waves, riding their silvery crests. The *malihini*, or newcomer, may learn the sport from the natives who are willing to teach it; or he may content himself with zooming over the clear, transparent waters in the unique outrigger canoe. If he is less athletically inclined, he may join in the smart, social swing at the celebrated Coconut Grove of the Royal Hawaiian Hotel or the Moana's Banyan Lanai, Mayfair of this mid-sea metropolis. There are so many things to do in Hawaii!

At the playground of the Pacific, choose your sport; the islands have it! Water sports naturally are the most popular: from sunbathing, where the waves lap upon the coral sands, to the vigorous challenge of monster game fish that stage their fierce struggles where the sea is deep. Harbor and offshore waters are ideal for yachting. Mountain streams lure the followers of Izaak Walton. Ducks, doves, pheasants, wild turkeys, wild pigs, sheep, and mountain goats make the islands a "happy hunting ground." And, of course, there are golf courses, some of the most extraor-

THE HAWAIIAN ISLANDS [213]

dinary in the world. Where else is to be found a crater like that of Kilauea, on the Volcano Course, into which to drive your old and over-worked golf balls?

Soldiers, sailors, and scholars of Uncle Sam are on the island of Oahu. Schofield Barracks, America's largest army post; the important naval base at Pearl Harbor; a radio station; and the large airdrome at Wheeler Field, form America's first line of defense in the Pacific. The University of Hawaii is America's westernmost center of higher education.

Nouano Pali and Waimanalo Pali, the great cliffs of Oahu, are but two of the many scenic wonders of the isle. Over the former, a twelve-hundred-foot drop, Kamehameha I hurled his enemies. The Rainbow Valley of Manoa, the Punch Bowl, the Blow Hole, Mount Olympus, Mount Tantalus, the Mormon Temple at Laie, the Sacred Falls of Hauula, Lalani Hawaiian Village, the great pineapple and sugar cane plantations, the Bishop Museum, and the Royal Palace—these are but a few of the other sights of Oahu.

HAWAII, THE VOLCANIC ISLAND

Realm of the Goddess Pele is Hawaii, largest and most southerly of the islands. Kilauea's tremendous molten lake, spurting liquid flame and red hot rock—dramatic, awesome, yet perfectly safe to watch—is the home of the goddess. Nearby, Mauna Loa

Courtesy H. T. Stearns, U. S. Geological Survey

MAUNA LOA WITH RECENT LAVA FLOWS

Courtesy Ruth Prazak
OUTRIGGER CANOE AND SURF RIDERS
AT WAIKIKI

rises triumphantly skyward; and a short distance away Mauna Kea, highest point in all the Pacific, sometimes wears a cap of snow on her head fourteen thousand feet above sea-level. Basking in the shadow of this majestic mountain lies the Kona District, last relic of very old Hawaii, where natives live as in olden times. Another attraction of this wonderland is Hawaii National Park. At Kealakekua Bay is the monument to Captain Cook, who died there in 1799.

MAUI, THE VALLEY ISLAND

Maui, the Valley Isle, is called the "Isle Supreme" by the natives. Dominating the island is Haleakala, the ten-thousand-foot extinct crater, largest ever measured by man. The immense cavity is reached by a new motor highway that winds its way through another unit of Hawaii National Park. Haleakala's height presents a view of stupendous grandeur; and its depth, a downward vista that fairly takes the breath away. At the opposite end of the island is Iao Valley, justly called Hawaii's Yosemite, with its special pride, the slim, green shaft of the Needle, towering twelve thousand feet above the sea. These two contrasting scenic highlights are connected by several motor drives of entrancing charm, threading through ever changing country of extraordinary beauty—jungles, waterfalls, gorges, lava flows, and sudden idyllic vistas of the sea. Just to the west, on the small island of Lanai, are the vast green fields of the great pineapple plantations.

KAUAI, THE GARDEN ISLAND

Kauai, the Garden Isle, is the oldest of the islands and the fourth largest. Her contours are softly rounded, her mountains deeply carved with brilliantly colored canyons. In her rich soil grows a wealth of flowering plants, as well as pineapples, sugar cane, and rice. Kauai, always joyous, in her lightest moments is almost frivolous; witness Koloa's sea geyser, the Spouting Horn, the Sliding Bathtub, and the Haena Caves. Scenic drives bring these and other phenomena within easy reach. Of the canyons, Waimea, south of Lawai Beach, leads them all. The red, turreted battlements, green stream beds, and purple cloak of haze of this natural sluiceway, three thousand feet deep, harmonize delicately with the rich blue of the sky and change their tints with every passing moment. There are those who claim that Waimea yields in nothing but size to its mainland counterpart, the Grand Canyon of the Colorado River.

The sands near Waimea bark beneath the footsteps of those who tread upon them. In Hawaii even the sands refuse to cling to established custom, and range in color from dazzling white to somber black. Variety and color, the unexpected and the exquisite, are all to be found on the Hawaiian Islands. Their rare beauty and the grace and charm of their people attract the traveler to their shores; delight and refresh him throughout his stay; and teach him the meaning of that joyous word, *"Aloha!"*

Courtesy Ruth Prazak

SUNSET ON WAIKIKI BEACH

Paul's Photos, Chicago

NATIVE PHILIPPINE DWELLINGS
First floors are built high above the ground so the owner's livestock may find shelter from the heat of the day.

THE PHILIPPINE ISLANDS

RICE TERRACES IN THE PHILIPPINES

One of the most delightful combinations of sophisticated civilization and charming native custom to be found in the world is in the Philippine Islands. In Manila one may meet titled nobility of the Old World, merchants and professional men from every nation; one may dance in the Manila Hotel and think himself in one of the smarter hotels of the Western Hemisphere. And without leaving the town one may see native women, in their lovely dresses with graceful long skirts and full, lacy sleeves, riding in calèches—tiny, two-wheeled carriages drawn by horses no larger than Shetland ponies. In other words, Manila is one of those fascinating oriental ports where anything may happen, and probably will.

MAGELLAN

Manila has felt the force of all the foreign influences to which the Philippines have been subjected, far more acutely than any other part of the islands. Magellan, when he discovered the Philippines, landed at Cebu, where interesting remnants of his occupation may still be seen. For fifty years the Spanish did not take Manila; but when they did, they made it their capital. Since that time Manila has been the dominant city of the archipelago.

A FRIENDLY OCCUPATION

For many years—in fact, until the last century—friendly relationships were maintained between the conquered and the conquering. The Spaniards did not disturb the native feudal system of chiefs, freemen, and serfs, but merely superimposed a governor-general upon the existing social and political hierarchy; and with the new political overlord came his religion. The various orders of the Catholic faith brought Christianity to the natives, who already had many different forms of worship, including the Mohammedan. Among some Filipino tribes, Christianity was eagerly accepted, and the people proved themselves to be pious and devout.

When other nations became interested in empire building, attempts were made by the Dutch and English to gain a foothold. The Dutch had the assistance of the Moros, who never did accept the Spanish rule peacefully. The Spaniards hated the Moros, who had held their country for so long; they considered them related to the Mohammedan tribes in the Sulu archipelago. Constant warfare and piracy were the order of the day, as long as the Dutch were powerful in that section of the world, and even afterward. The English managed to take and hold the islands for a year during the Seven Years War in Europe, but after peace was signed the islands went back to Spain and remained under that country until the United States took them over in the Spanish-American War.

INDEPENDENCE!

Even before the American occupation the more advanced Filipinos were agitating for independence. The greatest name in Philippine history is that of José Rizal, who was executed in the nineteenth century for his political activities. Another cherished name is that of Emilio Aguinaldo, who led the Filipinos in their rebellion against Spain immediately before Admiral Dewey's famous attack. And after the battle in Manila Bay, Aguinaldo continued his leadership as the Filipinos attempted to resist all occidental rule. The desire of the upper-class Filipino for political freedom still continues, but that desire does not permeate the population. According to one of the commoners, independence would mean: "The Chinese take all the money, the Japanese take all the land, the Moros take all the heads. What is left for the poor Filipino?"

A SHADY COCONUT GROVE IN THE PHILIPPINES

GREEN ISLE IN THE SEA

The most exquisite spot in the world is a little island off the mainland of Mindanao. Lovelier natural scenery cannot be found anywhere than that of the Philippines. The island rises from a brilliant blue, set in conical perfection to point its loveliness into an equally blue sky. It is a paradise of tropical bloom; luxurious orchids languish above the soft, bright green fernery which carpets the earth from which tower magnificent palms and other tropical trees. Fringing the island is a quaint, native village in which lives the Mohammedan priest who tends a shrine at the peak, which no white man has ever seen. As one leaves the island, he feels that he is leaving behind him a garden in which the events of *The Arabian Nights* actually took place.

And going back to Mindanao, one comes to the town of Zamboanga. From San Pilar, the old Spanish fort at Zamboanga, one can see at sunset the native vintas—outrigged dugouts—going out fishing. These vintas have gorgeous, multicolored sails which, reflecting the natural glories of the always magnificent sunset, make sea and sky unite in outdoing the splendors of the rainbow.

A MUD FENCE

Before we leave Zamboanga we must comment on the source of its romantic and exotic name. There is a local legend that when the Spaniards first landed at the town, it was nothing but a native fishing village composed of straggling nipa shacks—houses made of bamboo and nipa, a palm used for roofing. In spite of this unprepossessing appearance, they decided that it would make a good harbor; and thinking to establish a fort there, as they later did, they politely asked the first natives they met the name of the town. Those natives, being unfamiliar with the dialect used by the Spaniards, thought the question was "What are you doing?" and equally politely replied "Zamboanga," which means "making a mud fence." The new Spanish settlement and fort were accordingly name Zamboanga, although the name of the fort was changed to that of San Pilar. The change in name was due to a miracle which another local legend attributes to the Virgin Mary. It is said that she warned the Spaniards of a Moro surprise attack at a poorly guarded gate to the fortress. An extra guard was established just in time to stave off the attack. The gate was immediately walled up and turned into a shrine to which, on Sundays and feast days, beautifully dressed Filipinos go to make their devotions. The shrine is a rich one, for the statue of the Virgin has been decorated with jewels and other gifts, but, although it is in the open, there has never been a theft. Even the Moros leave it untouched.

A PATCHWORK OF BEAUTY

Sailing north from Mindanao, one threads his way through a veritable patchwork of beauty. Thousands of small islands—some less than one mile square—form bright spots of color which relieve the monotony of the sea and keep the traveler constantly on the lookout. Sometimes it will be only a coral reef; next there will be a small mass of green, refreshing and inviting; and again there will be an island which is a fishing center, where the coast is fringed with vintas—tiny boats—ready to be launched at a moment's notice, light, yet strong enough to brave a rough sea. At night the fascination of gazing at the phosphorescent wake of the ship is broken while one turns to watch the Filipinos fishing by torch light which blind the fish so that they may be speared.

CHURCHES

In Manila, where Old World and New, East and West, meet and mingle, one finds the old Walled City—all there was of the city at one time—with a moat that has been drained and made into a splendid golf course. Within the walls are some of the most exquisite churches in the islands. There is an elaborate and beautiful cathedral with sixteen altars in which there is always a crowd of devout men and women praying or listening to mass. The oldest church in Manila is the Augustinian. It is also one of the most magnificent, for it has a pure silver altar and a nave of gracefully carved marble. In contrast to this there is the Jesuit church where decorations are all of the beautiful native hardwoods, handsomely carved and glowing. But the most interesting church in all the islands is that of Las Pinas, between Manila and the naval base of Cavite. In this church is the famous bamboo organ built over one hundred years ago. No metal or any other wood was used in its construction, and it is the only one of its kind in the world. Nor is it merely a curiosity, for its tone is as clear and its melody as pleasing as that of any of the more orthodox organs to be found

Paul's Photos, Chicago

SANTA CRUZ CHURCH, A LANDMARK OF MANILA

elsewhere. And above Fort McKinley, the largest military reservation flying the American flag, as one follows the Pasig river into the hills, Antipolo is reached. There one finds the magnificent altar to the Mother of God, Our Lady of Good Voyages. The altar itself is an extremely rich one, of hammered silver, but the greatest glory of the church is the silver statue to Our Lady which is studded with jewels to the value of $125,000.

BATS

If one has so timed his trip to Antipolo as to leave for Manila in the early evening, Montalban Gorge and waterfall offer an amazing spectacle. For at this time thousands of bats leave the caves in the cliffs where they spend the day and start upon their nightly flights. In the same locality, though within a short drive from the civilized city of Manila, a traveler is quite likely to come upon grown men and women walking about perfectly naked except for American straw hats, which seem to fascinate the Filipinos in spite of the splendid hats of native straw which can be had so reasonably.

HEADHUNTERS

Near the center of the island of Luzon, surrounded by the Igorots who until recent years were inveterate head-hunters, is the summer resort of Baguio, where it is always cool, and where frost has been known. High in the mountains, it is the favorite resort of vacationers from Manila. The scenery here is quite different from that of other parts of the Islands in that it is less tropical, but this loss of a degree of sultry splendor does nothing to rob the spot of its beauty. Magnificent mountains, which by frequent rains are kept fresh and clear, suffice in themselves to make the resort popular without the interesting natives who live in the neighborhood and who are so different from most of the Filipinos in clothing, culture, and other characteristics.

PRODUCTS

Until recently when gold was discovered in Luzon (and this event had the usual effect upon the population and industry) the

Paul's Photos, Chicago

COCONUTS ON THE WAY TO MARKET
Hundreds of the nuts are lashed together in rafts, and expert boatmen start downriver with their cargoes.

main products of the islands were sugar, copra, coconuts, coconut oil, hemp, rice, tobacco, straw hats of the better sort, wicker work, and exquisite embroideries. In the mountainous regions of Luzon, rice-growing is an elaborate process for which stone terraces have been built. The hills of this region are so altered by the terraces that, instead of rough slopes on which nothing could be cultivated, there is level after level of fertile soil. The huge amount of water needed for the cultivation of rice is kept at the right level by walls of stone which prevent the water from spilling over to the next terrace until the first one is properly flooded. The heavy rainfall in the region maintains a sufficient supply for all the terraces. Agriculture itself is primitive, the water buffalo and handmade plow being used. Superstition also plays a large part, for in many sections the farmers always wear something white while tending the rice, so that it too may be white and firm. Conversely, when tending watermelon something red is always worn, so that the meat may be red.

The wickerwork is of the famous Bilibid sort, made in the Bilibid Prison, one of the most advanced and modern of oriental prisons. There is also the Pinpin wicker furniture, which is of high quality, though lacking the popular fame of the Bilibid. The embroidery and lovely linen and pina cloth work furnish one of the chief glories of the islands. No woman, be she six or sixty, can see the work done there and not wish that she were collecting a trousseau.

The Philippine Islands offer something of interest to every visitor. Whatever a man's or woman's particular bent may be —unless it is winter sports—there is some place or group of people to satisfy that interest. The Islands have a way of getting in one's blood and making departure difficult.

Paul's Photos, Chicago

STRIPPING HEMP IN THE PHILIPPINES

ISLANDS OF THE SOUTH SEAS

Paul's Photos, Chicago

NATIVES OF THE SOCIETY ISLANDS

THE SOCIETY ISLANDS

BETWEEN THE SAMOAN ISLANDS and the Low Archipelago island group, fifteen to twenty degrees south of the Equator, is a cluster called the Society Islands. Originally discovered by the Spanish in 1606, it was not until 1769 that Cook visited them to make certain astronomical observations for the Royal Society of London and named the group after the Society. English missionaries arrived in 1797 but they lost their influence to the French in 1844, when the islands were made a protectorate of France. The Society Islands consist of Tahiti, the Windward Islands, and the Leeward Islands, together with a vast number of atolls, which are circular coral reefs enclosing still-water lagoons.

NATIVE CHIEF-TAIN OF THE SOUTH SEAS
Society Islanders are men of magnificent physique, as this picture shows.

Paul's Photos, Chicago

TAHITI

Most important of all the Society Islands is Tahiti with its capital city of Papeete. The island has been immortalized in literature, painting and song, and rightly so, for it is one of the most beautiful of tropical paradises in the world. More travelers visit it than any other island in the entire South Seas.

Known by the natives as Otaheite, the island of Tahiti was first discovered by Quiros, a Spaniard, in 1606. In 1774 the Spaniards attempted to colonize it but they were unsuccessful. Later, various explorers found their way to its shores. Word of this heathen paradise reached England and missionaries were sent out in 1797 to convert the natives. It was to Tahiti, in 1788, that Captain Bligh brought the good ship *Bounty* for bread-fruit trees, word of which had been brought back to England by English explorers. Later, in 1836, some French Catholic missionaries

ANOTHER TYPICAL NATIVE OF THE SOUTH SEAS
The radio tubes given him by a white man are worn as ornaments.

Paul's Photos, Chicago

arrived but they were driven away by the natives. This, naturally, brought French warships to Tahiti, and a treaty giving the French the right to settle and missionize was obtained. Later, when the English and the French disputed about whose possession Tahiti was, Queen Pomare decided in favor of the French and, from then on, it has been a French colony.

Many authors and artists have traveled here to enjoy the glorious climate and mode of living. Many remained. It was to Tahiti that Robert Louis Stevenson first came. Gaugin, the French painter, came and stayed the rest of his life here, painting all of his colorful canvases of South Sea life. Pierre Loti, Robert Keable, Herman Melville, Frederick O'Brien, Gouverneur Morris, Jack London and, most recently, Nordhoff and Hall, the two men who wrote *Mutiny on the Bounty*, have written of the charms of Tahiti.

WATER DWELL-
ERS OF THE
SOUTH SEAS
Boat and ladder are
essential in reaching
this home.

Paul's Photos, Chicago

PAPEETE

The harbor of Papeete is full of submarine coral reefs which make it dangerous for ships to enter the harbor. Passengers are sometimes delivered to the island by launch. Along shore the piers are crowded with the small boats of the pearl and copra fleets. Shops with warehouses looming up between them line the waterfront. Behind the city are vast masses of green tropical vegetation and behind this are the solid hulks of mountains rising up to the Diadem, the highest peak on the island. As is the case with all islands where boat landings are infrequent, many natives await the arrival of tourists, particularly those with things to sell. The native women, colorful with *leis* of woven flowers, extend a hospitable greeting.

Here in Tahiti, the Chinese have infiltrated so that pure native blood has become a rarity. The French who have discarded all feelings of caste in their territories, allow the Chinese to intermarry with the natives. In Tahiti about half the population is Chinese and most of the business is done by them. The early morning market in Papeete is supposed to be one of the most picturesque sights on the island. Here are displayed the many-colored fish that swim in the clear South Sea waters. Eaten raw with lime juice some of these fish have an excellent taste.

Papeete, itself, is a modern seaport. It boasts a movie, cafés, night clubs and the usual fare to attract tourist trade. But a trip over the Broome Road which goes into the interior is one that should be taken by all. Starting at the Fautaua Bridge, the scenery is one glorious picture after another. Riotous color in reckless profusion is scattered about prodigally: black sand, green grass, purple bougainvillea entwined over the walls and roofs of the houses, and flamboyant scarlet, orange and white hibiscus flowers.

MOOREA

The island of Moorea, in full view from Papeete, is notable for its skyline of high, jagged volcanic mountain peaks, green with forests of trees on their slopes. At the entrance to the bay, on one of the many coral reefs, are the remains of a French ship which foundered there. The usual thatched huts are to be found on the island, but, in addition, there are gorgeous gardens of scarlet hibiscus flowers, iris and flame trees.

THE INTERIOR OF TAHITI

At Pare, on the Broome Road not far from Papeete, is the grave of Tahiti's last king, Pomare V. The monument at Point Venus locates the place where Captain Cook made his astronomical observations for the Royal Society of London. On and on the road leads, through sugar plantations, palm groves, up valleys, down hills and passing many tiny lacy waterfalls. At Orofara is the island's leper colony. Throughout the trip, native villages, like Fautire, of corrugated tin and wooden frame houses, are to be seen filled with little naked, brown-skinned children, tall bronzed Polynesian men and lithe, graceful women colorfully garbed in their red and white skirts. And over the whole scene are the overpowering odors of jasmine, *tiare,* and the yellow pandanus.

UNFORGETTABLE TAHITI

Tahiti is no place for the tourist who desires to see ancient churches, art galleries, imposing monuments, hoary fortresses, castles, magnificent residences of modern architecture, and vast mechanical projects. Tahiti has none of these attractions. But Tahiti has something more, something that few places possess. Tahiti has an atmosphere. That is the only way to describe it for it is something intangible, something that can only be felt. It has a charm, a subtle *something* that creeps into you and sticks. The natives know this. They have a proverb which says: "He who eats of the *fei* (the wild banana) will never leave Tahiti." And as you stand by the rail of the ship that is taking you away from this paradise of the Pacific, a wreath of *tiare* and yellow pandanus petals around your neck, the pathos of the Tahitian's farewell songs in your ears and the odors of Tahitian flowers in the air, you will know that, although your body is leaving, your memories will remain forever in Tahiti.

A YOUNG SOUTH SEAS HUNTER WITH KNIFE AND SPEAR

Paul's Photos, Chicago

HERE COMES THE FLEET!
Society Islanders, in their outrigger canoes, are real sons of the sea.

FIJIAN GIRL WITH COCONUTS

A TYPICAL SOUTH SEA ISLAND

Bora Bora (pronounced Bola Bola), one of the Leeward Islands, is like all other South Sea islands with the exception, perhaps, of its mountain chain which rises in grotesque shapes over the island. When a boat anchors in the bay, the natives come out in their catamarans, native boats, and sell brightly colored hula costumes embroidered with white *puka* seeds. On land, they can be induced to put on their dances. Attired in grass skirts and decorated with crowns and necklaces of woven flowers, and tiny sea shells, they do the *hula* and other dances while musicians play on drums, tin cans, and guitars. At one time, Bora Bora was quite prosperous because of the rise in price of vanilla beans. But, of late, because of the decline, the island people have stopped ordering modern, expensive radio sets, sewing machines, and knick-knacks.

THE "SEA-RAIDER"

It was near the island of Raiatea, another of the Leeward Islands, that Count Felix von Luckner, the German sea-raider, was beached by an enormous tidal wave. Von Luckner and his crew were saved but, later, when he rigged up a sailboat and got to the Fijis, he was captured and imprisoned in New Zealand. Boats which anchor in the harbor of Raiatea are met by the natives skimming over the water in their *vahaas*, outrigger canoes, twenty to thirty feet long. Utaroa, the village on the waterfront, is one of the largest in the Society Islands. Its white and Chinese population is greater than on any of the other islands. The Chinese handle most of the trade here, as they do all over the South Seas. Copra, dried coconut meat, is the chief export. In a clearing of a coconut grove nearby the natives put on one of their unique fire-walking performances. As the drums beat a mystic tom-tom in the night, the dancers wriggle and twist and leap in a frenzy of dancing. Then, finally, the leader goes to a pit of glowing logs over which hundreds of flat stones have been resting for hours. First he, himself, walks over the hot stones with his feet bare. Then he takes his young daughter with him, and they are followed by all the dancers with flaming torches in their hands, but silent now.

SAMOAN ISLANDS

Almost midway between Honolulu and Sidney, Australia, in the South Pacific Ocean are the Samoan Islands. Of these, Savaii and Upolu islands, formerly owned by Germany and now under the mandate of New Zealand, are known as the Territory of Western Samoa. The Manua Islands, Tutuila and Swain's Island, called American Samoa, have been a United States possession since 1899.

The first white man to visit the Samoan islands was probably the Dutch explorer, Roggeveen, in 1772. Because of a native massacre of Laperouse's French expedition, in 1787, white men avoided the islands. It was not until 1830 that missionaries of

ISLANDS OF THE SOUTH SEAS [233]

Paul's Photos, Chicago
ON THEIR WAY TO THE BARBECUE
Natives of Pago Pago truss up a live pig and carry it to the place of the barbecue.

the London Missionary Society arrived and began to convert the Samoans. Eventually, Great Britain, the United States and Germany took a three-way possession of the islands. Later, Great Britain withdrew and the islands were divided between Germany and the United States. After the World War, Germany lost her interest and its two islands became a British possession under New Zealand rule.

"RAIN" IN PAGO PAGO

The city of Pago Pago (pronounced Pango Pango), on the island of Tutuila is American Samoa's only port. Surrounding the city and the harbor is a chain of mountains, their slopes green with verdant forests. The famous Rainmaker mountain with its flat table-top is supposed to be the source of the continual rainfall which deluges Samoa monotonously day after day. In fact, this city was the scene of Somerset Maugham's short story *Sadie Thompson* from which the famous play *Rain* was dramatized. The house in which the action was supposed to have taken place still stands in Pago Pago with the sign "Sadie Thompson's Inn" hung over the door. Most houses in Pago Pago are simply four poles with a roof overhead to keep off the sun and draw-blinds to lower when the weather is inclement.

The Samoans have remained pure Polynesian and, as a result of American methods in dealing with them, have actually increased their population in a pure strain. What is more, no land in Samoa is owned by foreigners. White people can be found only on the island of Tutuila. Even the police, about one hundred of them, are Samoans, tall and graceful and colorful in their short-sleeved white undershirts and lava-lavas, which is a sort of wrap-around skirt hanging down to the knees. Stripes around the bottom indicate the length of their service in the corps.

INTO THE INTERIOR

A road following the harbor line and going into the interior of the island is well worth traveling if the visitor desires to see Samoa as it really is. In many forest clearings can be seen native villages which are clusters of oval thatched-roofs held up by wooden posts, open on all sides. Quite often the natives will perform one of their dances. Instead of the customary wild dances one finds in these parts, they do a graceful sort of swaying, accompanying themselves with the clapping of hands, and chants. Farther in the interior is a Mormon mission, a frame house in the center of a group of huts, in which Samoan children are educated.

Paul's Photos, Chicago

NATIVE SAMOAN HUT IN ITS GROVE OF PALMS

The village of Vaitonga, still farther in the interior, is typical of Samoan villages. From a black lava cliff beetling over the ocean's rim, the visitor can obtain a beautiful view of the coastline and the almost limitless stretch of water.

Of especial interest are the *siva-sivas* which the natives perform. In the sitting *sivas,* a group of them seat themselves with their legs crossed in front of them. Then, led by a *taupo,* an unmarried girl chosen for the position because of her beauty, they perform graceful motions with their hands, arms, and bodies while a drum taps out the rhythm, and accompany themselves with handclaps.

All in all, the slow-moving, tropical life of American Samoa is refreshing because of its utter simplicity, and because of the color and grace and congeniality of its inhabitants.

STEVENSON AND SAMOA

It was this same easy-going existence that attracted Robert Louis Stevenson to the Samoan Islands. He purchased the Vailima house in 1890, after having come to Samoa merely on a cruise. But the climate was so beneficial to his tubercular condition that he decided to remain. He died four years later and was buried on the top of Mount Vaea—"under the wide and starry sky," as he had wanted to be.

APIA

Entrance to Apia, the largest city in the Samoan islands, is hazardous because of the many coral reefs which treacherously underlie the harbor's waters. The skeleton hulk of the German ship, *Adler,* is still to be seen on the beach, a grim reminder of what can happen if boats cannot get away from the reefs when a sudden gale blows up. During the gale that beached the *Adler,* five other warships, British, German, and American, were so seriously damaged as to make them unseaworthy and worthless. These warships had been sent by their respective countries because of friction between the two countries in regard to the handling of the Samoan situation. The result of the hurricane was that, by the Berlin pact, England withdrew and left the islands to the United States and Germany. During the World War, a British fleet seized the German Samoas and New Zealand has, since then,

PRIMITIVE PAPER MAKING
Samoan women weave bark into papyrus.

held mandate over them. Conditions, however, are not as ideal as they are on the American Samoas. Bitterness and dissatisfaction between the New Zealand authorities and the natives have been the cause of much dissension. Although the natives do not desire complete independence from Britain, they would still like to have an autonomous crown colony of their own.

Because these islands are peopled by the same Polynesians found on the American Samoas, their culture is practically the same. The houses in Apia are like those in Pago Pago, as are the native huts in the villages, and the dances and *siva* presentations are the same.

COOK ISLANDS

Avarua, the port of Rarotonga, the largest of the Cook Islands, has a harbor which, because of its coral reefs and constantly blowing winds, cannot accommodate ocean liners. On reaching shore by means of a launch, the visitor finds himself beleaguered by natives selling hula costumes, colored beads and various ornamental pretties made of pearl shell. The native houses here are not made of wood and bamboo, but are neatly built of plaster and whitewashed boards. No Chinese or Hindu laborers are allowed on these islands. A trip to the interior over the motor road reveals the usual palm-tree groves, limpid pools and native villages. Ancient ceremonial places called *marae* are scattered about the island and are interesting relics of Polynesian religious customs. Here, too, the natives are expert dancers and perform dance-dramas in which they act out mythological scenes of their history.

FIJI ISLANDS

A thousand miles south of the Equator, five thousand miles from San Francisco and nearly three thousand miles from Sydney, Australia, is a large group of about two hundred and fifty islands, called the Fiji Islands. Most of them are small coral reefs, but other larger ones are volcanic cones, thrust up from the floor of the Pacific Ocean. Only about fifty are inhabited. Viti Levu, the largest, is about one hundred miles long and about seventy-five miles wide. Suva, the capital city, is on this island. The Fiji Islands are now British possessions. During a Fourth of July celebration, in 1849, the American consulate at Nukulau was destroyed by fire and the American government claimed indemnities of forty-five thousand dollars of Thakombau, king of the Fijis. With no cash treasury, the king offered his sovereignty to Queen Victoria if she would authorize payment of Fiji's debt to the United States. When she refused to consider the offer, King Thakombau offered to turn the islands over to the United States to clear the debt. But, being involved in a civil war, the almost disunited United States did not even deign to make reply to the offer. In 1874, reconsidering its first refusal, Great Britain took over the islands and it became a British possession.

CAPTAIN BLIGH

The first white man to sight the Fijis was Abel Janszoon Tasman, Dutch explorer and discoverer of Tasmania and New Zealand, in 1643. In 1774, Cook cruised around the southeastern islands. The notorious Captain Bligh in 1789 passed between two of the islands with his longboat after he was cast off by the *Bounty* mutineers. Although he and his men were practically starving

Courtesy Mason Warner

FIJIAN NATIVES IN THEIR "SUNDAY CLOTHES"

and without water, they decided not to land because of the stories they had heard of the cannibalistic Fiji Islanders. Their boat was chased by canoes full of savage natives. The Chinese came in later for sandalwood and *beche de mer*, the latter being used to flavor their soups. Survivors of ships wrecked on the treacherous coral reefs were eaten by the natives. A few, though, managed to save themselves from the stew-pots. It is said that one, an Irishman named Paddy Connell, lived forty years after having been shipwrecked, by telling the Fiji chiefs a new story every day.

WILD AND WOOLY FIJI ISLANDER

A conspicuous characteristic of the Fiji native is the mass of long, wiry hair that grows in a curly, crimped, outstanding bush on his head. Otherwise he has the usual Melanesian facial lineaments. Of the entire population, 90,000 are native Fijians, 70,000 are East Indians imported by the British to work on plantations, 5,000 are Europeans, while the balance of about 12,000 are a mixture of half-castes, Chinese and Japanese. Because of the efforts

Courtesy Mason Warner

THE POT IS LARGE ENOUGH FOR BOYS AND PIG

FIJIAN GIRLS WITH BREADFRUIT (UTU)

of missionaries who began their work as early as 1835, cannibalism has practically been eradicated. Most of the natives have adopted the Christian faith. Instead of being a wild and warlike people, the Fijians are now mild-mannered and peaceful.

SUVA

When the boat docks at the wharf in Suva, it is met by a flock of shrill-voiced, chattering women selling coral that has been plucked from the bottom of the ocean. The city itself is quite attractive. In the main, the houses are simply one-story affairs. The better-class residences are to be found in the surrounding hills where the white population lives. The Government House, built of white stucco, is one of the largest buildings. Nearby is the parade ground where the natives perform weird dances, chanting meanwhile, clapping their hands on fans and brandishing war-clubs and spears. Occasionally, in mock battle, they vanquish the enemy and, like Tarzan, scream out a fierce shriek of victory.

After the dance, *yangona,* an infusion made of chewed-up *yangona* root, is served. No matter how unappetizing it might appear to be, the visitor must sip of it, for to refuse it would be insulting.

A motor trip over the main road reveals an interior that is colorful and definitely tropical. Huge trees tower around the road in great forests. Enormous ferns shoot out of the underbrush. Parrots and cuckoo birds and doves chirp and coo. Plantations of sugar cane, citrus fruits, bananas, coffee, rice, rubber and cacao are to be seen. Occasionally, the road leads through a native village of thatched huts. From the road also can be glimpsed the corrugated tin houses of the East Indians who labor on the plantations. The Fijians, in the main, are lazy and are disdainful of all labor, leaving that for the Indians who also work as servants and shop-keepers. The Hindu caste system, so prevalent in India, has been done away with in the Fijis mainly because of the scarcity of Indian women.

A visit to the native museum at Suva should afford the visitor an insight into the customs and traditions of the early Fijians before the advent of the white man. Here are to be found native boats, idols and other exhibits. Particular pride is placed in the German flag of the sea-raider, Count von Luckner, who was captured by the British during the World War in the Bay of Wakaya Island, one of the Fiji group.

Other islands of the Fijis are Vanua Levu, Taveuni, Kadavu, Koro, Gau and Ovalau.

Courtesy Mason Warner

BALINESE DANCING GIRLS

DUTCH EAST INDIES

Courtesy The Art Institute of Chicago

THE TEMPLE OF BÔRÔBÔDÛR, IN JAVA

TROPICAL ISLES

THE TROPICAL ISLANDS of the Dutch East Indies, little known until the beginning of the sixteenth century, have since that time attracted ever increasing attention. They are among the richest colonies in the world and are unsurpassed for oriental glamour and beauty. Most of the inhabitants, like the natives of the Philippines, are of Malayan stock. Over two thousand years ago the Hindus came from what is now British India and brought their culture and religion to the primitive people of these islands. After 800 A. D., magnificent Hindu temples were built in Java, Bali, and elsewhere, the ruins of which can still be seen. Somewhat later, about 1200 A. D., came the Arabs, whose missionary zeal converted many of the East Indian people to Mohammedanism. As a result, Mohammedanism is the prevalent religion of the Dutch East Indies today, although some Hindus are still found on Java and Bali.

At the beginning of the modern era the European countries heard about the wealth of the East Indies. The famous Marco Polo had visited Sumatra about 1292. Portugal sent ships to the East Indies around the Cape of Good Hope in 1510-12. Trading posts were established by the Portuguese on Sumatra and Java, and especially at Molucca (the Spice Islands); and a flourishing trade in spices brought much wealth to Portugal. In 1602 the Dutch organized the Dutch East India Company and established trading posts in East India. Soon the Portuguese and Spanish were driven out, and Holland gradually extended its control, acquiring more territory as time went on. To accomplish this result, many bitter wars were fought with local sultans and with the famous Malayan pirates and headhunters.

Multatuli, the Dutch writer, whose novels inspired many reforms in the Javanese colonial service, called Dutch East India "the glorious realm that winds yonder around the equator like a girdle of emeralds." Its proximity to the equator and its fertile soil are conducive to the rich growth of tropical verdure. Rare plants and animals strange to other parts of the world are found in the thick forests. Extensive plantations produce coffee, rice, sugar cane, indigo, rubber, and coconuts, on Java and Sumatra. Rubber and oil from Borneo rank highest among present exports. The population of Dutch East India is about sixty millions, while the Netherlands, the ruling country, has only eight millions. Most of the population of East India is concentrated on Java.

JAVA

Java is a typical island of the tropics. Its cultivated fields, amazingly rich, were won from the jungle, whose massed, tangled growth of ferns, vines, orchids, mango trees, bamboo, and palm encroaches whenever cultivation ceases. The strange contrasts are unforgettable: roadsters on the highways pass carts drawn by water buffaloes or bullocks. Dutch missions and Mohammedan temples; fox trots in the Hotel des Indes and fascinating Javanese shadow plays in the native theaters. Trade bustles in the ports by day; and at night the incredible stillness of the jungle returns.

Batavia is the capital of Java and also of all of the Dutch East Indies. Its Dutch section is as Dutch in character as is Amsterdam, with immaculate houses built along canals in which natives do their washing. The Arab quarter, the Chinese quarter, and the native bazaars where one can see glorious batik done by the natives, are all fascinating to the stranger. The gardens of Buitenzorg, not far from Batavia, include a collection of orchids that is known all over the world. The old town hall, built in 1710, has prison dungeons below it. The fortifications, which are now in ruins, were once besieged by Javanese sultans. Not far away lies

A RICE FIELD OF JAVA

a large old cannon half buried in the mud, around which superstitions have gathered. The natives believe that it has the power to cure sterility, and childless women make their humble offerings before it. Other important places of interest on Java are the Bromo Crater and the Sand Sea; the hot springs at Songgoriti; the Water Castle; the leather, brass, and batik industries; and the Sultan's croton at Djokjakarta; the temple ruins and native dancing at Prambanan; and the Borobodur, the most famous of all Buddhistic remains in Java—a colossal eighth-century structure, 394 feet square, 115 feet high, with over two miles of carvings.

BALI

Enchanting Bali, a small island rising abruptly from the sea, is adorned with vegetation of such startling beauty that it seems unreal as one approaches it. The fields are separated by lanes of high palm trees and are fragrant with flowers. The native women, whose forms are of surpassing beauty, wear only the long embroidered *sarong* or native skirt, leaving their golden bodies bare from the waist. With graceful carriage they bear heavy burdens on their heads. Little touched by western civilization, the people have an ancient, complex culture, and a deep faith in many gods. Each member of a family has his own tiny temple, built near the small family house, where he makes daily offerings of rice, bamboo tassels, shell carving, or silver work to the god of the particular day. The natives throng to the great and strikingly beautiful temples, bearing offerings to the gods of the sun and the soil. At Penelokan is a wonderful panorama of Batur—both the lake and the mountain, which holds an active volcano. Den Pasar is the center of Balinese native life, with musicals, dances, and an ethnological museum. Not far away is the sacred forest Sangeh. Other points of interest are the rock convent, the royal tombs, the temple, and the sacred fountains at Tirta Empoel.

BORNEO

Borneo is the third largest island in the world and is situated in the South China Sea, east of the Malay Peninsula and Sumatra, north of Java, west of the Celebes Islands, and southwest of the Philippines. One of the least-known islands of the Pacific, its largest and most valuable part is owned by the Dutch. The other three portions, which include the northern end of the island, are British North Borneo; Brunei, a Malayan sultanate over which the British have a protectorate; and Sarawak, which is ruled by a hereditary English rajah, with Britain in charge of foreign relations. As early as the seventh century there were trade and tribute connections between China and Borneo. In the sixteenth century the Portuguese and Spanish were both successful in gaining trading privileges, but no attempt was made by a European nation to gain territorial control until 1779 when the Dutch acquired authority. Great Britain also managed to establish a degree of control, though her power is not so active as that of the Dutch, who develop the oil deposits of the island as well as its other natural resources, such as gold, copper, iron, and coal.

THE LARGEST FLOWER IN THE WORLD

The island is a mountainous region but with only one strikingly high peak, that of Kinabalu, a beautiful mountain in the extreme northern part of the island. The rivers of Borneo, prominent among which are the Barito, the Kapuas, and the Sambas, are the principal avenues of communication and trade with the interior. The coasts are marshy and in many places fringed with treacherous mangrove swamps, the vegetation of which looks like huge serpents writhing out of the thick mud. In contrast to this sinister type of coast line there are spots where the island rises from the sea in sharp, red bluffs of great beauty. In the interior one finds exceptionally luxuriant tropical forests, remarkable for the towering Tapang trees. These trees are extremely tall and straight, with no branches or forks between the base and the top, where they suddenly branch out into a ceiling of green. In keeping with such magnificent dimensions as these, the Rafflesia, the largest flower in the world, grows in Borneo. Here also grows the Durian, a fruit of delicious flavor, whose popularity the stranger can never understand because of its nauseating odor. But once a man musters enough courage to take the first bite he is enchanted, for then the odor is not noticeable, and the taste well compensates him for his effort.

THE WILD MAN OF BORNEO

Living in a primitive country inhabited by the orangutan, the python, the rhinoceros, the crocodile, and the elephant, the famous wild man of Borneo is really a likable chap, unless he happens to want someone's head. He is content to live a simple life, weaving mats and carving wood, tatooing his body, and cultivating his terraced rice fields. Ordinarily the natives do not deliberately go to hunt for heads but collect only those of slain enemies. The heads are greatly revered and are an important part of many religious activities, chiefly in funeral rites. With the inroads made by alien cultures the use of the heads has become merely formal, in the main, and the objects are lent about among the tribes to save bloodshed. The actual practice has almost died out, except among the Ibans, who were always the most active and offensive of the hunters; even among the men of this tribe headhunting is known only in rare instances.

Philosophically enough the Borneans realize that death is inevitable; and they have, therefore, incorporated it into their religious beliefs as a thing of little consequence. To them the life after death, *Apo Leggan,* is merely a continuation, with little change, of this life, and consequently they have absolutely no fear of it. They are a curious group of races, including Chinese, Malayans, Negrito pygmies, Dayaks, and others, with varying religions, and customs.

[248] UNIVERSITY OF KNOWLEDGE

Acme photo

A MISSION VILLAGE IN NEW GUINEA

NEW GUINEA

NEW GUINEA, lying north of Australia, from which it is separated by Torres Strait, is one of the last strongholds of savagery left in the world, in spite of the fact that it was discovered as early as 1526 by Dom Jorge de Meneses. Apparently the empire-building nations of western Europe did not think the large island, exceeded in size only by Greenland, desirable, for it was not till 1793 that any nation made an attempt to claim it. In that year the English East India Company annexed the island. In 1928 the Dutch claimed part of the territory, and a little more than fifty years later Britain, Germany, and the Netherlands came to an agreement recognizing one another as possessors of the various parts of the land. After the World War, Germany's territory was made a mandate of the League of Nations and placed under the jurisdiction of Australia.

The western half of the island is owned by the Netherlands, and the eastern and more civilized half by Britain and Australia. For many years there has been little reason for the nations of Europe to quarrel about ownership, for not much is known of the resources of the island. Limited commerce and industry exist and there are only a very few small settlements, which are occupied by government appointees, missionaries, and enough traders to supply them. The largest settlement in South New Guinea is Merauke, whose nearest neighboring town is Kaimana, five hundred miles away. In Fak Fak, the largest of the western settlements, the natives have become semi-civilized because of outside influences.

CANNIBALISM

Generally speaking, the natives of western New Guinea are small, frizzy-haired and ferocious. Head-hunting is practiced to some extent and cannibalism exists, chiefly in the Dutch area in the west. Since the island is plentifully supplied with wild sago, coconuts, sweet potatoes, and sugar cane, there is little need for land cultivation, and the natives lead indolent and carefree lives. They supplement the vegetable diet by spearing fish, harpooning dugongs, and hunting the kangaroo, wild boar, and other animals. Much of their time is spent in religious observances and in savage feuds with other local tribes.

The several ports of call, Mabudauan, Samarai, Daru, Port Moresby, and others, offer the traveler opportunities rarely found in a civilized world. Without making perilous ventures into the interior of isolated islands, he may actually see primitives living in their stilt houses, chewing the betel nut, and wearing bone ornaments through their pierced noses.

A trip to New Guinea is worth while if only to see the gorgeous birds of paradise, which are one of the exports of the island, along with rubber, copra, cacao, and cotton.

JAPAN

Courtesy N Y K Steamship Line

SKATING AT FOOT OF MOUNT FUJI

THOUGH MODERN in her business, her commerce, and her world relations, Japan's culture is like a lovely old fan or vase. Her people are quiet, extremely polite, dignified in their associations; they show regard for one another's feelings and a rare, pleasing tactfulness. The country itself has a beauty in keeping with such a national character. The serenity and poise of famous Fujiyama symbolize the dignity of the people, while the fragile loveliness of Japanese cherry blossoms is nature's version of their delicacy and charm.

The principal port at which travelers arrive in Japan is Yokohama, a modern seaport surrounded by the glories of nature and the shrines of old gods. Approaching through the Uraga Channel from the Pacific, the first sight which greets one is the island of Oshima with its active volcano Mount Mihara. By day this volcano is exciting enough, with smoke and sparks constantly pouring forth; but by night there is nothing more magnificent. Against a dark sky a mighty glow rises into the heavens, giving one the feeling that even yet Lucifer is attempting to make good his vows against his God.

FUJIYAMA GREETS YOU

Beyond the blazing glory of Mount Mihara stands Mount Fuji, calmly gazing upon the violent performance of his brother Mihara, as though quietly smiling at the whole show. The word magnificent is well applied to Fuji, for there is probably no mountain in the world which can vie with this one for sheer serene, majestic beauty. It is a perfect cone whose corrugated sides rise in simple symmetry to the peak.

Still farther in the bay is Uraga, the beach celebrated for being the scene of the first arrival of Commodore Perry in 1853. About two miles down the coast is the place where the shoguns (feudal barons of old Japan) received the letter which the famous Commodore brought from President Fillmore. Today that spot is marked by a monument, which commemorates not only the arrival of Perry but also the entrance of Japan into the modern world of commerce and international relations.

Very near Uraga is Yokosuka, today an important naval station. A relic of the near past is the old battleship *Mikasa,* which was the flagship of Admiral Togo in the most important squadron of the Russo-Japanese War. But the naval fame of Yokosuka goes much farther back than the nineteenth century. On the shore is the memorial tombstone of Will Adams, the "first Englishman in Japan." Reaching Japan in 1600, as a pilot on a Dutch ship, Will was kept captive for a time. His captivity was far from unpleasant, however; for he enjoyed the full confidence of the Shogun Iyeyasu, who used his talents in ship-building and in western inventions, in return for which he gave him everything a man could desire. Adams married a Japanese woman and remained in Japan until his death in 1620.

"BRISTLING WITH A THOUSAND MASTS"

After these interesting sights are passed, Yokohama comes into view. The first sight that greets the eyes is that of the bristling masts of hundreds of ships of all sizes, shapes, types, and nationalities. Opened to foreign trade as the result of Commodore Perry's negotiations, Yokohama has in less than eighty years changed from a tiny fishing village of eighty-seven houses to the foremost trade port of Japan. It now covers an area of more than fifty square miles and has a population of 620,000. Although the

Courtesy N Y K Steamship Line

YOKOHAMA HARBOR

city was practically wiped out by earthquake and fire in 1923, within two years it was rebuilt; and it soon attained its earlier rank in population and importance. The Earthquake Memorial Hall both commemorates those who lost their lives in the catastrophe and glorifies Japanese progress.

On the seashore at the edge of the thriving city is one of the loveliest sights in all Japan. The Sugita Plum Garden is a vision of delight, especially about the end of February when the trees are in bloom. By the miraculous intervention of the gods of beauty, the earthquake, which so nearly ruined everything else of value in the city, did nothing to harm this garden; and the trees continued blooming as though they were trying to compensate the aesthetically acute Japanese for their other losses. Many of the trees are gnarled and twisted with age, some of them being two hundred years old; but that age only enhances the exquisite charm of the fragile, white blossoms which cling to the boughs like delicate old ladies to old men, half seeking strength and half giving it.

TEMPLES AND FARMS

The trip from the pier at Yokohama to the center of Tokyo, eighteen miles, is packed with interest. The two cities adjoin and the ride is between almost unbroken lines of small business houses and homes, surrounded by tiny Japanese farms, curious for their lack of fences or hedges, for they are separated only by the irrigation ditches which keep the paddy rice fields deep in mud the year round. The city limits of Tokyo are entered unawares unless some one who knows points out the boundary line of Yokohama. Specific spots of interest on the trip are the Sojiji Temple at Tsurumi. This temple is the headquarters for the Zen Buddha sect, otherwise known as the Soto sect, and is one of the most notable structures of its sort in all Japan. And not far away is the Daishi Temple which is connected with one of the founders of esoteric Buddhism in Japan, the famous priest Kobo Daishi, who lived from 774 to 834. Beyond that is the Ikegami Honmonji, a well-known temple of the powerful Nichiren sect. Continuing, you get a glimpse of the remains of the forts which were built in the middle of the last century as a defense against warships of foreign nations.

Courtesy N Y K Steamship Line

ROWS OF CHERRY TREES EXTENDING OVER TEN MILES ALONG THE RIVER KAJI, NEAR NIIGATA

Courtesy N Y K Steamship Line

MAIN ENTRANCE TO THE IMPERIAL PALACE, TOKYO

THE HOME OF THE EMPEROR

Then you are in Tokyo! The capital of the Japanese nation, the home of the Emperor, the third largest city in the world, with more than five million people, covering an area of over two hundred and thirteen square miles, Tokyo is as interesting as any city you could possibly find. The character of Tokyo is evident the minute you leave the station. The station itself is a thoroughly modern building in perfect western tradition, and opposite it are commercial buildings of similar design; but when you look down the broad street which leads from the station you see the grounds of the centuries-old imperial palace. With feudal walls towering above the antiquated and no longer useful moat; with pine trees, actually fascinating by virtue of their age, the palace and its grounds bring to mind old, old Japan.

The combination of age-old tradition and modernity is found throughout Japan. It is more strongly felt in Tokyo, however; for although modern business methods have thoroughly permeated the Japanese nation, western culture has left untouched the older culture of the land of the rising sun. That culture, more delicate and fragile on the surface, is, in essence, enduring and strong. The Japanese, realizing its virtues and its significance to the national spirit, have retained it and have superimposed the commercialism of the West, to increase the potency of their country.

FROM YEDO TO TOKYO

Named Yedo in the twelfth century, after the great Yedo Taro Shinenaga who chose the site of the present city as his headquarters, Tokyo rose to prominence in the sixteenth century, when Tokugawa Iyeyasu rebuilt the old castle of the city and made it his residence and the seat of government. Because of his policy of requiring all his vassals to keep their families in the city as hostages against ill behavior, the city quickly acquired powerful population. The shogunate of Tokugawa continued powerful until 1868, when the imperial regime spread its influence over the area. At that time Yedo was selected as the capital of the empire instead of the old capital Kyoto, and the name was changed to Tokyo, meaning Eastern Capital. The old shogun palace became the imperial residence, and Tokyo became the imperial seat of the Japanese Empire.

"NŌ" PLAYS AND "NŌ" DANCES!

An understanding of the national character of the Japanese people is of necessity based upon an understanding of their culture. Even a cursory glimpse of this culture explains much of the Japanese character which would otherwise be lost to the observer. Among the traditional examples of the growth and significance of this culture, which can be viewed easily, and with slightly more difficulty be appreciated by the interested and sympathetic spectator, are the Nō Plays and the Nō Dances. Tokyo has several theaters where these traditional performances may be seen. The origin of the Nō Plays is lost in antiquity; but it is known that most of those that are performed today were written during the fourteenth and sixteenth centuries, when more than a thousand were written. Of the eight hundred which survive today, only two hundred and forty-two are performed on the stage. The word Nō means ability or accomplishment, which shows that the play is a dramatization of the hero's achievements. The play itself is so utterly foreign to the western training that even with the

SCENE FROM A "NŌ" PLAY
The "Nō" dramas, written in prose and verse, include a chorus, music, and dancing. Nearly all were written in the fifteenth century and have been handed down unchanged.

recitative chants of the chorus and the gesticulation of the actors it is generally not understood, while even the Japanese would not know what was going on without the chorus. But a knowledge of the plot is not necessary to an appreciation of the beauty of the drama. The elaborate costumes and masks of the actors; their gestures and intricate steps; and the low, melodious, albeit archaic, recitations are sure to hold the aesthetic interest of anyone.

Japan, in taking up what she considers best of Western civilization, has built a Coney Island in the city of Tokyo. The Asakusa Park is daily thronged with pleasure-seekers who go there to enjoy roller coasters, slides, games of chance, puppet shows, movies and other modern amusements. But even in such a place as a noisy and giddy amusement park, Japan does not go far from her traditional culture. In the park is the Kwannon Temple, an old shrine founded as long ago as the seventh century. It is dedicated to the Goddess of Mercy; and every day almost as many people come to pay her reverence and to ask her benevolence as come to the park for lighter purposes.

STONE LAN-
TERNS OF ASA-
KUSA TEMPLE
Paul's Photos, Chicago

CHERRY BLOSSOMS

As interesting and beautiful as Tokyo is at all times, it is loveliest in the spring of the year when the cherry blossoms are in bloom. Every park and every garden that is large enough for a single tree has at least one cherry tree. In the spring these trees blossom, and the entire city is a mass of delicate pink. The Japanese make a cult of the cherry, and cultivate it with such loving care and such true skill that it is inevitable that the blossoms are exquisite. Soft, pink petals of unbelievable fragility surround the less delicate yellow centers of the flowers, which are so perfectly set against the black, shining boughs of the trees.

JUJITSU

As representative of Japanese culture as the cherry blossoms is Jujitsu, the art of self-defense without weapons. Kodokan is a school devoted to the training of young Japanese in this art. Strangely enough, all classes of men attend the school; and the director of it is a very refined gentleman. Jujitsu is to the people of this delicate country an art on the same plane as fencing, rather than mere physical exercise. Every gentleman should be expert at the technique, even as in the old world years ago every gentleman had to know how to fence, even though he might never fight a duel. Most Japanese cities of any size have such institutions as the Kodokan, to which cards of introduction are issued by the Japan Tourist Bureau. The one in Tokyo is considered the most representative of all and is certainly one of the most interesting.

THE IMPERIAL UNIVERSITY

The Imperial University of Japan, at Tokyo, is the oldest and most important of all the Japanese universities. The campus was in feudal days the estate of the important Maeda family, and it has a very favorable location and great beauty. The only relic of those days of military glory is the impressive gate, which is now preserved as a national art and historical treasure. It was built in the eighteenth century by the head of the government of Yedo, the Shogun Tokugawa Iyenari, in honor of his daughter's marriage to the lord of the Kaga clan, Nariyasu Maeda. The style is "Goshuden-mon," which could be used only by the greatest lords

Paul's Photos, Chicago
YOUNG WOMEN OF TOKYO WATCHING AN ECLIPSE OF THE SUN

of the empire. Almost as large as an ordinary house, its red lacquered walls, curved silver roof, and gold decorations give it a majestic and rich appearance. Age and the soft tone of the lacquer have increased the mellowness until the Akamon, as it is called in Japanese, seems, except for its state of perfect preservation, to be far more than two centuries old. After viewing it you can easily understand how the emperor decided to make a museum piece out of the dignified old gate.

Another important institution in Tokyo is the Nautical College. Founded in 1875 and maintained by the government, this school is an example of Japan's earnest and successful endeavor to make up in a short time for her many years spent in isolation. The college has a group of handsome buildings appropriately situated on the waterfront, where young Japanese, instead of romantically "running away to sea," take a well-planned course of training which fits them to be skilled mariners. Anyone who has ever traveled on a Japanese ship can testify to the efficiency of these young men. But efficiency is not the only aim of the college; the graduates must not only know how to perform their own technical duties without mistakes, but they must also be courteous gentlemen who are glad to make an effort for the comfort of the passengers on their ships.

THE MEIJI SHRINE

The Meiji Shrine, a Shinto shrine dedicated to the great Emperor Meiji, is one of the holiest and most frequented pilgrimage shrines in the Japanese Empire. Every year millions of pious Japanese go to worship at the sacred place, which is all in purest Shinto style. The oratory, which is the main building, is constructed of hinoki wood; the roof is made of the bark of the same tree; and the whole is decorated with gilt copper. Most of the other edifices of the shrine are of the same type of architecture and materials. The oratory houses a complete ensemble of sacred costumes, with two sacred swords and two sacred mirrors, while behind it is a treasure house dedicated to the care of relics of the Emperor Meiji, including his carriage. Two main glories of the shrine for those who do not go there to worship are the particularly fine and varied irises grown there and the large *torii*, or gates. The torii on the grounds are among the largest and most magnificent in Japan, standing nearly forty feet high, with pillars four

JAPAN   [261]

Courtesy N Y K Steamship Line

DANCING GIRLS AND CHERRY BLOSSOMS IN THE
GARDEN OF THE HEIAN SHRINE, KYOTO

feet in diameter. But most interesting are the torii at the entrances which are made from hinoki wood brought especially from Mount Arisan in Formosa. This wood is over seventeen hundred years old.

THE SILENT HALLS OF DEATH

Leaving Tokyo behind, you reach Kamakura in less than an hour. Kamakura is little more than a village, although it is one of the most interesting towns in Japan because of its memories and its relics of past glories. One can not help but feel that he is in the silent halls of death as he wanders among proud old witnesses to the greatness of the city in the thirteenth and fifteenth centuries. The ancient shrines, nearly empty now, are eloquent tribute to the devastating effects of war which caused the deterioration of the once powerful city.

[262] UNIVERSITY OF KNOWLEDGE

Courtesy N Y K Steamship Line

MEIJI SHRINE, TOKYO, DEDICATED TO THE GREAT EMPEROR MEIJI

Courtesy N Y K Steamship Line

"DAI BUTSU," OR GREAT BUDDHA
AT KAMAKURA

DAI BUTSU, THE GREAT BUDDHA

The Great Buddha, Dai Butsu, which is one of the main sights of Kamakura, was erected in 1252. The fifty-yard-square building which originally enclosed it was carried away by a tidal wave in 1494, after which the Buddha was left in the open, where it stands today, silent, superb, and calm. An idea of its size may be had from the width of his eyes which measure three feet and four inches. Towering forty-eight feet high, huge, the symbol of placidity and endurance, the great Buddha is truly an impressive sight.

OJIN, THE JAPANESE MARS

Also in Kamakura is the Hachiman shrine, originally built in 1063 and dedicated to the Emperor Ojin, who lived late in the third century. This emperor, from his martial career and successes, is popularly called the god of war. Although the original buildings do not now exist, the shrine is of particular charm and beauty, especially because the approach from the station is lined with cherry and pine trees. At the left of the stone steps is a tremendous gingko tree, beside which, in 1219, the Shogun Sanetomo was assassinated by his nephew, the chief priest of the temple, who waited in ambush behind the tree. Adding to the interest of this shrine are many old swords, pieces of armor, and masks, which are among the national treasures of the realm.

FUJI THE MAGNIFICENT

Leaving Kamakura to dream of her faded power and former glories, you go on to Mount Fuji, whose glory will never fade. The highest mountain in Japan, the "National" mountain, Fuji is known the world over for its flawless beauty. The simplicity of line and the perfection of the cone which towers over twelve thousand feet above sea-level, are a striking proof that frills and gaudiness do not make true beauty. Once a fearful and active volcano, Fuji has neither erupted nor given cause for alarm since 1707, when Tokyo, seventy-five miles away, was covered with six inches of ashes, and the thundering noise held the inhabitants trembling with fear. Since that last show of power, Fuji has been content to awe its spectators by its majestic beauty rather than to terrify them with molten lava and flames. It allows only a faint bit of steam to escape occasionally as a reminder of its dormant power.

From earliest times this volcano has been considered by the Japanese as a sacred summit. No woman was allowed to attempt the climb to the peak until 1868, when the ascent was made by Lady Parkes, the wife of the second English minister to Japan. Since that time many women have climbed the beautiful slopes of the mountain; and every year many women are numbered among the fifty-seven thousand or more pilgrims who reach the summit and look inside the fearsome crater.

In the summer Mount Fuji has only a ring of glistening snow around its summit, but in the winter the whole of the smooth cone is wrapped in a mantle of white. At such times it looks even less real, but to those who enjoy winter sports it is a very real source of pleasure. The Japanese, who have taken up skiing with enthusiasm, have found that the slopes of this magnificent mountain are ideal for rapid, down-hill runs; and every winter many athletes throng to the neighborhood. Almost as popular are two of the five famous Fuji lakes, Yamanaka and Kawaguchi, which offer especially fine skating. Foreigners, who usually picture Japan as a tropical country whose people sit quietly in quaint costumes, drinking tea, are usually amazed to see young Japanese girls in European skating dress, their black hair shining against the whiteness of the snow, skimming as easily over the ice as though they had been reared in Scandinavia.

Courtesy N Y K Steamship Line
MOUNT NEKODAKE SLOPES, CELEBRATED AS A SKIING RESORT, SUGADAIRA

The beautiful Fuji, however, is not so popular as a winter sports center as are the Japanese Alps. Kirigamine, a skiing ground, which is within easy access of Tokyo, is so well attended in the winter months that from a distance it looks for all the world like a sugar bowl full of ants. Everywhere one sees people on skis. Some of them are flying down the hills as though on wings; others plod their way up that they, too, may fly down; many beginners, hardly able to stand, struggle over the flat surfaces; but all have the time of their lives. The Japanese have taken the Alpine sport to their hearts and turn out to enjoy it as soon as the snow is right. And from the beginning of fall until spring the department stores, which one would think would deal in obis of costly brocade, in damascene, and in tea pots, have large sections devoted exclusively to ski clothes and to winter sporting goods in general.

NIKKO

The Japanese have a saying "Do not use the word magnificent until you have seen Nikko." That saying is well justified; for against a background of extremely beautiful natural scenery—mountains, rivers, waterfalls and cascades, lakes and ancient trees which seem to be coeval with the mountains themselves—are some of the most beautiful temple buildings in all Japan.

Crossing the Daiya River is the sacred bridge Mihashi, first built in 1636, but destroyed by floods and rebuilt in this century according to the original plans. The bridge is used only by imperial messengers on ceremonial occasions and by the governor when he makes his annual visit. It spans the river in a single graceful curve at the spot where Shodo-Shonin is reputed to have crossed the river on the back of two huge serpents. The bridge is lacquered in a brilliant red, ornamented in gilt metal, and rests on granite supports in the shape of torii, one at either end of the span. Since you are probably neither an imperial messenger on ceremonial business nor a governor making your annual visit, you must cross the ordinary bridge which parallels this sacred one 100 yards away if you wish to see the shrines on the other side.

The son of Tokugawa Iyeyasu, the founder of the great Tokugawa shogunate who died in 1616, built the greater part of the magnificent Nikko Mausoleum in honor of his illustrious father.

THE SACRED BRIDGE AT NIKKO

No limit was set upon the cost of the shrine and mausoleum, and the finest artists and most expert craftsmen of the country were called to devote their best talents to the monument of filial piety. An equally free hand was used with regard to materials, the amount of gold leaf in the buildings being estimated as enough to cover nearly six acres.

The Gate of Sunlight, or Yomei-mon, at the top of an impressive flight of stone steps, is more popularly known as The Twilight Gate, because twilight invariably overtakes those who try to inspect the whole and really appreciate its beauty. This gate represents the height of decorative art expressed by the Japanese artistic temperament. It is by far the most beautiful gate in all Japan, a land where gates are considered as aesthetic rather than as utilitarian edifices. On it was lavished all the skill which was developed in the Momoyama period. An eight-columned, two-storied structure, gabled and balconied, the Yomei-mon is vari-colored and has hardly an inch of uncarved surface on its whole exterior. All sorts of birds, flowers, and beasts have been used in the *decor,* such as dragons, lions, tigers, and giraffes, geese, and chrysanthemums. Gold and white are the outstanding colors, although red lacquer has been introduced into the design to render a striking note of contrast and to give focal points in the midst of intricate carvings.

Among the columns there are two of particular interest. One of the center ones is decorated with the carved figure of a tiger, the natural grain of the wood very cleverly representing the hair of the animal. Another is the Upside-down Column, or the *Mayoke-no-hashira* (Evil-averting column), which is entirely carved in patterns purposely placed bottom side up, because of a superstitious belief that such a flaw would avert the jealousy of evil spirits who might envy and covet the beautiful gate.

One of the most interesting buildings at the mausoleum is the Smiling Hall. The hall is really the sacred library, but it is given the delightful nickname because of the wooden images in the front, of Fudaishi and his two sons, all three smiling so broadly that they are called the Laughing Buddhas. The library contains nearly seven thousand of the Buddhist Sutras and represents a collection of great worth. These books are kept in a large revolving

Courtesy N Y K Steamship Line

YOMEI-MON OF THE TOSHOGU SHRINE, NIKKO, MOST RESPLENDENT GATE OF ITS KIND

A FAMOUS LAUGHING BUDDHA OF JAPAN
One of the popular images in Japan. He is held in high regard as a god of good fortune.

bookcase, supposed to have been invented by the chief of the Laughing Buddhas, Fudaishi. Also worthy of notice in the library are a bronze candelabrum, a bronze lantern, and a revolving lantern which were presented by the Dutch government in 1636, before Japan closed her doors to all foreign trade.

The outer hall of the main shrine, the oratory, is another of the rare and exquisite buildings of this group. Metal steps lead up to the antehall; the lacquered pillars are openwork covered with metal casings, on which dragons writhe. Above three gold *gohei* is hung the sacred mirror, around which cluster small lacquered tables bearing caskets of Buddhist texts. Black lacquer has been used in the oratory more lavishly than has the red, while the ceilings are done in a bluish color to provide an excellent background for the dragons painted there.

KARUIZAWA

After you have sufficiently—though that seems impossible—feasted your eyes on the strange beauties of the Nikko group, you will probably go to Karuizawa, which is as different from Nikko as any place in the same nation could possibly be. Karuizawa is a summer resort of delightful coolness. The thermometer never rises above eighty degrees Fahrenheit in the hottest weather; and the surrounding country is so lovely that the popularity of the resort is not surprising.

A splendid view of Mount Akagi, an active volcano, may be had from any spot in the town; but most people prefer to go to the slopes of the mountain itself to view it. There, at times, the visitor almost forgets he is in Japan, for the herds of horses which pasture on the hillside with the range of mountains in the background make him think of the American western states, until he sees a Japanese, or a distant shrine, or gets a faint whiff of volcanic smoke. Then he knows that he is still in Japan, and that he is merely seeing another aspect of this delightfully varied country.

IKAO

One of the most famous of Japanese spas is the celebrated Ikao, which is built on a series of terraces on the northeast slope of Mount Haruna. The hot spring, which contains iron and sulphate of soda, is believed to be particularly beneficial. The location at the foot of a wooded mountain makes the place very lovely, and gives excellent opportunity for long walks in the forest to several points of peculiar interest to resorters. Among them is Miharishi, a bold, bare-faced bluff which looks out over the surrounding territory and gives an exciting view. Lakes, rivers, plains, and mountains can be seen, the pattern stretching away into a misty distance.

SENDAI

Largest and most important of all the cities in northeastern Japan, Sendai is also one of the most interesting. It has been a center of learning and culture for over three hundred years and is noted for its educational institutions. Most important of these is the Tohoku Imperial University; but there are also several secondary schools of a very high standard. Until recently Sendai rested on its laurels as a cultural and intellectual center; but lately it has turned to the manufacture of silk and other textiles, carved objects, beer, and *saké*. *Saké* is a Japanese wine of pungent flavor. It is sold in tiny half-pint porcelain bottles which look more like vases than wine bottles. It is invariably served hot, and the steam which rises from the little flat bowls is as fascinating as is the bouquet of fine old brandy. The Japanese have a penchant for taking their *saké* to the top of a mountain and drinking it there while philosophizing.

DATE MASAMUNE AND THE POPE

At about the beginning of the seventeenth century a great lord, Date Masamune, headquartered at Sendai. He was the son of a petty chieftain; but he rose by his own strength and cunning to the position of the most powerful lord in northern Japan and terrorized the central government. His domain was the largest north of Tokyo, but that did not satisfy him. He dreamed of foreign conquest. Consequently, he saved from persecution in Tokyo some Christian missionaries from Europe, in order to learn from them about the lands he intended to seize.

After learning all he could from the Christians, Masamune ordered a certain Hasekura Tsunenaga to go to Europe on a tour of investigation. Setting out in a Japanese boat modeled after an English craft which had been wrecked on the Japanese coast, Hasekura went as far as Mexico. From there he was taken to Spain in a Spanish boat. As the first Japanese to be seen in that country, he was well received by Philip III. In 1615 he was converted to Christianity and baptized. Proceeding to Switzerland, he was enthusiastically welcomed by the president of the Swiss Federation. He then went to Rome, where his triumphal entry was magnificent, and he was the honored guest of the pope, Paul V. He returned to Japan with a portrait of his Holiness and a letter as gifts to his master. Although he lived in Japan until his death he never gave up his occidental religion. The two existing portraits of Hasekura, one in the possession of the Date family in Tokyo and the other in the Vatican, show that Hasekura was a singularly intelligent and attractive gentleman. Although Hasekura reported to Masamune that the European conquest would not be too difficult for one so powerful as his master, the plans fell through because of the isolation policy of the government at Yedo. Near the crest of Mount Aoba stand two massive old gates, all that remain from the once mighty castle of the great war lord, Masamune.

JAPAN [271]

Courtesy N Y K Steamship Line

MATSUSHIMA OR PINE ISLANDS, ONE OF THE SCENIC TRIO OF JAPAN, NEAR SENDAI

THE PINE ISLANDS

Matsushima, meaning Pine Islands, is on the coast of Matsushima Bay, which is full of delightful islands, all pine-clad and green. It is one of the spots chosen in the classical antiquity of Japan as lovely enough to be a member of the scenic trio, or the three most beautiful places in Japan. Every visitor should take at least one day for a boat trip around the islands; for not only are they beautiful in themselves, but they give an insight into the civilization of the time at which they were chosen to be among the scenic trio. And if you have the time you should certainly give a part of it to a protracted visit to Tomiyama and Otakamori, two of the most interesting spots about this attractive bay.

Otakamori is a mountain only a fifteen-minute walk away from the city. From it you may see the entire bay, and much of the surrounding land; and on clear days, far out to sea. Near the summit is the Daikyo-ji Temple, which is said to have been founded by the famous general Tamuramaro who subdued the northern part of the island before he died in 811. A wooden statue of him is still preserved in the temple. Although the shrine is not lavishly magnificent, it is one of the most interesting, because of its age and because of the lovely view of the bay of Matsushima, which it commands.

LUCKY-ROCK TEMPLE

The Zuigan-ji Temple, meaning the Lucky-Rock Temple, is also near Matsushima and is even more interesting. Not only is it judged by connoisseurs to be a splendid example of the art of the Momoyama period; but it is nearly as old as the Daikyo-ji Temple, having been first built in 828. Little of the old temple remains, but it was rebuilt in even greater beauty by the powerful Masamune in 1609. An avenue of Cryptomerias leads to the temple itself; and even more fascinating to the foreigner are the smoke-begrimed caves past which it leads. They were used as dwelling places by student priests who studied at the temple, because the famous abbot Heishiro was so popular that room could not be found in the temple to house all the scholars eager to sit at his feet.

The whole temple is rich in memories of the great Date Masamune. In the beautiful Peacock Room is a wooden statue of the general in armor. Interesting to note is the extreme lifelikeness of the statue. One of the eyes is missing. Masamune lost an eye in an engagement in his youth and was always proud of that proof of his valor. Close by, as though ready to serve again as soon as the lord wakens from his sleep, is one of Masamune's war drums. Going down the last corridor you will find many blue tablets on which are carved the names of all his lords who committed *hara-kiri* (suicide, as proof of loyalty) at Masamune's death. In the same corridor is a pair of cut glass candlesticks, which Hasekura brought to Masamune from His Holiness Paul V.

LAKE TOWADA-KO

Due north of the Pine Islands and not far away lies Lake Towada-Ko, in an old crater. The lake is notable for its size, its many pine islands, and for the woodlands and cliffs which surround it. It is almost exactly circular except that on the south side two promontories jut into the water dividing that part of the main lake into three portions of almost equal size. They are known as the West, East, and Central lakes while the portion north of them is called the Great Sea, a name well applied. The lake is well stocked with trout.

PAUL BUNYAN AND ST. GEORGE

There is a legend that toward the end of the ninth century Hachiro Taro, a woodsman whose size rivaled that of the legend-

JAPAN

LAKE TOWADA, THE HEART OF THE NATIONAL PARK KNOWN AS TOWADA PARK

Courtesy N Y K Steamship Line

ary American Paul Bunyan, was fishing in the region, which was then solid land except for a small stream running through it. Becoming thirsty, he drank from the brook and was immediately turned into a tremendous dragon. Since even a dragon must live, he converted the pleasant valley into a lake in which he made his home. Shortly thereafter the priest Nansobo was presented with a pair of iron sandals by the god Gongen, who instructed him to go on a pilgrimage and not to stop till the sandals wore out. As soon as Nansobo reached Lake Towada, his sandals broke and he knew that he had reached the spot where Gongen had intended him to build a shrine. But before he could do so, he was attacked by the dragon. In the battle, which was as exciting as that between St. George and his dragon, the priest was triumphant. Today you may see at the shrine a statue of Nansobo, who is now the patron saint of the region; and also the iron sandals which he wore.

Descending a sheer face of rock from the Nansobo Shrine to Central Lake, by means of a chain and an iron ladder, you arrive at the Japanese Delphi, Ouranaiba. From the most ancient times it has been the custom for those particularly anxious to find out if their prayers were to be answered to place copper coins on twists of paper in the water. Tradition has it that if the coin sinks immediately, the prayer is certain to be answered. Recently, to test the faith of his flock, a Shinto priest hired a diver to recover the money which ages of pious Japanese had dropped into the water; and coins to the value of two thousand yen were recovered.

SOUTHERN JAPAN

But you have been in northern Japan all this time, and the lure of the south is strong. So you will probably take a *maru*—boat, and go along the western coast of the country admiring the mountain ranges in the distance and the wooded and coved shore line. It is a treat to have such beautiful scenery stretching out before your eyes, constantly changing and constantly more entrancing, while you merely sit in a comfortable chair and rest from your exertions of active rather than passive sight-seeing on the shore. And just as you begin to feel that you would like to move about and do your own sight-seeing again you reach Nagasaki, the oldest open port in the nation. Incidentally, this interesting city is in a fortified zone, and photography is prohibited. The importance of the city dates from the twelfth century when it was given to Nagasaki Kotaro, from whom it takes its name, by Minamoto Yoritomo, who founded feudalism. But the real significance of the port was attained in the sixteenth century, when it became engaged in foreign trade with European nations.

Great galleons came from Portugal, Spain, and Holland to buy the exotic products of the unknown but fascinating Japan; and this was also the home port for all Japanese trade with the Philippines, China, Formosa, Siam, and other countries. In 1637, with the beginning of the closed-door policy, Spain and Portugal were forbidden entry; the Dutch were confined to the tiny island of Dejima in the bay; and only the Chinese were allowed perfect freedom of trade. But all during that period of isolation foreign influence and learning managed to filter into Japan through Nagasaki. For this reason this city was a very popular center for students who wished to profit by the advances made in culture in other countries. But when Japan again became a member of foreign trade groups, other and larger ports welcomed this learning; and the popularity of Nagasaki diminished.

But Nagasaki is nevertheless interesting, not only for the memories which it brings of the great exploration period in Europe, but also for its sights. The most impressive of these is the fine bronze *torii*, one of the largest in Japan, which is to be seen in the Suwa-jinsha. This graceful gate stands over thirty-three feet high and is a most impressive sight. At the same place is a bronze horse, a votive offering, which stands in the courtyard of the shrine built around the torii and the horse.

THE HEART OF OLD JAPAN

Kyoto, the center of Japanese culture and for over a thousand years the capital of the country, is great in historical glory. It is the center of Buddhism in Japan and the origin of those arts for which Japan is famous the world over. Gracefully situated in the center of a group of mountains which protect the old city, Kyoto is rich in appeal and in interests.

Since wisteria is considered the flower which best represents the spirit of Japan and is the flower which the geisha girls are

FRAGRANT BLOOMS OF THE WISTERIA, REGARDED BY THE JAPANESE AS A SYMBOL OF IDEAL WOMANHOOD

Courtesy N Y K Steamship Line

taught to arrange beautifully, it is natural that Kyoto, the city which best represents the spirit of Japan, should boast some of the most beautiful specimens of the plant. But Kyoto, a beauty-loving city, does not devote itself exclusively to this one flower. It has also fine gardens in which grow azaleas, peonies, irises, and plums. Nor are chrysanthemums neglected; but they finish off the year with a blaze of glory, as they are shown in the Maruyama Park in October.

In the eighth century the city that is today known as Kyoto was chosen as the capital of the empire and was called Heian-kyo, or the City of Peace. Later the name was changed to Miyako, meaning imperial capital; and still later to Kyoto, meaning capital. Years of war left the city in desolation and great poverty. It was not till the sixteenth century that the city was restored to its former glory by the famous Oda Nobunaga, who entered the city in 1569 at the head of his forces and immediately decreed the rebuilding of the imperial palace and the rest of the city. His successor carried on the work, and it was not long until Kyoto was a city suited to be the head of the empire of Japan. In spite of the removal of the administration to Tokyo, Kyoto is still the classical capital of the nation, partly because of the clause in the constitution which requires that the coronation or ceremony of enthronement of each new emperor be held in that city.

The imperial palace is closed to the general public, only the highest ranking Japanese being admitted. Foreigners, however, may get permits through their consuls in Tokyo, which will admit them to most of the rooms, providing they observe the customs and rules: to go in morning coat and leave shoes and hat at the door; not to smoke inside the palace itself; and not to take photographs or make any sketches of the place. The palace itself is situated in the center of the Imperial Park, which was once filled with the residences of nobles of high rank and favor with the ruler. The palace, which dates from 1856, is surrounded by high walls. The original was built in 794, but was destroyed by fire in 1788, after which it was rebuilt in the same fashion. Again in 1854 flames gutted the impressive building. And again it was rebuilt in the original style, which is one marked by great simplicity and beauty of line.

One of the most important rooms of the palace is the throne room, which is used for the most impressive ceremonies and functions of the state. Two of the affairs which took place there were the enthronement of the emperor and the New Year's audience. In the center of a large hall, seventy-two by one hundred and eight feet, is the throne covered with the finest of silk draperies; while on each side of it are stools for bearing the imperial treasures, the sword and the jewel. On one side of the door is planted a cherry tree and on the other a citrus tree, representing the archers and horsemen who in ancient times stood on guard at these posts. Almost the only decoration of the room is provided by the painted panels along the walls which were done by the famous Kano Sukenobu—in an attempt to replace those which had been done in 888 by Kose no Kanaoka and later destroyed. This hall, as is the entire palace, is decorated with dignified simplicity.

THE NIJO PALACE

Kyoto is a city of many palaces. Besides the group originally intended for the emperor, there are many which have come under the imperial sway. Outstanding among these is the Nijo Palace, built by the first Tokugawa Shogun, Iyeyasu, in the early part of the sixteenth century, as a residence for himself when visiting in Kyoto. After the restoration, the palace was temporarily used as an office building for the prefecture; and an appalling amount of damage, some of it beyond repair, was done to the rare objects of art there. Since that time the palace has become another imperial palace; and much has been done to restore the former glories of the Nijo.

This palace is quite different from the main imperial palace, as it has the most prolific and extravagant decoration. All the public chambers, where the shogun received his courtiers and his master's messengers, are in this elaborate tradition. Fine paintings, many of them of unusual size and boldness of design, vie with skilful carvings for attention. But when you reach the private room of the shogun, you find more subdued though even more elegant and refined decorations.

The garden is still interesting, although it is not as it was in the days of the great shoguns. They had a beautiful garden, but without trees, because the falling of the leaves was an ever-present and unpleasant reminder of the transitoriness of life. Since that time, however, trees have been planted there.

HERO'S SHRINE

West of the Imperial Park is an old Shinto shrine, which is dedicated to Wake no Kiyomaro, an eighth-century courtier who barely escaped being murdered and was sent into exile because he would not assist a usurper to overthrow the emperor. Eventually affairs were straightened out and the emperor recalled his faithful retainer and sent the villain into exile. The returned hero was heaped with honors for his loyalty and was placed in charge of much building in Kyoto.

GEISHA GIRLS AT THE KABURENJO

On the west bank of the Kamo is the Ponto-cho, a street well known as an amusement center. The Kaburenjo is celebrated for its geisha girls who do the famous dance, the *Kamogawa Odori*. These girls are artists of entertainment. Trained from youth in the graceful posture dances which are a part of Japanese tradition, in the art of flower arrangement, and in social conversation on an intellectual plane, they constitute one of the institutions of old Japan. Utterly refined, quiet and well-mannered, they provide companionship on an elegant and moral plane for the gentlemen of Japan. Their status is a high and honorable one, and after practicing their profession for a long enough period to provide themselves with a dowry, they usually marry into a higher circle of society than that from which they came.

A. T. Palmer photo, Berkeley, Calif.

DANCE OF THE CHERRY BLOSSOMS

OSAKA

We travel on to Osaka, one of the most important cities of Japan. Osaka traces her history back to the third century when the Emperor Ojin built a palace on the hill on which the castle now stands. In the fourth century Nintoku built one on the same spot. This Emperor Nintoku, so they say, while looking down on the village about the foot of the hill, one evening, noticed a sign of hard times. The fires in all the houses were burning low. Truly interested in the well-being of his subjects, he immediately remitted taxation for three years in order to give his subjects a chance to recover their financial status. It was not till the sixteenth century that Osaka really began to develop as a commercial center, but since that time it has grown steadily, and today it is one of the most important of Japanese industrial cities.

THE PUPPET SHOW

In feudal times Osaka became the drama center for the entire nation, and today it still retains a high position. It is partially due to the puppet theater that Osaka claims this eminence. It has the only puppet theater in Japan which performs continuously and carries on an age-old tradition. In the early part of the eighteenth century puppet shows were the most popular form of drama in Japan. They had been developed to such a state of artistic perfection that their appeal was almost as great as that of real actors, while their popularity was greater. Slowly the public began to tire of the artificial aspect of the puppets, and drama became once more a performance of persons. At Kyoto, though, the puppet stage has been kept alive, and today you may see the puppets giving splendid performances under the skilful management of their manipulators.

OSAKA CASTLE

On the edge of a clear green lake stands the Osaka Castle. Rising from the waters in which it is reflected and surrounded by trees, the castle looks more like a pleasure residence than a military edifice. But it has a deceiving appearance of gentleness. Closer inspection reveals the foundation and walls made of granite blocks, capable of withstanding a siege. Most of the old castle

Courtesy N Y K Steamship Line

OSAKA CASTLE

has disappeared, and only the innermost citadel remains to tell of the bloody battles, the assaults and repulses, and the successful attacks connected with its history. The double line of towered walls and moats is gone; and other buildings have gone. There remains a towering building of white, with many gables, which broods as it looks into its reflection in the water and sees that it has passed its period of usefulness.

KOBE

This time we depart for Kobe, the only port in the country that vies with Yokohama for the position of largest open port. Kobe is not an old city, although the town of Hyogo, which it absorbed, was the center of government as early as the twelfth century. Hyogo throughout its history was a fairly prosperous town; but when the country was thrown open to trade in the last century, it did not take Kobe long to rise and surpass the rival city. Sixty years ago Kobe was only a fishing village, and today it is one of the most important commercial and manufacturing cities in the entire nation.

With a continuous line of mountains as a background, Kobe lies in a long strip on the coast. The business section is along the waterfront, while the residential section is slowly mounting the slopes of the mountains behind. It is an attractive picture from

FUJIYAMA, THE MOST FAMOUS MOUNTAIN OF JAPAN

Courtesy Japan Tourist Bureau
MOUNT ASO, AN ACTIVE VOLCANO 27 MILES EAST OF KUMAMOTO

THE CLASSICAL "KABUKI" PLAY

Courtesy of the Japanese Government Railways
A JAPANESE FAMILY AT BREAKFAST

the bay or from an airplane, with the thriving waterfront contrasting the luxurious and peaceful group of graceful homes surrounded by their gardens, little or big, according to the wealth of the owner.

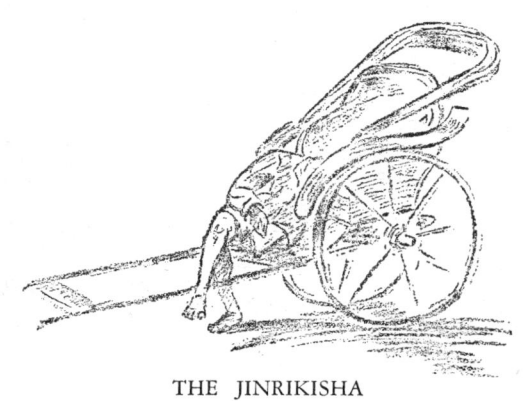

THE JINRIKISHA
In narrow Japanese streets, this man-drawn vehicle is the only wheeled conveyance allowed. Each 'riksha carries but one passenger.

THE JINRIKISHA

The Motomachi, one of the busiest streets in the city, is most unusual. It is the shopping center of the town, but the streets are so narrow that motor traffic is prohibited. The only conveyance allowed is the jinrikisha, the most typically Japanese of all vehicles. To do any shopping, and surely you will, or at least you will want to look about, you must get one of these oriental taxis. And remember to hold tightly to the sides or you will regret not having done so. They are small and carry only one person at a time; and as soon as that one person is seated, however insecurely, the tiny human horse trots off. At first everything seems fine. You are comfortably seated in a smooth-rolling vehicle with a perfect view of the whole street. Then the little man stops, and unless you have been holding on, you will find yourself catapulted forward in undignified haste onto the back of your jinrikisha man,

MIYAJIMA, ONE OF THE GREATEST SCENIC BEAUTIES OF THE COUNTRY

Courtesy Japan Tourist Bureau
THE AOI FESTIVAL IN KYOTO, HELD ON MAY 15

JAPAN

A SHINTO TEMPLE FESTIVAL
Children carrying traveling temple in Shinto festival,
an ancient custom.

who will do nothing to stop your fall. But after about two of these sudden stops you get the knack of the riding and decide that it is a most enjoyable way to get from one place to another.

"ISE, THE SOURCE OF NIPPON'S SOUL"

Before we leave Japan we must go to Ise where the Sacred Mirror is kept. This mirror was one of the three gifts, of which the other two were the sacred sword and a necklace of strangely carved jewels, by which Amaterasu Omikami, the Great Sun Goddess, gave the Japanese tangible proof that they are a chosen people and that their ruler is of divine descent. When she made these gifts to her heavenly grandson, she sent him from paradise to conquer and rule over the islands which make up Japan. Although the sword and jewels are held in high honor, they do not approach the mirror in importance and significance in the eyes of the Japanese. Amaterasu Omikami told her grandson that when he gazed into that mirror he would see her soul. Out of reverence for the soul of so great a goddess, no human eye has seen his mirror for all these centuries; but every year thousands of devout Shintoists from all parts of Japan go to the simple shrine to pay tribute to divinity and to their emperor.

Because of the Shinto horror of pollution, a new shrine is built every twenty years for the housing of this national and religious treasure. So ritualistic is the building of a new shrine that it takes eight years before the mirror can be transferred from its old home. When it is moved, there is a great ceremony. After sundown, to the accompaniment of wailing reed flutes, the procession, lighted by pine torches, leaves the old shrine. At the head are princes and government and court officials in elaborate and rich court dress; following them, in ancient Japanese costume, come musicians and priests; and after them, sword bearers and archers. But the heart of the procession is contained in four billowy walls of whitest silk that hide the men who carry the casket containing the Sacred Mirror, which is the very soul of the Japanese people and represents their ageless, changeless, and enduring loyalty. Every twenty years for more than two thousand years this ceremony, the Shikinen Sengusai, has been performed, and each time it has meant far more than the mere moving of a mirror. It has exemplified the immutability of an ideal.

CHINA

STREET SCENE IN SHANGHAI

SHANGHAI, THE POPULAR PORT OF ENTRY

IN PEACEFUL TIMES, the traveler in China usually selects Shanghai as the city from which to start his journeys of exploration because of its central location and easy accessibility.

It is a good thing that Shanghai is a modern and cosmopolitan city. One needs a base of operations that will give one a return to normalcy after wandering in China's back regions. Yet even Shanghai is not entirely commonplace.

On Nanking Road, near the great department stores of Wing On and Sincere (where in warfare so many have been victims), there is a small door set unobtrusively in a gray brick wall. One can go through that door without challenge but one will not stay there. The inner courtyard, reached by crossing a small outer courtyard, is a mass of humanity, on cold days a mass of humanity and chicken feathers. Members of the Beggars' Guild sleep and rest in that courtyard; men, women, children, deformed, diseased, starved.

TEA HOUSE NEAR SHANGHAI

There is a temple farther toward the Bund, opening off Nanking Road, where the incense burns day and night and at regular intervals the Buddhist priests chant songs and beat gongs while the worshipers kneel in silence, touching their heads softly against the worn stone floor.

ROMANTIC BYWAYS

It is easy to leave the prosaic shopping sections of Shanghai in the International Settlement and the French Concession, the wide tourist streets lined with a hodge-podge of shops, all displaying goods designed to attract the foreign tourist, and to become lost in the back streets, in some of which the tourist has to walk down the middle of the street to avoid the many stalls of merchandise set out to entice the coolies and working Chinese who inhabit these byways.

Set in the midst of these narrow, dirty streets is a cemetery circled by a high iron fence. The gate is always open and inside are old graves, many unattended these long years. Near the gate is the grave of a father, his photograph set at the headstone inside a glass case, and in a row beside him lie four smaller graves. He died on his coast steamer at the beginning of the century. The first mate brought his body to his home in Shanghai and while it lay waiting for the funeral his four little children died of diphtheria. They were buried together and the bereaved wife and mother was left alone in the great house.

Near these graves is a huge wisteria vine which in the spring turns its trellis into a glorious mass of purple. The trellis is the remains of a fire tower of the early Shanghai days and the bell which once hung in the tower is now in Jessfield Park in the outskirts of the city. There was a day, not so many years past, when one could go on a warm Sunday to Jessfield Park and there see an old, old lady, all misshapen with disease, sitting near the bell. She was the widow of the sea captain—it was she who was left alone in her youth and freshness.

Later she married the chief of the volunteer fire department and bore more children. One cold and sleety night the bell in

Paul's Photos, Chicago

SHANGHAI HARBOR ON THE WHANGPOO RIVER

STREET SCENE IN SHANGHAI
Picture shows Edward VII avenue in British section, with skyline of modern Shanghai in background.

the cemetery rang wildly and the fireman went to his duty. They brought him back to her in the morning, and now he lies near the old tower, under the wisteria vine.

THE CITY NOW

In those days, near the end of the nineteenth century, the foreign part of Shanghai was isolated; wide muddy streets lay near the Whangpoo River, and some distance away was the walled Chinese city of Nantao. Now the foreign parts of the city stretch on and on, wide and narrow streets reach back from the river over the old swamp lands and the old "Chinese City" is one with the rest of the town.

The Bund is a wide and busy street running along the Whangpoo River waterfront, with huge office buildings and hotels on the landward side. The ocean liners lie to in midstream or dock far up beyond the city, the naval boats of the various nations are at anchor nearby and, across the river where once only birds and plants of the swamps lived, are factories, docks, and other appurtenances of modern industrial life.

CHINA [291]

The main streets of the business district, directly back of the Bund, ceaselessly carry heavy traffic, and here one feels at home no matter what his native country. Business, banks, shops, traffic, pleasure, all go on in the customary modern manner. Only at night, perhaps, these commercial streets look a little different from the streets of European or American cities. Nanking Road, the Bund, Szechuen Road, all the main streets are flaming with signs bearing Chinese characters in red neon. Chinese characters are picturesque to begin with but done in red neon, glowing against a black sky, they are superlative. The night life that goes on during these dark hours of beauty is a story unto itself.

WHERE BOMBS KILLED HUNDREDS IN SHANGHAI

Paul's Photos, Chicago

There are many more Chinese living in Shanghai than there are foreigners, but the foreigners dominate the life of the International Settlement. A mixed court handles many of the cases coming up within the area, and the stories of this court provide amusement and tragedy for the residents. Rickshaw pullers are brought there to settle their arguments by law rather than fist and serious affairs are arbitrated. One such serious case was that of a house boy who was discharged by a European music teacher for incompetency. The night after his discharge he broke into her apartment and attacked her with a dagger, deliberately endeavoring to mutilate her hands so she could no longer play the piano. The court dealt justice but the foreign community held a benefit theatrical performance to get money for her aid.

In former times even Chinese of position were not allowed in the foreign hotels but in more recent years they have used all the facilities of the city in common with the other nationalities. The result is that hotel and restaurant life is far more colorful than in most other cities of the world. Nothing is quite so decorative as a native Chinese girl in her long, close-fitting gown.

UP FROM A MUD FLAT

Shanghai is more than a charming return to the not-too-ordinary for the sensation-weary traveler in interior China. It is a huge and still growing city of vital importance to the rest of China and to the world. It has grown in population and in size with astounding rapidity. Once it was a tiny fishing village. Then, in the middle of the last century, it became a small, unimportant port for the import and export trade. Now it ranks among the first ten ports of the world for volume of trade and is becoming more and more important every year.

Cotton and silk are produced in nearby provinces and raw materials are brought from interior China and from abroad to be manufactured into commodities and to be distributed throughout China and abroad. What once was a mud flat on the shores of the Whangpoo River is now the center of China's commercial, industrial and cultural life. Yet, despite all this solemn importance, there are tiny peasant cottages set in the midst of farms within the metropolitan area, and meandering canals carry little boats past huge modern factories.

Courtesy Robert R. Farman

BOATMAN ON A RIVER IN CHINA
The rivers of China are crowded with strange-looking craft. Much native commerce is carried on through the use of small boats (sampans) such as this one.

Courtesy Robert R. Farman

CHINESE JUNKS (SAILBOATS) ON SOOCHOW CREEK

Courtesy Robert R. Farman

SCENE ON SOOCHOW CREEK, WITH THE SHANGHAI POSTOFFICE IN THE BACKGROUND

Try as one will to think of Shanghai as a great, fast-moving business center, concerned only with the problems of trade, one cannot do so. A walk through the outlying or semi-outlying districts shows too many quaint contrasts: a naked child standing in his courtyard watching the smartly garbed foreign women dashing past on thoroughbred horses, or an exquisitely arranged Chinese garden hiding behind a brick wall with heavy traffic roaring over the nearby highway.

WAYS TO REACH PEIPING

The trip to Peiping may be made by several routes each involving a different means of transportation. For the hardy traveler with plenty of time on his hands the old ways of travel are by far the most interesting.

He may take a river boat up the Yangtze to Chinkiang, where the Grand Canal crosses the Yangtze River, and there transfer to a canal boat propelled by sail or a barge pulled by a steam launch. On this trip up the canal, as the boat slowly pushes its way past the flat banks, he may walk along the shore, seeing the farmers at their work and watching the wild ducks settle in flocks on the many small lakes. He can continue thus on the canal, to at least Tsingkiangpu, where the salt canal branches off to go to Haichow, which is on the seacoast eighty miles to the northeast. He may be able to go much farther north on the Grand Canal but, if the water is low, he will find it necessary to proceed by sedan chair, wheelbarrow, ox-cart or on foot. Motorcycles or bicycles are especially satisfactory for this backroads travel.

Another way, and easier, is via coast steamer, stopping at various towns along the way north. These steamers are on the whole reasonably comfortable and along the northern coast there is less danger, from both typhoons and pirates, than along the coast from Shanghai south.

The last stages of this journey may be made by rail to reach Peiping itself. One can go by airplane also from Shanghai to Peiping, a short and simple journey made in half a day. But the usual way, and perhaps the most satisfactory for the average person, is by rail. The train runs from Shanghai to Nanking in about eight hours. After crossing the Yangtze by ferry to Pukow, one boards another train which goes straight through to Peiping. This stage of the journey lasts about two days and a night but may

Homer Smith photo, Chicago
GOLD MOUNTAIN TEMPLE AT CHINKIANG, CHINA

easily be several hours to several days longer. Travel in China's interior is sometimes restricted by bandits, wars, floods, and other unpleasantries.

PEIPING—CITY OF GRACIOUS LIVING

One comes upon Peiping, majestic city of the ancients, after passing through endless miles of flat, monotonous country.

The first view of the city gives one the impression that everything is walls, great and high and blank. The inside of the city is the same—streets and streets all lined with walls. The shopping areas have open-front stores, but the residential sections are tantalizing in their reticence.

After washing off the dust of the journey and eating a good foreign meal in one of the completely modern and comfortable hotels, one can set forth to see the city with a little more receptivity. The discomforts of the train journey, present even if one has taken a private compartment, enormously increased if one has traveled with the Chinese in second or third class, are forgotten. The soft chairs in the hotel have removed the memory of the springless benches of the train and the good meal has wiped out an empty feeling occasioned by the several days' rations purchased in the dining cars attached to the train.

CHINA [297]

Paul's Photos, Chicago
MAIN STREET IN SUICHING, CHINA

Courtesy The Art Institute of Chicago
SUMMER PALACE NEAR PEIPING

Paul's Photos, Chicago
SIDE VIEW OF CHIEN MEN GATE, PEIPING

Without half trying, one is bound to come upon a market place which turns out to be a riot of color and noise, hundreds of varieties of fruits being drenched in brilliant sunlight and all sorts of magicians, vendors, pedestrians, adding to the gaiety by talking loudly about themselves. The wise tourist buys nothing to eat or drink in native Chinese markets, for there is always present the lurking danger of dysentery.

Here one may see cricket-fights lasting two or three minutes—exciting battles ending by the vanquished insects lying down in a corner with his antennae meekly lowered. Here the candy man performs his miracles, making enchanting dragons, horses, birds, people, out of brightly colored sugar. Here the traveler may see noodles cut in all shapes and colored, or chickens and ducks roasted a lovely shiny brown. Fruits are on sale here, brought from all parts of China. Perhaps the most appealing are the huge golden grindstone persimmons, raised in the country nearby and kept through the winter in flat pits, where the freezing weather is said to give them an especially delicious flavor. Yet the experienced traveler is not tempted.

Surfeited with noise and motion, one gladly goes into the Forbidden City, wherein dwelt the emperors and royalty of China for nearly six centuries, or to some of the ancient palaces or temples, where there is quiet and exquisite beauty. The old builders of China outdid themselves in the perfection of these structures. They utilized line and space, sunlight and shadow, to produce a feeling of expanding thoughtfulness. They have laid gorgeous color over woodwork and tiles till one is sometimes shocked by the near garishness of the scene. These temples and palaces are a taste of the true spirit of Peiping, one of gentle living, intensely interesting and appealing to all. The discerning person stays as long as he possibly can, savoring the art of living which is so highly developed here among foreigners and Chinese alike.

AN EXILED TRIBE

It is with great reluctance that one leaves Peiping for even short visits to such well-known places as the Western Hills and the Great Wall. By going a little farther afield one may see the Valley of the Lost Tribe, about a hundred miles west of Peiping.

Here five thousand or so Chinese live in poverty, until recently dressing and living as did their forebears in the Ming Dynasty. In 1644 the Manchus were trying to invade China through the pass at Shanhaikwan. A Shensi general took the opportunity to seize Peiping and, when the last of the Ming emperors hanged himself on the top of Coal Hill within the city limits, the Shensi general proceeded to set up his own private dynasty in Peiping. Unfortunately he also took one of the favorite and most beautiful concubines of Wu San-kuei, the chief Ming generalissimo. Naturally enough, the latter was thoroughly aroused and immediately joined forces with the invading Manchus to oust the Shensi general. They succeeded easily.

Some three hundred of the Shensi men escaped from the city with a good deal of silver metal and hid themselves in the barren, wild region west of Peiping. The Manchus followed them and shut them up in the most inaccessible valley, with guards at the exits. The only kindness was to allow the victims to import wives from their native Shensi.

Eventually, when the enforced retirement ended, they had gotten so used to the valley that they stayed on. Their descendants raise as much grain and vegetables for food as they can, utilizing every fertile scrap of land. Incense wood used in the region round about Peiping is one of their products.

BY RAIL THROUGH THE NORTH PLAIN

Peiping has been the center of China's political, intellectual and cultural life these many centuries. One leaves it to go southeast to Tientsin, important only because of its location. The country between the two cities, like nearly all the country seen by rail north of Hsuchowfu, is flat, endlessly flat. In winter everything is one common shade of brown, in summer a study in shades of green.

Here the peasants cultivate every bit of land, their thousands of little mud huts connected by footpaths which border their rectangular fields, their dead buried in graves marked by circular mounds scattered helter-skelter through the neatly tilled fields of wheat and kaoliang, soybeans, and vegetables. Summer and winter the farmers work in their small fields. All are dressed in cloth dyed with indigo. Some of the garments are shiny with dirt, others faded pale from long use. Day in and day out the seemingly humble, actually often vicious, little donkeys carry heavy loads from one place to another, the oxen pull the wooden plows, and the squeaking wheelbarrows toil back and forth from the fields to the villages.

The brown landscape is relieved occasionally by a neat grove of evergreens planted to keep the sharp north winds from the ghosts of long-dead persons who were able to squeeze a little more money than usual out of the land. Among the fields are stone or wood tablets erected to the memory of one individual or another, each standing on a tortoise, symbol of long life, his face turned to the south. The farmers are obviously very poor, scarcely able to force a living from the worn soil. Since the fertility of the soil is so low, they use every sort of manure, and every scrap of dried grass is gathered to use as fuel.

TIENTSIN, STRICTLY A BUSINESS CENTER

Tientsin lies at the junction of the Haiho and Peiho rivers and the Grand Canal, some forty miles from the sea and eighty miles from Peiping. It has become important because it is one of the best of the poor harbors of this part of China. In spite of the Taku Bar across the mouth of the Haiho, and in spite of the difficulty of keeping the river channel open, it is a growing city with a promising future.

A SECTION OF THE GREAT WALL OF CHINA

An astronomer is reported to have said that if some one on another sphere were studying the earth the one thing noticeable would be the Great Wall of China, erected in the third century before Christ. This immense wall stretches over mountains and valleys along the northern boundaries of China for fourteen hundred miles. The wall is about twenty-five feet thick at the base, and fifteen feet at the top; rises in height from twenty to thirty feet, and has towers which are forty feet high and are placed about three hundred yards apart. Between these towers there is a driveway about ten feet in width on the top of the walls.

There are many foreigners here and a constant coming and going of produce. Dried egg powder is shipped from here to be used in the bakeries of the United States. Foreign commodities enter here to be distributed to the huge hinterland which reaches as far as distant Sinkiang in western China. It is interesting to sit at the waterfront and watch the traveling families, Chinese and foreign, with their many children and many more suitcases, baskets, bedding rolls, bundles, and boxes. Travel to a resident of China is serious business—the whole household must go along, including the pet bird.

TSINGTAU, GATHERING PLACE OF LOVELY WOMEN

Traveling south from Tientsin by rail the tourist passes through more monotonously flat country. At Tsinan he changes trains to go east to the seaport of Tsingtau.

Tsingtau was developed by the Germans from an insignificant fishing town. It lies on the edge of a beautiful harbor where the swimming is excellent. Many foreigners come here in the summer and the beach is constantly dotted with charming women from all parts of the world. It has been controlled by the Japanese and the Chinese in turn since the Germans lost it during the World War.

A great deal of shipping goes on through its harbor but the interest to the traveler is in its delightful parks, its varied shops, dealing in goods chosen to entice the tourist, and in its military history.

"IN THE WHITE WINDY PRESENCE OF ETERNITY"

On the way back to the main rail line it is easy to take a trip to Tai Shan, the most ancient sacred mountain in the world. It is said that the Emperor Shun made sacrifice on this mountain in the twenty-third century before Christ. A peak over five thousand feet high reaches up from the comparative level of the plain. On its summit is the temple to which go pilgrims wishing to do honor to Confucius. Buddhists and Taoists also do reverence at Tai Shan. Some ride up in sedan chairs, some walk, and some, to gain special credit, go up the thousands of steps on their knees. Eunice Tietjens, in her poem, "The Most Sacred Mountain," best expresses the feeling inspired by this revered shrine.

BURIAL CHAMBER IN AN ANCIENT CHINESE TOMB
The body was placed in a pit in the center of the cross-shaped bottom.

JEWS AND MOHAMMEDANS AT KAIFENG

Back at the main railway, one proceeds to Hsuchowfu, where the Lunghai railroad, running east and west, crosses the line from Tientsin to Pukow. Here one takes the train to go west to Kaifeng, the city where once flourished a Jewish colony. This colony was established at the time when the silk trade between Europe and China was at its height. Merchants from Europe who carried on the business used Kaifeng, among other cities, as headquarters. The Jewish merchants set up synagogues and through the years many Chinese were converted to their faith. Some of the few existing relics of the Jewish synagogue at Kaifeng are still there, mostly at the Trinity Cathedral. Descendants of the once strong Jewish group now are held together only by kinship, there being no longer any religious ties. There are now in Kaifeng several Mohammedan mosques. Chinese Mohammedanism borrowed from Chinese Judaism in the past and has continued whereas Judaism has died out. Many and strange are the intricacies of China's culture.

The city of Kaifeng lies some miles south of the present bed of the Yellow River. There are dykes near the city walls which show that once the river passed close by. The walls of the city enclose a great deal of extra space, including a lake on which wild-duck hunting takes place. In the center of this lake, joined to the mainland by an artificial causeway, is an island on which stands a series of buildings. In the innermost of these is a carved stone, said to have been used as a throne by emperors during the different periods when Kaifeng for strategic or political reasons served as the capital of China. Nearby is the Iron Pagoda, so called because the glazed tiles and porcelain used in its construction are of a peculiar iron-rust color. The slender spire dominates the town and, seen against the setting sun, is a thing to impress one with the strength and delicacy of China's architecture.

There is a great deal of silk manufacture in the city and in the surrounding region a particular sort of wood is cut into blocks and shipped via the Lunghai Railway to Tientsin and thence by ship to Japan, where it is used for outdoor shoes. Here, too, eggs are dried to be shipped as powder to the United States and other countries. In Kaifeng is a university, many years old. In the old days examinations for advancement were given here. The hundreds of examination cells, in which the aspirants to higher and

CHINA

yet higher learning were locked to spend days composing philosophical essays upon the classics, are now mostly destroyed, and the university has been developed along more modern lines.

Perhaps because the city has for so long been a center of intellectual life, it is now a place where all sorts of writing paper are manufactured.

DUST STORMS AND SHENSI CLIFF DWELLERS

Great dust storms come out of the west and north to cover Kaifeng with clouds of misery. The winds that bring them often shift the sand dunes which lie to the north of the city, sometimes piling them against the city walls till it is possible to walk directly from the wall onto the dunes. Most of this dust comes from nearby Shensi Province, which is composed largely of loess. The loess is so thick in Shensi that the road beds are often forty feet below the level of the plains, for when once a track is started, the water from the torrential rains follows the depression and wears away more and more of the fine, wind-laid soil. The peasants

Paul's Photos, Chicago

COACH STATION AND INN IN SHANSI, CHINA

often dig their homes in the side of loess cliffs. The rooms thus formed are comfortable and cheap, but when a landslide or earthquake occurs the loss of life is very high.

Living is difficult in this loess region and the farmer has all he can do to raise food for his family. If the climate were more favorable, it might be possible to cultivate the fields so that there would be more than enough food for all. As it is, the farmers live in their snug little cave-rooms, housing the few animals they possess in similar dugouts, and raise what grain and vegetables they can on what really might be termed their roofs. There are practically no trees in the whole area so every bit of grass and straw has to be gathered for fuel. In spite of all the poverty, the people of this area, as of all China, are satisfied and content with what they have, rather than complaining because they have not more. The land near Kaifeng is composed of this same loess mixed with silt brought by the Yellow River.

This means that the soil is better for crops and does not have the quality of standing in cliffs along the edges of permanent or temporary streams. The climate around Kaifeng, which is in Honan Province, is more gentle than that of Shensi Province, making it less difficult to grow sufficient food.

HAICHOW, AN UNTOUCHED NATIVE CITY

The Lunghai Railroad takes one back from Kaifeng to Hsuchowfu, and through Hsuchowfu on east to the sea. Twenty-five miles from the sea the railroad runs within two miles of Haichow, a native city as yet scarcely changed by foreign influence yet easy to reach. It is the residential town of a business city four miles away and lies near a tidal river.

The city has a wall around it which is kept in good repair because the area has for many years suffered from ceaseless bandit raids. The wall is of great gray bricks and granite blocks. Set into the top of the wall are stone gutters which were used in the old days to pour melted lead on invaders. There is a moat all around the city, each of the four gates having a drawbridge. The water gate, formerly used, is now closed. Inside the wall, there is a bank which reaches up to the battlemented top of the wall and one can walk on this around the city. The slope of the bank is used for truck gardening and there are other empty areas within the city. During long sieges these places were used to grow food.

CHINA							[307]

As one walks on the wall one sees that the poorer homes of the city huddle along winding streets while here and there the courtyards of the richer homes form geometrical patterns of neatness. The temple courtyards are neat, and the courts of the officials are lined with soldiers on guard or waiting to go out into the country on bandit-exterminating journeys.

From the West Gate to the East Gate runs the main shopping street and in the center of the city lie the markets, the cross streets of shops and the local business houses. From the North Gate to the South Gate runs a main street, lined part way with shops and intersecting the main shopping center.

CHINESE WOMAN VENDOR OF PEANUTS

Paul's Photos, Chicago

A WALK AROUND THE CITY ON TOP OF THE WALL

The North Gate of the city opens onto the end of the canal which runs southward to join the Grand Canal eighty miles away at Tsingkiangpu. The road to the business city of the area runs northward out of this gate, so all day long laborers are staggering in and out with loads of merchandise going to the south and north, or being brought in from those sections. There is always a soldier or two at the gateway, keeping an eye on affairs.

The East Gate opens onto a residential district outside the walls of the city composed mostly of homes of poorer people who, in common with the people living around the southern and western parts of the wall, carry on truck gardening and poultry raising to supply the needs of those living inside the city. The East Gate region is hilly but there are more hills as one goes toward the South Gate, until one comes to the Little Mountain which is a bare granite hill two or three hundred feet high.

Between this hill and the South Gate of the city runs a stream which is full of rushing dirty water during the rains, but which usually is a wide gravel bed with several clear streams winding aimlessly. Here the women of the city come to do their washing. Rows of them sit by the little streams and beat their clothes against rocks while they talk long and loud about absent neighbors. The water is clear and sweet when it comes down the stream to this sections, but it is blue and full of scum and dirt when it leaves. In this gravel bed the men dig holes and, when they are filled with water, carry it into the city for drinking, cooking, and household use. The children play in the water of the stream when the weather is warm, and the old men sit leaning against the city wall during winter days, sunning themselves while they smoke and look at the running streams.

There is a well near this river from which people take water when the stream runs dry in times of drought. When the well is full it looks like any other well but, it is said, when the water is low one can see, if one looks carefully, that near the bottom are two great dragon's heads, spouting water day and night. No one knows how long the well has been there or who built it.

As one goes on around the wall of the city one comes to the West Gate where there are numbers of shops outside the city walls. It is here that the story-teller sits all through the day, recounting his endless tales of the heroes of old who, like the Greek heroes, ate, slept, and fought; then ate, slept, and fought again.

CHINA   [309]

The houses outside this gate are many and extend over an area of a square mile or more. The hospital, built in 1914, lies here, and next door to it are the houses of one of the big bandit families of the region. Everyone knows the family gains its living in the wicked ways of banditry, but the members have such political power and bribe the control of justice so expertly that they are never hampered in their actions.

BANDITS

These bandits and others of the same variety have for years harried the whole neighborhood of Haichow. It is customary to see, on a dark night, the glow of burning villages in the country. The bandit gangs swoop down on a village, loot the houses, kill the inhabitants who are not fortunate enough to have fled, and set fire to the houses and what crops they cannot carry away. A little later the men of the village thus treated are apt to retaliate on the village of the bandits or attack some other group of houses.

Bandits living near Haichow are defiant because they can flee to safety among the hills, but they, too, have their troubles. The military officials wage constant warfare on the bandits. The

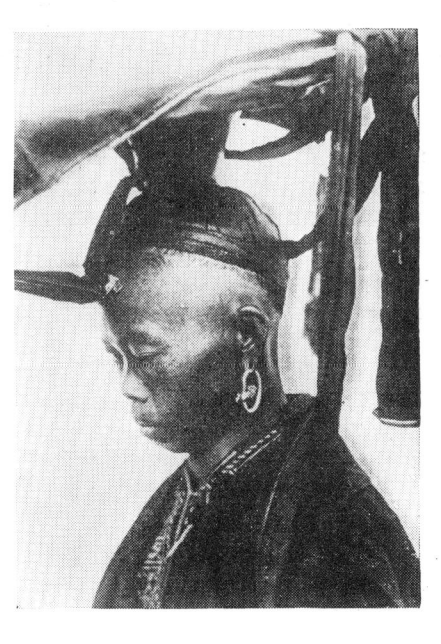

FESTIVE HEADDRESS OF CHINESE WOMAN

Paul's Photos, Chicago

degree of success depends upon how well the local soldiery was bribed to guard the wrong villages. When the soldiers of the local general are serious about capturing some particular bandit group, they do a thorough job, but usually they would just as soon not catch the offenders. When a bandit is caught he is jailed and usually beheaded. His head is then hung in a basket on the city wall at the West Gate so that all may see what happens to bandits who are caught.

A MUCH-USED HILL

The Little Mountain, the hill lying just south of the city of Haichow, has no vegetation upon it. At the base, away from the city, lie graves all crowded against one another and in the midst of these graves is the official execution ground. Here bandits and other criminals are executed. Families may, if they wish, remove the bodies. Otherwise the dogs of the city attend to the matter of disposal. Here, too, the paupers' bodies are left and the bodies of all dead babies.

The base of the hill on the side toward the city is occupied by a temple which is the center of the great spring fair. In May the farmers and villagers come from miles around to sell the produce peculiar to their own sections of the countryside. There are farm tools made of willow wood and cast iron, baskets of willow wands, toys of willow gaily painted, mats of reeds, endless varieties of articles made from willow-wood or reeds. In one stall are sold cuttings of plants, seeds, and potted plants; in another trinkets of tin and brass and sometimes of silver, often of pewter. Here are clothes made from cotton brought from the more southerly parts of China, woven locally and usually dyed with the ever present indigo. There are mud toys painted with brilliant colors, and dishes baked to a glowing brown-red. All the things ordinary people need to carry on their work and live their lives are brought together for all to see and all to buy. For a week the whole countryside thinks of nothing but the annual fair, and all ordinary business is laid aside.

The Little Mountain is easily climbed. Just above the fair ground is a cave in which the beggars sleep. Near the cave the rocks are covered with carvings, writings put there by unknown men many years ago. There is a flight of tiny steps cut into a sloping rock, leading from nowhere to nowhere. There are all sorts of odd-shaped holes cut into the rocks. No one knows why these

GIANT BUDDHA OF WU CHOU SHAN
A fifty-foot rock sculpture of Buddha.

carvings were made or what purpose they once served. Most of the mountains and hills of China have these various strange carvings. Sometimes the meaning is known.

Within a short distance of Haichow, on the canal which leads from Haichow to the Grand Canal, is a granite hill much like this hill near the city. On the hill are bas-relief carvings of Confucius and his seventy disciples. They are there, so the story goes, because once Confucius stood on that hill and looked southward, seeing white horses outside the gates of Soochow, some hundreds of miles away.

THE COUNTRY AS SEEN FROM ABOVE

A mile and a half farther south of the city of Haichow lies the Big Mountain, a long ridge of granite running east and west and rising to a top height of thirteen hundred feet.

This mountain, if such it may be called, is partially covered with pine trees, for the wealthy landlords, who own most of the mountain as well as most of the countryside, have made valiant efforts toward reforestation. The pines stand in orderly rows and offer welcome shade to the person trying to reach the highest part of the mountain, the Horse's Ears. The Horse's Ears are formed by two jutting cliffs of granite and from their summit one can see twenty or thirty miles away on all sides. To the north lies Haichow, at this distance a unit of houses surrounded by a wall with more houses clustered near the outside of the wall. Between the city and the Big Mountain lie the Little Mountain and the fields of broomcorn, wheat, small grains and vegetables. The houses of the farmers are clustered together among the fields, and every so often a dark green rectangle shows where the grave of some well-to-do person lies surrounded by evergreen trees.

North of the city of Haichow lie more flat fields through which winds the river; and far away, if the day is clear, one sees the ocean. Eastward from the top of the Big Mountain one sees the granite ridges of more mountains. Higher than any others in the region, they border the sea. In their recesses lurk bandits and pirates. Between the Big Mountain and these distant mountains are the flat alkali plains where salt is gathered. The Lunghai Railroad crosses these plains to reach the sea.

CHINA

A RAILROAD AWAKENS A SLEEPING VILLAGE

The terminal of the Lunghai Railroad as yet bears no settled name. The line reaches the Yellow Sea at a fishing village which has always been called Lao-yao.

Before the rails were laid this village and the surrounding farm homes drowsed out their lives in silent peace. The granite hills come sharply down to the sea here, and the tides wash the golden sands among the granite boulders. The villagers have always carried on their lives with little concern for the rest of the world. Each season several ocean-going junks were loaded with fish which were taken down the coast to Shanghai for sale. The farmers raised and shipped grain and vegetables. Sometimes pirates captured the returning junks and took the money collected in Shanghai. At other times bad winter storms destroyed many of the boats. But nothing really changed from decade to decade.

Then suddenly the construction gangs of the railroad came to Lao-yao. Within a few weeks the sleepy village became a roaring railroad town, with hotels springing up along the crooked streets. Real estate boomed in the surrounding area. The construction of the railroad continued, the golden sands were dirtied with refuse, the quiet mountains echoed to commercial development.

CHOPSTICK ARTIST AT A ROADSIDE RESTAURANT

Paul's Photos, Chicago

A FUTURE METROPOLIS?

There are those who say that this place, once so quiet and isolated, will become a city larger than San Francisco.

They say that the Lunghai Railroad and the railroads which it crosses in its long journey from the west part of China reach millions of potential customers for the goods of the world and that the things grown and manufactured in these regions are of untold value to the world.

If they are right, the great city which will grow at the terminal of the Lunghai Railroad will be one of the most interesting places in any country—a city with no past, developed entirely during the twentieth century, yet a city placed in a country with the longest continuous history of any in the world.

TRAIN TRAVEL AGAIN

The traveler returns to Hsuchowfu by rail and there changes to the north-south Tientsin-Pukow line in order to return to Nanking. Hsuchowfu itself is an old city, becoming more and more modern each year as the traffic on its two railroads increases. The train leaves Hsuchowfu, set in its flat plain, and goes southward through more flat plains.

Before long there are glimpses of small hills, the country becomes slightly rolling, and occasionally there are real hills. During the growing season one notes more rice fields and fewer grain fields, but the vegetable patches are still there. The farmers still wear dark-blue, and miniature donkeys carry the same enormous loads.

CHINESE GIRL OF THE POORER CLASS SEARCHING AN ASH PIT FOR UNBURNED BITS OF COAL

Paul's Photos, Chicago

CHINA

Homer Smith photo, Chicago
CARVED CAMELS ALONG THE ROAD TO THE MING TOMBS

There are more water buffalo working in the fields as one goes farther south, and there are more men carrying burdens on the ends of poles, laid over their shoulders. Many deep pits are scattered among the fields where water accumulates to be used for irrigation. Those seriously wishing to commit suicide go to these pits. Many young girls have died in their green depths.

The people here have traits of both the North and South, but they are still northerners at heart. The true southerners live south of the Yangtze River. They are the ones who suffer if they don't have rice to eat. These farmers north of the Yangtze like wheat and millet, and rice is a feast-day luxury.

NANKING, THRICE CAPITAL OF CHINA

At Pukow one again crosses the Yangtze by ferry to reach Nanking. The hills in and around Nanking are the foothills of the Central Mountain Belt, that range which rises between north and south China and through which the Yangtze has made its way. The Yangtze River has since earliest times, since life first came to the earth, separated the northern and southern sections of China. Nanking, set among little foothills, partakes of the North and of the South. Three times has this city been the capital of China.

Here, since the city first was built centuries ago, North and South have met. The tall northerners have mixed with the smaller men of the South. The many dialects of the two sections are spoken in the streets of Nanking.

Once the city rivaled Peiping in beauty and splendor of architecture. Those were the days when the Southern Sung and Ming Emperors chose Nanking for their capital city, in the times before Columbus reached America. The glory of those days was destroyed in 1853 during the Taiping Rebellion. The only remnants of its early splendor are the Ming Tombs which lie far outside the city.

The city has little industrial but great political importance. The population has nearly doubled since Nanking was again made the capital of China in 1929. Educational work had long been carried on in the city and it has now become the center of all sorts of schools, universities, and other institutions.

Nanking has been influenced by foreign customs and has been changed to conform with modern ways of living. A large section of the city wall, once the longest in all China, has been removed and a wide motor-road built on its site. Streets able to carry modern traffic have been constructed and there are hotels with contemporary conveniences. Here one buys the famous Nanking tapestry, by the yard or in complete pictures ready to hang on the wall. Here beggars roam the wide modern streets, clutching bits of food cast aside in the markets, collecting cigarette butts from the gutters; and, finally, resting against a convenient sunny wall, they meditatively pick the lice from their clothes.

WUHU, GEESE AND TOYS

River steamers go up the Yangtze River at all times of the year but the traveler will enjoy the trip most if he goes during the fall or early winter. Then the weather is stimulating and the scenery is at its best. Accommodations on the steamers are comfortable and the trip is an opportunity for a rest.

The first stop up the river from Nanking is at Wuhu, center of the goose-raising industry. One may be lucky enough to see hundreds of geese being floated down the river to the larger cities. They are driven into Wuhu from the surrounding country, their feet coated with tar and sand so that they can make the long trip successfully; then they are herded into the water. They are guided on their way by herders in boats.

Homer Smith photo, Chicago

TEMPLE OF THE REVOLUTION IN NANKING

There are always two or three United States and British gun boats at Wuhu. The doctors on board these boats have an arrangement of flag signals whereby the hospitals of the city let them know when some interesting operation is to be performed. The men then go ashore and attend the clinic.

One can purchase all sorts of children's toys in Wuhu, miniature grindstones, gay baskets, tinkling bells.

KULING, MOUNTAIN RESORT

All the way up the Yangtze to Kiukiang the banks of the river are low and the wide river seems to flow slowly on its yellow-brown way. The current is faster than it seems and, at times of high water, rushes past the low banks sometimes breaking through them. Kiukiang means "Nine Rivers." The name is taken from the number of outlets the river has in the vicinity of the city. These outlets lead into Poyang Lake, south of the river. This lake is very low during the dry season but, when the water is high, it serves as a safety valve for the Yangtze, catching the extra water and helping to prevent serious floods. It is this same water that overflows the plain around Kiukiang during the rains and into which one's baggage is apt as not to be set by carriers to whom one has given not quite enough of a tip. Fishermen line the banks of the river, lowering their nets into the yellow water, raising them filled with the silver catch. The nets are held open by bamboo poles so that when they are raised they look like spiderweb-thin baskets, dripping and frail. Kiukiang has long been a center for the making of porcelain.

Tourists leave the steamer at Kiukiang to go fifteen miles overland to a mountain resort to the south, Kuling. Here, amid tree-covered hills, are the summer houses of foreigners and Chinese. The resort is used more and more during the winter and is well worth a visit at any season. A room in a hotel or private home may be obtained to serve as headquarters for walks and camping trips into the adjoining hills. There are swimming pools in the mountain streams and the views of the surrounding flat country are exceptionally lovely. One enormous cliff looks down over Poyang Lake. The mountainside drops down with scarcely a break to the plain, which stretches away to the lake lying there all hazy-blue in the distance. There are temples or shrines at every vantage point. The ancient Chinese believed in supplying comforts for the sightseer.

THE DEATH-DEALING GORGES

As the steamer continues up the Yangtze, one notices that the mountains seem to be crowding in on the river. This continues until, at Ichang, a thousand miles from the sea, the huge cliffs are

Paul's Photos, Chicago

IRON SUSPENSION BRIDGE OVER A GORGE IN CHINA

CHINA [319]

so close together on either side of the water that they seem to touch overhead. Here are the Yangtze Gorges, famous for their grandeur and their danger. More than one boat has been overturned in the rapids here, and many lives have been lost. The river makes no exception of foreigners when it starts upsetting boats.

The adventurous traveler will go on from Ichang, through the gorges, to Chungking, in the fertile and fascinating province of Szechwan, and from there he will go, by whatever means he can find, on and on up the Yangtze, till he has to walk along the border of the river; on and on, all the three thousand two hundred miles of the tremendous river clear to Thibet.

THE DOWN-RIVER JOURNEY

However, the average traveler will be ready enough to go back down the river once he has reached Ichang. The trip down river is somewhat faster than that up, as the current helps the steamer. One is reluctant to see the mountains of Kuling fade away, the last reminder of those ranges farther west.

The flat plains on either side of the river resume their regularity below Kiukiang and one is impatient for the journey to end. The steamer stops at various towns to take on cargo, sometimes to discharge tea or wood-oil or other up-river commodities. One need not get off at Nanking to return to Shanghai. It is more interesting to stay on board until Chingkiang is reached, some hours later.

Chingkiang is on the south bank of the river, and here the Grand Canal crosses the Yangtze. The city is old, the streets are narrow and tortuous, but modern conditions have necessitated the widening of many. Fishing boats, canal boats, river junks, congregate along the water front. In the Yangtze River just out from Chingkiang is Silver Island with several old temples. The priest shows travelers the stone carvings which tell of different ancient heroes. Carved into the rocks of the island are poems written by men of long ago. One can buy rubbings made from these stones, mounted on scrolls to hang on the wall. There is one which pictures three bamboos and an oddly shaped rock, with a poem that tells of the beauties of a sunset on the Yangtze.

When one is back on the steamer, going on down the Yangtze to the Whangpoo River, where the boats turn in to go to Shanghai,

WESTERN ENTRANCE TO WINDBOX GORGE ON THE YANGTZE RIVER

one imagines the poet's ecstasy when he wrote the poem. Sunsets on the Yangtze are very beautiful. But perhaps the rising moon is even more lovely. The moon of China is more fascinating than the too familiar moon of one's own country.

BY MOTOR TO THE SUMMER HOME OF EMPERORS

The long trip up the Yangtze will have given the traveler such a thorough rest he will be glad to hire a car to drive to Hangchow. The trip from Shanghai to Hangchow, toward the southwest, may be made in a few hours.

Hangchow lies on the banks of West Lake. It is a city proud of its past and present. The streets now are wide and clean, but the past is of more interest. Once it was the summer capital of China and at that time the emperors built an artificial lake, complete with little islands and flawless landscaping. A causeway runs out into the center where the largest island houses a temple and tea houses. One can hire a tiny boat and go from island to island, admiring the sweep of the tea-house roofs and the arrangement of the weeping willow trees.

At one end of the lake is the ruin of the Thunder Peak Pagoda which collapsed some years ago, its ancient base having been weakened by the constant picking of souvenir hunters who wanted bits of the enormous old tiles to take away with them. At the end of the lake is the Needle Pagoda, built for beauty and as an observation tower for the astronomers. The strange instruments they used are still there, rusting in the open weather.

On the side of the lake away from Hangchow is a well-known Buddhist temple which was restored by the substitution of Oregon pines for the original supports. The temple was falling into ruin some twenty years ago because the main pillars had decayed and China had no trees large enough to replace them. An American business man of Shanghai had pines brought from Oregon and they were installed in place of the Chinese pillars. Now the temple is visited every year by thousands of Chinese pilgrims, each with his pilgrim's bag, and by scores of foreign tourists, each with his camera. There is ample material for photography. The temple

THE FAMOUS PAGODA AT HANGCHOW

A. T. Palmer photo, Berkeley, Calif.

UNIVERSITY OF KNOWLEDGE

IN THE INTERIOR OF CHINA
Members of a Scientific Expedition as guests at one of the strange monasteries in the interior of China.

grounds are tremendous—the courtyards go on and on, each offering some new arrangement of flowers or trees; each opening into some of the hills in and around the temple is covered with inscriptions cut by pilgrims and holy men through the past centuries. Vendors sell all sorts of foods, some for the pilgrims themselves, some to be offered as sacrifices. Other vendors sell snakes, beetles, lizards, birds, to be purchased by devout pilgrims and released to gain merit. Most of the creatures promptly go back to the vendors, having been trained to do so, so everyone is satisfied, and business is brisk.

On the way back to the city, if one looks carefully through every open gateway, one may manage to see tea gardens where rows of tea plants stand sheltered from the sun, their leaves growing to just the right stage of perfection for picking. Silk worms are grown here too and the mulberry trees, the leaves of which they eat, fill many courtyards. In the spring the hills are covered with low-growing azaleas, turning the slopes to rose, pink and gold. The peasant cottages are neatly white-washed and on the gable ends are often found painted scenes from legends, the colors kept bright and clear by yearly repainting.

In the city itself there are many shops where silk may be purchased. There is a huge native medicine laboratory where deer, snakes, scorpions, and insects of all kinds, are to be seen, and where many herbs are grown. The medicines are made from these and from imported ingredients, by men and boys who work in dark, pungent-smelling rooms. The finished medicines are sold on the spot or shipped to all parts of China.

One can spend days in Hangchow and its vicinity. The city is considered one of the most beautiful in China, and rightly so. From Hangchow one may return to Shanghai by train or by car. There the traveler may take a cargo-passenger boat to visit the cities on the southern coast of China.

NINGPO AND CHINA'S QUIETEST TEMPLE

The first stop is at Ningpo, near to Shanghai. This is the city of fishing guilds and Ningpo varnish—an old trading city where foreigners have carried on business for years. In the old foreign cemetery there are seven graves, one the grave of a tough old English merchant of the bygone days, the others the graves of his wives. On each of their headstones is inscribed, "We wait till he comes." He outlived them all.

OLD NORTHERN GATE IN THE WALL AT CANTON
The tower is imposing, but the entrance is rather small for modern traffic.

Paul's Photos, Chicago

Outside of Ningpo is a hill and on that hill stands one of China's most beautiful temples. One reaches the first gate of the temple after a steep ascent through waving bamboos. Inside the first courtyard is a great iron bell, to the clapper of which are attached many strands of long black hair. Women go there to pray for sons, and each woman fastens a strand of her hair to the clapper before she tolls the bell to wake the god of fertility so that he will be sure to hear her request. The next courtyard is reached by a flight of steps and in it are flowers and dwarf trees standing silent in their perfection. The courtyards and buildings which open on them go on up the hill, each building filled with different images. One building is filled with vividly painted figures representing all the tortures of hell. Another contains the living quarters of the quiet grey-clad priests. The topmost courtyard of all opens from the building where the Buddha is housed.

From the door of this building one looks out over the walls of all the other courts, down to the gently rolling plain, where farmers everlastingly work in their fields, the same farmers, one would think, who were working in the fields of north China. They are clothed in the same dark blue and go about their labor in the same patient way. Every bit of land which can be tilled is in use and the same tiny footpaths wander among the fields, going from one cluster of houses to the next. Here are many rice fields, and we see water buffalo in every field, but the vegetable gardens are the same as they were in the north and as they were around Shanghai.

CHINA   [325]

From Ningpo the steamer goes on south, stopping at various ports along the way. The coast is rough, hills come down to the water, and there are many small harbors where local fishing boats come and go. Foochow, up the Min River, is busy with importing, exporting, and fishing. Amoy is alive with commerce. Swatow is active. Hongkong is a busy British colony. Macao, the Portuguese island and business city, is always occupied with its gambling.

MODERN CANTON AND UNBELIEVABLE SIGHTS

The city of Canton lies up the Pearl River, eighty miles from Hongkong. It is an easy journey from Hongkong by either railway or river boat. Canton is the third largest city of China and is the one which has known foreign trade the longest. Vessels of the United States went there when our country was in its infancy. It has always been a progressive city. In China's history rebellions have repeatedly originated with the Cantonese and they have been leaders in all sorts of new movements throughout China.

A TYPICAL STREET IN HONG-KONG

A. T. Palmer photo, Berkeley, Calif.

A CHINESE WEDDING PROCESSION, PEIPING
Bride and groom are carried in this elaborate sedan chair.

Modern Canton has several broad, paved streets. Fortunately, most of the old characteristics have been preserved. One street, now wide and smooth and lined with modern Chinese shops, still has ancient carved stone arches. Their elaborate pillars obstruct traffic, to be sure, but who minds that when a tie-up in vehicles gives one time to examine chubby stone lions and delicate flower tracery? The traveler has all too little time for minute examination of such detail.

Rising from rice fields near Lingnan University, one of Canton's best schools, is a nine-storied pagoda. It is old; trees known to have been full-grown over a hundred years ago writhe from the walls, and hundreds of birds nest in its openings. Yet it is only slightly dilapidated, so well was it built. Modern structures, gay and neat now in their day of newness, will not outlast it. In ancient times a monument, or even a dwelling, was constructed for permanency. In a city like Canton, where New China is so overwhelming, one is moved to wonder about the real value of much that is "modern."

The traveler is therefore glad to find, on going into the country nearby, that modernism does not penetrate far beyond the city limits. Here are the farmers again, working now in rice fields, using water buffalo entirely, but still patient and slow, dressed in blue, moving along the footpaths around their rectangular fields.

Canton lies in Kwangtung Province. Nearby is Kwangsi Province, reached by the West River. Kwangsi and its northern neighbor Kweichow Province are well worth a visit. In fact, though the going is not too easy, the traveler who makes the effort to visit this region will have seen a rarely visited section of China. His friends at home will not believe the stories he tells; they will say his photographs are faked. In these provinces are the limestone hills which have so influenced Chinese painting. Foreigners say that Chinese art is weak because of lack of perspective. The foreigner who has seen these fantastic hills and isolated peaks will feel that perspective is superfluous. Why bother with depth when before one stands a gold and green column, towering four hundred feet into the air, slender and abrupt? Trees cling to the crevices and fling their weather-twisted branches in silhouette against a matchless sky. Faint in the distance more hills outline themselves, jagged peaks rising from steep foothills, producing a skyline surrealist in its impossibility. But there it is. One takes a photograph, because one can't believe one's eyes. The hills are full of grottos, ravines, even natural tunnels extending through, so one can walk through a six-hundred-foot hill rather than have to circle or climb it.

Needless to say, these weird mountains are filled with temples, shrines, tea houses. At the foot of one cliffed hill is a covered bridge, of which there are few in China. It is centuries old and looks as though it would last centuries more. There are dozens of interesting things to see, the strange methods of fishing, the big round hats, the odd costumes of the isolated tribes back in the mountains.

One spends as many days or weeks as one can, wandering here and there; then one goes back to Hongkong or Shanghai, where one can take a steamer to go on to Europe or America. The traveler's stay in China is ended, but in all likelihood he will be back some other year, really to see the country. And that means he will return again and again, for one never "really sees" China.

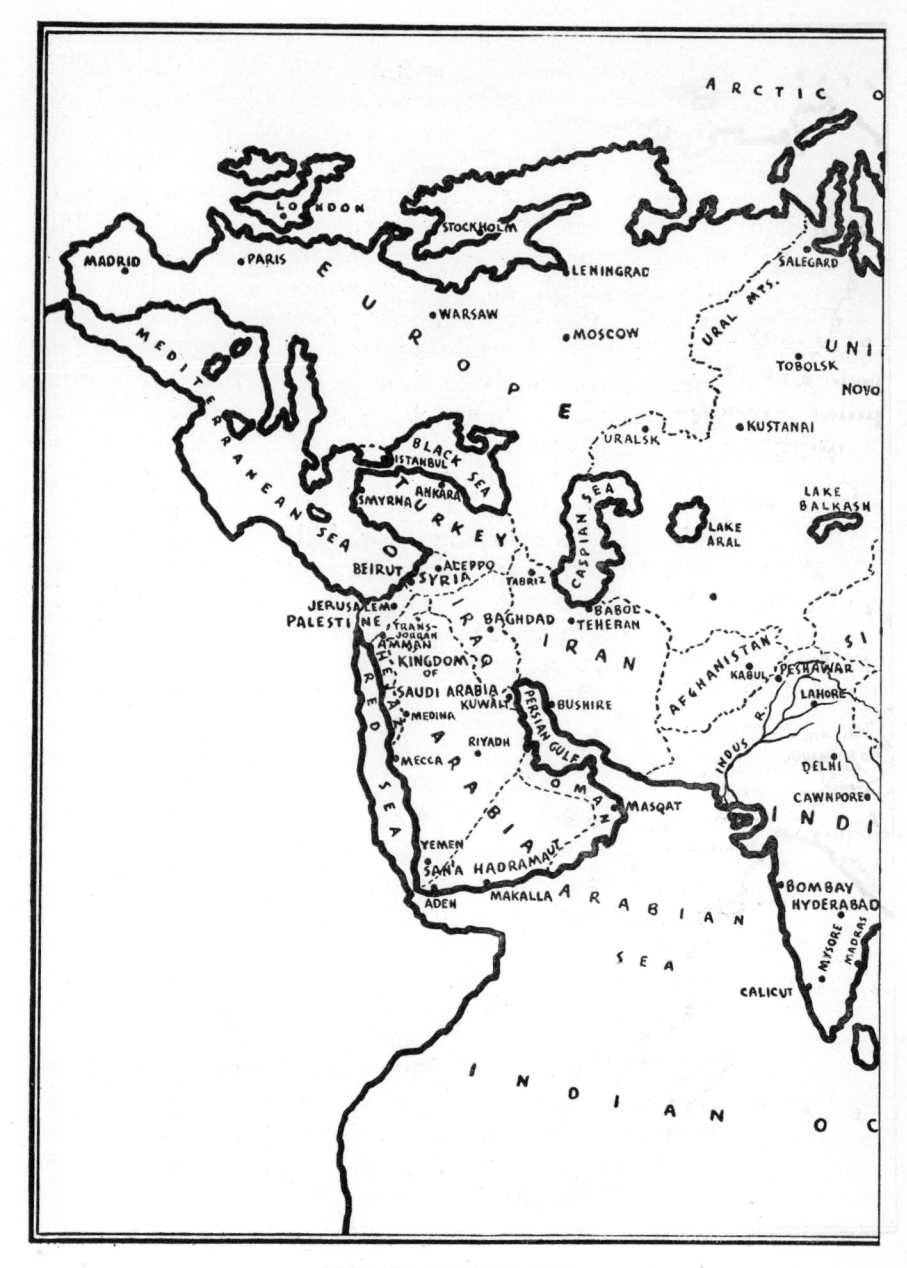

MAP OF EUROPE AND

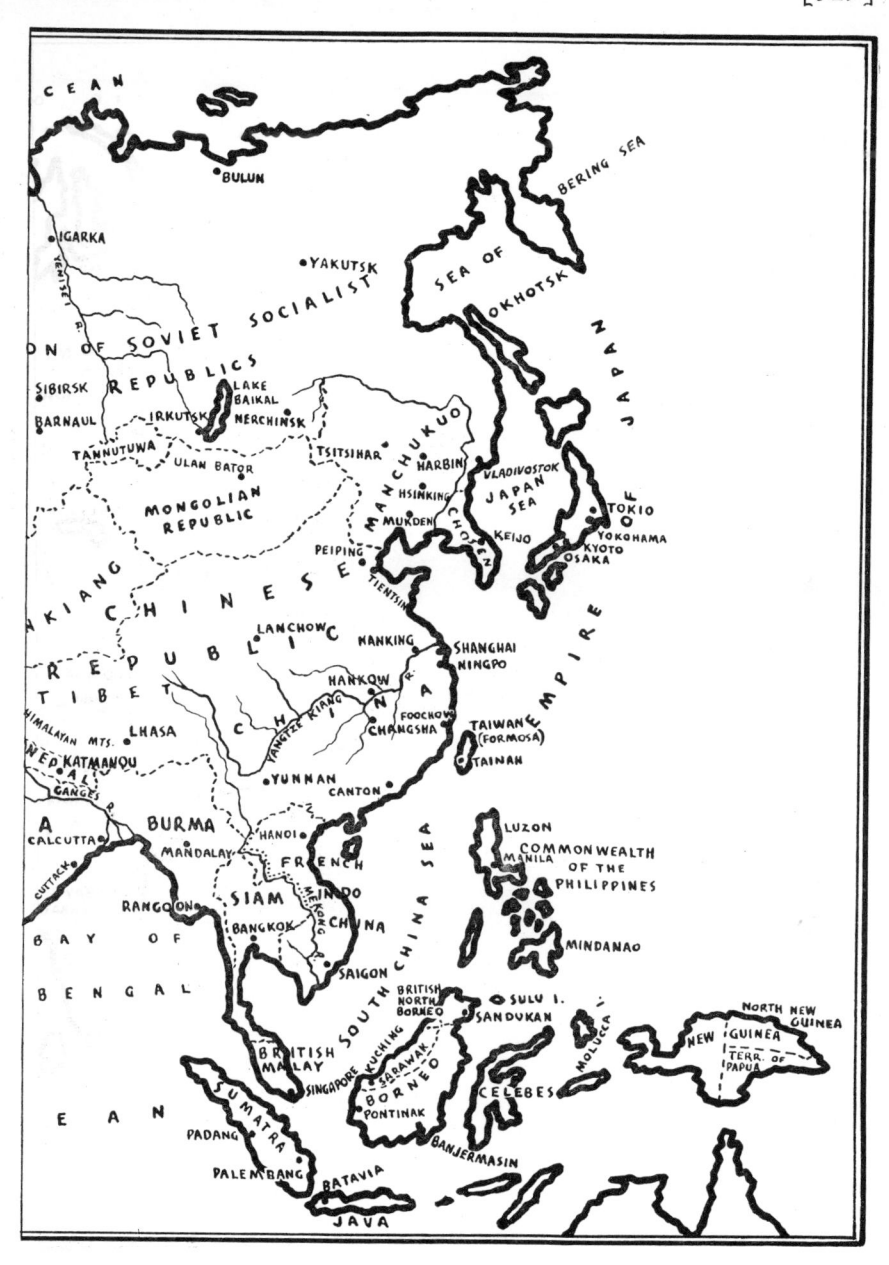

ASIA IN 1938

Courtesy Mason Warner

THE "TEMPLE OF HEAVEN" AT PEIPING

RUSSIA

THE MUSEUM OF THE REVOLUTION, LENINGRAD
This store-house of art objects and relics of the revolution is now one of the chief centers of Soviet culture. It was formerly a royal palace.

A CHANGING COUNTRY

STRETCHING across one-sixth of the earth's surface, the Union of Soviet Socialist Republics, modern successor to Russia, encompasses the most varied and vivid scenic panoramas and the most dramatic and swift-changing civilization in the world today.

From the Baltic to the Pacific, from the Arctic Ocean to the semi-tropical border of Afghanistan, 170,000,000 Soviet citizens, of 180 races, live, build factories and till the soil in every type of topography and climate known to man. Here are vast, dark canyons and sharp-peaked, snowy mountains, including the highest in Europe, Mount Elbrus, and the "Roof of the World," the Pamirs of Asia; frozen Arctic tundra and torrid sub-tropical deserts; wide, monotonous steppes and countless miles of sea coast ranging from the icy cliffs of Polar oceans to the warm, sandy beaches of the Black Sea.

A RUSSIAN
RURAL SCENE

Paul's Photos

Against this magnificent background, Russia's millions are rushing through five centuries in two decades. Since the Revolution of 1917 they have transformed Russia from a semi-medieval empire, its people half-barbaric, to a modern industrial commonwealth, creating new frontiers in twentieth-century technology and culture. They have achieved this gigantic metamorphosis while experimenting with a social system never before tried in modern, industrial society—planned development of resources and production of goods in place of the capitalistic system of individual enterprise and *laissez-faire*.

THE OLD IS PRESERVED

Yet, in the midst of feverish industrialization the old is not destroyed—indeed, wherever it is beautiful or historic, it is consciously preserved. Exotic onion-bulb churches flank super-dams and canals of glistening concrete, and modernistic apartments tower over wooden peasant cottages. On the streets of Moscow and Leningrad, factory workers jostle bast-sandaled peasants and brilliantly-gowned and turbaned cotton farmers from far Turkestan.

So swift is the pace of industrialization, so rapid the changes in culture that travelers who return to the Soviet Union from year to year must take their bearings anew each time. Cities, landscapes, people, food, clothing, even hotel accommodations, assume new forms almost week by week. Somnolent, romantic old Russia has become a land of endless physical, economic, and spiritual revolution.

INTOURIST, OR HOW TO SEE THE SOVIET UNION

Breathless pursuit of technology, via the famous five-year plans, has kept Russia keyed to an almost wartime discipline. To industrialize a backward nation in the minimum period of time, every aspect of life is rigidly organized. Even tourists are organized. There is little chance for vagabond roaming. The average traveler cannot motor or cycle or hike his way across mountain, steppe, or desert, or attempt to "do" Russia on a dollar a day.

To compensate for this, through the service of Intourist, official Soviet travel organization, he is given access to factories, schools, courts, collective farms, nurseries, and other facets of day-by-day life not available to tourists in most countries. Intourist buys his railroad tickets and registers him in and out with the militia in every city—now a necessary formality in many European countries; both invaluable services in a country where red tape rolls abundantly and the language difficulty is formidable.

In most cases it is necessary to arrange for an Intourist tour in order to secure a visa to the Soviet Union. A tour may be arranged for as extended a stay as is desired in any of the following cities in which Intourist maintains hotels: Moscow, Leningrad, Kiev, Kharkov, Minsk, Rostov, Odessa, Sevastopol, Yalta, Batum, Kislovodsk, Sochi, Ordzhonikidze (formerly Vladikavkaz), Tiflis, Baku, Erivan, Stalingrad (formerly Tsaritsyn), and Gorky (formerly Nizhni-Novgorod). For the time being, other parts of the Soviet Union are accessible to foreigners only through special arrangement with Soviet consular authorities.

For the traveler who wants a planned itinerary, Intourist offers forty-two tours, ranging from five to twenty-eight days in length. They comprise visits to the cities mentioned above, voyages on the Volga or the Black Sea, or mountain climbing in the Caucasus.

Intourist provides three categories of travel accommodations: first class at fifteen dollars a day, second or "Tourist" class at eight dollars a day, and third or "Hard" class at five dollars a day. These rates include hotel rooms, three meals, one sightseeing tour and a certain number of kilometers of rail travel which the tourist may or may not use as he chooses. Third-class rooms compare favorably with second-class hotel rooms in America. Meals are varied and well cooked. "Tourist" and "Hard" menus combine such typical Russian dishes as borsch, *bliny* (pancakes stuffed with cheese or jam), sour cream, with American-style ham and eggs, roasts, and ice cream. First "category" accommodations are more luxurious, the meals including caviar and wild game.

Applications for visas are made by Intourist through its Moscow office. They are free unless cable service is requested, when the fee is two dollars. The so-called consular visa, secured at the Soviet consulate in New York, permits a stay in Russia without Intourist service. It is granted usually only to foreigners employed by the Soviet government, press correspondents, and, in exceptional cases, to persons desiring to study some particular phase of Soviet life. Unless the traveler has a job awaiting him in Russia or is plutocratically equipped, vagabonding via the consular visa is inadvisable. The present rate of exchange of the ruble is five to the dollar. All prices to non-Intourist travelers are high. The buying power of one ruble is, to cite a representative case, half a small sandwich of doubtful quality.

There are five main approaches to the Soviet Union: Leningrad, port of entry from the Baltic; Negoreloye, at the Polish frontier, where travelers entrain for Moscow; Odessa, on the Black Sea, the gateway to the Crimea and the Caucasus; and Vladivostok, the Soviet's Pacific port, and Manchuli, where the Chinese Eastern railway meets the Trans-Siberian, near the Manchurian border, doors to Siberia and Central Asia.

LENINGRAD—A CITY OF STRIKING INDIVIDUALITY

With the development of passenger service on the Soviet merchant marine, Leningrad is becoming an increasingly popular port of entry. A trip from London to Leningrad on a Soviet ship gives a brief and complete introduction to Russian customs, food, and workers' life.

LENINGRAD IS THE SCENE OF MANY COLORFUL PARADES
SUCH AS THIS ONE

THE KREMLIN, MOSCOW
On one side is the most famous square of tsarist Russia, now a place sacred to the Soviets. Here is the tomb of Lenin, father of the Soviet Revolution. It is called Red Square and has become the center of great demonstrations by the Soviets.

No city in the world has a more striking individuality than Leningrad, the capital of tsarist Russia, now the second largest metropolis in the U. S. S. R. In its wide streets and classic eighteenth-century buildings it resembles a European city, but its onion-domed churches, its fortress and its stone signal towers guarding the Neva River give it a semi-oriental air.

Leningrad was built in 1703 by Peter the Great as his "window toward Europe." It shows its character as a planned city in the orderly way it is laid out around the winding Neva and the canals built by Peter's engineers to drain the swamps on which the city originally stood. Its broad thoroughfares, full of light and air, converge on the Admiralty building, the slender gilt spire of which dominates the city.

Modern Leningrad is an important industrial center of the U. S. S. R. and a nucleus of cultural and scientific activity, world-famous for its ballet and its art galleries. It is also a great living museum. On the banks of the Neva stands the huge red Winter Palace, home of all the tsars from 1762. Today it serves as a Palace of Art.

FORTRESS, CATHEDRALS, AND HERMITAGE

Across the Neva on an island are the stark gray walls of Peter and Paul fortress. This medieval-looking prison, Leningrad's first building, was constructed by Peter to guard the city. Later it lost its military importance to Cronstadt Fort and became a state prison where political offenders were kept in close confinement. Today it is preserved in its original form, a grisly museum of tsarist methods of punishment.

Three great cathedrals give Leningrad a glorious skyline. St. Isaac's is a granite pile with a mammoth dome which commands a vista of the city and countryside as far as the Gulf of Finland. It is now an anti-religious museum. The austere Kazan Cathedral a few blocks away is the world's leading museum of religious history, tracing the rise of every faith. The "Church on the Blood" stands on the spot where Alexander II was killed by terrorists. It is an authentic, if bizarre, version of early Russian church architecture, its spiraled bulb domes and its façade painted in garish red, blue, green, and yellow.

On the Neva shore, adjoining the Winter Palace, is the huge building of the world-famous Hermitage Fine Arts Museum

"Intourist" Photo

HALL OF COLUMNS, HERMITAGE, LENINGRAD

founded by Catherine the Great. Its collection in its entirety ranks with those of the Louvre and the National Gallery in London, and its Rembrandt group is the most famous in the world. Leningrad has also an excellent Russian Museum and the world's first Museum of Arctic Exploration. The museums of Leningrad attract more than 3,000,000 visitors annually.

The hotels for foreigners, in the heart of Leningrad, were once beehives of aristocratic life, where the nobility of St. Petersburg held their balls and receptions. Their central location makes them excellent starting points for strolls around Leningrad. This city lends itself to the gentle sport of sightseeing on foot. It is only a few minutes' walk from the center to its shops, churches, theaters, parks and quays. Its river promenades offer the best view of Leningrad's skyline and the gayest cross-section of its life. The wharves are crowded with workers and students. In June, during the "white nights," when the sky is dark only for an hour or two near midnight, the city is especially festive.

Within short bus rides from Leningrad are Peterhof, Peter the Great's gorgeous summer palace, and Pushkino, formerly Tsarskoye Selo, with its two magnificent palaces. Behind the white and gold palace at Peterhof, a series of gold-encrusted fountains, gorgeous copies of those at Versailles, range across a terrace sloping down to the gray Gulf of Finland.

At Pushkino the Catherine and Alexander Palaces are the chief objects of interest. Both have been turned into museums and rest homes, and the summer houses of the nobility have been remodeled into children's palaces. The Catherine Palace, favorite residence of Catherine the Great, is famous for its splendid halls done in gold and amber and its lawns and forests, now used as public parks. The Alexander Palace is interesting for the wing which has been kept exactly as it was left by Nicholas II and his family in 1917—even to the clothes hanging in the closets.

MOSCOW—THE HUB OF THE SOVIET UNIVERSE

He who has seen Moscow has seen the Soviet Union in miniature. Moscow is at once a fascinating old Russian city and the most vigorous of modern metropolises, the hub of the universe for 170,000,000 Soviet citizens, the nerve center of the Communist experiment. In this city of 4,000,000, the largest in the country, everything that is taking place throughout the country is shown on a small scale.

International News Photo

WHERE LENIN RESTS
The magnificent tomb of Lenin stands out impressively in the background of this picture. In the foreground are masses of Red soldiers.

The eight centuries of Moscow's history are recorded in its city plan, which resembles a spider's web. The hub is the Kremlin, at the founding of Moscow in the twelfth century a walled city of wooden huts, today a perfectly preserved fifteenth-century fortress. From the Kremlin Moscow expanded into the walled Kitai-Gorod (China Town), then the White City, also walled. As successive suburbs developed beyond the White City, earthworks were erected. Today Moscow's principal boulevards follow the lines of these old walls. The trade roads which radiated like the spokes of a wheel in all directions from the Kremlin have become the city's main streets.

The Kremlin with its grim walls and nineteen medieval towers is the seat of the Soviet government. Its palaces have been converted into offices and apartments for Stalin and other government leaders. Its three ancient cathedrals are preserved as museums, although the Kremlin has not been open to the public for several years.

THE RED SQUARE AND LENIN'S TOMB

The triangular Kremlin is flanked on one of its three sides by the Moscow River, on another by the Red Square, the heart of the Soviet Union. In the Middle Ages the square was a trading center and the scene of the tsars' public executions. Today it is the stage for Soviet Russia's greatest celebrations: the gigantic parades on November 7, anniversary of the Bolshevik revolution; and on International Labor Day, May 1.

In the center stands the tomb of Lenin, a truncated pyramid of gleaming red granite. At one end towers the nine-domed Cathedral of St. Basil, a symbol of the richest part of Russia's past.

Contrasts between the old and the new Russia are vividly drawn all over Moscow. Across the river from the ancient Kremlin rises the "battleship gray" modernistic apartment house for government employees, the largest in the country. Throughout the city other modernistic apartments and office buildings overshadow ancient, baroque Russian churches and the classic mansions of former nobles. In 1937 work was under way on the new Palace of Soviets, Russia's first skyscraper. This many-tiered office building, to be surmounted by a statue of Lenin, will be higher than the Empire State Building in New York City.

AMUSEMENT, CULTURE, REST

The brilliance of Moscow's theaters is known the world over. Classical drama, modern plays, and the new Soviet drama emphasizing Communist themes are covered by the repertories of the celebrated Moscow Art Theater, the Kamerny, the Vakhtangov, the Meyerhold, the Realistic, the Maly, the Theater of the Revolution and numerous smaller theaters.

At the Bolshoi State Theater of Opera and Ballet, historic home of the Imperial Opera, the great tradition of Russian opera is ably carried on. As in the theater, both the classics and the works of Soviet composers are presented.

Virtually every aspect of man and his world is portrayed in Moscow's 170 museums. The finest are the Museum of Modern Art, with a collection of modern paintings rivaled only by those in Paris, and the Tretyakov Gallery, with superb exhibits of

Courtesy Intourist, Inc.

GRAND OPERA THEATER, MOSCOW
The Soviets have given much attention to the theater, which receives national aid. This building may be spoken of as the center of Soviet entertainment.

European and Russian Art. But there are also museums of Russian history, of the revolution, of the theater, of toys, of Lenin, of Tolstoi, of almost every phenomenon in art, history, and contemporary life.

There is a Park of Culture and Rest in every Russian city, but the most notable is Gorky Park in Moscow. Occupying hundreds of acres along the Moscow River, it is a vast network of sports grounds, parachute jumping towers, dance halls, cinemas, outdoor theaters, children's playgrounds and theaters, and riverside restaurants. On "rest days" it is crowded with Russians in vigorous pursuit of relaxation or amusement, and it is as worth visiting for its picture of Russian life as for its beauty.

In Moscow, Intourist offers its most interesting excursions into day-by-day Soviet life: tours of factories, courts, schools, nurseries, clubs, rest homes and collective farms. With the insistence of travelers that they want to see a typical rather than a model institution, average factories and ordinary schools attended by children in the lower income levels have been selected.

Moscow's inadequate busses and street cars, notorious for their crowding and discomfort, have been relieved of much of their burden by the city's new Metro subway, twelve kilometers long, acknowledged to be the finest in the world, with its palatial stations done in richly-colored Ural marbles. Extensions of this underground railway are under construction.

THE VOLGA—A RIVER OF SONG AND BUSTLE

The Moscow-Volga canal, one of a chain of new waterways, makes the journey to Gorky (formerly Nizhni-Novgorod) a delightful steamer trip.

Gorky is the chief northern entry to the Volga. Here the mighty river, which rises in northern Russia, becomes broad and full and starts the most interesting part of its 2,325-mile flow to the Caspian.

Gorky is an ancient city built around a medieval Kremlin, or citadel. In the last century it was celebrated throughout Europe and Asia for its annual fair, which attracted traders from as far east as China and Mongolia. Today it is a great industrial center. Its huge automobile plant is one of the basic units of the Russian motor industry. A new Palace of Labor, the Lenin Radio Institute, and a local regional study museum give it cultural significance. Splendid views of the Volga countryside may be obtained from the Kremlin and from the high hills that border the river.

A four-day steamer trip down the Volga to Stalingrad is one of the most attractive Intourist tours. The scenery ranges from flat steppes to the rolling heights of the Zhiguli mountains.

THE LAND OF TATARS

The first port of call is Kazan, the capital of Tatar Autonomous Soviet Republic. In its skyline the towers of the Kremlin and the belfries of the Russian churches mingle with the minarets of Tatar mosques. Kazan was founded by the Tatars in the middle of the fifteenth century and was captured by Ivan the Terrible in 1552. In the eighteenth and nineteenth centuries it expanded as a trading point and cultural and industrial center.

[344] UNIVERSITY OF KNOWLEDGE

Courtesy Intourist, Inc.

CAFE SCENE IN GORKY STREET, MOSCOW
This street has been named after Maxim Gorky, famous Russian author who has been honored by the Soviets. He is looked upon as the leading cultural figure of Soviet Russia.

It is famous for its university, where Tolstoi and Lenin studied, and for its House of Tatar Culture.

A few miles below Kazan is Ulyanovsk, formerly Simbirsk, the birthplace of Lenin, whose real name was Vladimir Ilyich Ulyanov. Ulyanovsk is in the heart of the Stenka Razin country —the great plains that saw the conquering march of the Cossack rebels against the tsar in the seventeenth century.

The steamer proceeds to Samara and Saratov, the capitals, respectively of the middle and lower Volga regions. Attractively situated on a succession of terraces, both were founded in the sixteenth century to protect the Russian frontier and are now flour-milling centers, linked by rail to the grain-growing regions to the east. Saratov has a Museum of Volga Workers, which depicts the life and labors of the "Volga boatman" through the centuries.

Stalingrad, (formerly Tsaritsyn), where the voyage ends, is one of the liveliest centers of infant Soviet industry. Its chief claim to fame is its gigantic new tractor factory, built with the help of American engineers and workers. With the cutting of the Volga-Don canal, another link in making Moscow a seaport, Stalingrad is expanding rapidly as a shipping center.

THE CAUCASUS—CRUCIBLE OF RACES

Stalingrad stands at the edge of the Caucasus, the broad strip of mountains and plains between the Caspian and Black Seas, the dividing line between Europe and Asia. The Caucasus begins as a fertile wheat-growing steppe, but toward the central region it rises to a magnificent mountain range, the crowning peak of which, Mount Elbrus, is the highest in Europe. Some of the wildest races of Europe still inhabit Daghestan and other regions of this range.

Since the beginning of history the Caucasus has been fought over, conquered, and ruled by all the races of Asia in their westward migrations. Today it is undergoing a great industrial, agricultural, and cultural renaissance. Mechanized agriculture is making its steppes a great wheat-growing center. Exploitation of the wells in the south is converting it into an oil-producing region. It is inhabited by forty-five tribes, each speaking a different tongue. Its government and institutions are examples of the new Soviet policy of encouraging minority groups to retain their old languages and cultures while building a modern, industrial society under a socialist government.

ANNUAL DANCE FESTIVAL IN THE CAUCASUS
The people in this area enjoy the vivid dances of their country.

Rostov-on-Don, the political, economic and cultural center of the North Caucasus, is one of the most interesting examples of a Soviet industrial city. It is an important river port, a large railway juncture, and the administrative headquarters of important Caucasian trusts, banks, syndicates, and collective farms.

Near Rostov is the *Gigant* (giant) State Farm, founded by the Soviet government to demonstrate the benefits of large-scale farming and complete mechanization of agriculture. It is four times as large as the Campbell ranch in the United States, hitherto considered the largest in the world.

The Gigant's most interesting neighbor is the Seattle Commune, founded by American workers from the Pacific coast in 1921-22. One of the largest and most successful experiments in communal agriculture, it has become a center of the collective farm movement in the North Caucasus.

THE SPAS IN THE FOOTHILLS

South of Rostov-on-Don, in the foothills of the mountains, lies the Soviet Union's spa center. Around more than fifty mineral springs, polyclinics and resorts have been built by the score. Outstanding is Kislovodsk, the only place of its kind for persons suffering from heart diseases. It is also an excellent climatic station and a point of departure for excursions into the Mount Elbrus region.

A MODERN CANNING PLANT AT KRYMSKAYA STATION

Courtesy Intourist, Inc.   Photo by Ignatovich
THE GORKY THEATER IN ROSTOV-ON-DON
Soviet Russia's newest and most modernistic theater.

Courtesy Intourist, Inc.
AUTOMOBILE ROAD BETWEEN SOCHI AND MATSESTA
Sochi is a well-known health resort for sufferers from lung and bronchial affections. It has an almost tropical climate, with many sunny days throughout the year.

West of Kislovodsk on the sunny shores of the Black Sea is Sochi, a garden town and a health station for persons suffering from tuberculosis and chest and throat congestions. With an almost subtropical climate, an average of 161 cloudless days a year and an excellent bathing beach, Sochi is also a popular recreation and sports center. In the summer it is crowded with actors and actresses from the Moscow theater and opera. South of the watering district lie Mount Elbrus and its surrounding peaks. Elbrus is a great double-headed cone, the result of tremendous volcanic processes. The western and highest peak towers 18,470 feet. During the summer attempts at ascent are made almost every day by Russian and foreign tourists. Planned ascents involving a stay of several days on the mountain are arranged by Intourist.

Beyond Elbrus is Ordzhonikidze (formerly Vladikavkaz), the administrative center of two of the small autonomous districts of the Caucasus—Ingushetia and Northern Ossetia—and therefore an excellent place to see the Soviet methods of developing a backward mountain people culturally and politically. The clubs and schools of various nationalities, the Pedagogical, Agricultural and Research Institutes show the rapid rise of a new civilization.

From Ordzhonikidze the magnificent Georgian Military Highway leads to Tiflis, the oldest and most important city in the Caucasus. Intourist travelers traverse it in swift open cars. The highway leads through the main range of the Greater Caucasus by a series of gorges, some of which are sheer 5,000-foot drops from the road to the foaming Terek River.

TIFLIS THE ORIENTAL

Tiflis (now officially called Tbilisi), the capital of the Georgian Soviet Socialist Republic, is at once an ancient and a modern city. At first glance the quaint old quarter catches the eye with its crooked streets, flat-roofed little houses and jutting balconies —the Asiatic city of the Middle Ages. But alongside these are straight new streets, large modern houses, theaters, museums, art galleries, shops, modern office and apartment buildings.

Nothing in Tiflis is more attractive than the people themselves. Although there is a cosmopolitan intermingling of races, the dominant group is the Georgians, an ancient people of the Caucasus. They are a handsome race with tall, robust figures and dark hair and eyes. Several Soviet leaders come from their ranks—

Courtesy Intourist, Inc.

A VIEW OF MOUNT DAVID FROM TIFLIS
The old and once almost impregnable fortress that crowns this hill of Tiflis overlooks a picturesque city and gives an imposing air to it.

Stalin, the late Sergei Ordzhonikidze, Commissar of Heavy Industry, Mikoyan, Commissar of the Food Industry, and others.

Tiflis is a nucleus of Georgian culture, its schools and museums showing the development of this ancient race which has given Russia some of its most brilliant dramatists, poets, and painters.

BAKU'S OIL

It is only a short journey southeast from Tiflis to Baku, on the Caspian, center of a great oil-producing region. Baku is the capital of the Republic of Azerbaijan, a semi-desert region lying along the western shores of the Caspian. Of Azerbaijan's 2,000,000 inhabitants, more than half belong to the Turkic group of Transcaucasian peoples, an old and primitive race. Under Soviet rule they are leaving their farms and handicrafts to enter factories, schools, and colleges.

Baku has preserved the ruins of a fortress of Arabian architecture built in the ninth century and the palaces of the former khans, with a mausoleum of a dervish, two mosques and a tomb, all illustrating Arabian art.

Modern Baku is known for its university, technical schools, conservatory, and museums, the latter devoted to exhibits of regional culture. There is also a Turkic theater and a Palace of Turkic Culture.

ARMENIA'S GARDENS

Bordering Azerbaijan on the west is the Armenian Soviet Socialist Republic, with its semi-oriental capital of Erivan, now being rebuilt as a garden city. Near Erivan rises Mount Ararat, according to Biblical story the mount on which Noah's Ark ran aground.

With a rich countryside, Armenia is a land of cotton plantations, gardens and vineyards, now collectivized and run on scientific principles. It is also being industrialized with the growth of a copper trust, cotton-ginning factories, a textile mill, and canning factory.

The last point of call in the Caucasus is usually Batum (officially called Batumi), a subtropical health and pleasure resort on the shores of the Black Sea. Palms, camphor laurels, eucalyptus,

Courtesy Intourist, Inc. Photo by Amursky
STREET SCENE IN TIFLIS
This capital of the Georgian Soviet Socialist Republic is a thriving city of over a half million population and has many modern factories, as well as famous old museums and monuments.

the magnolias line its splendid boulevards. Its sanatoriums offer treatment for heart and lung troubles. Its excellent bathing-beach makes it a popular sports resort, and its salubrious climate, particularly golden and warm in October, is typical of the Caucasus.

Batum is also the chief port on the eastern coast of the Black Sea and from here the traveler may embark by Soviet steamer for the Crimea.

THE CRIMEA—RUSSIAN RIVIERA

A land of semitropical sunshine and glorious vistas of mountain and steppe, of ancient temples and medieval walled towns, the Crimea is one of the most interesting and beloved regions of the Soviet Union. The beauties of this jagged peninsula in the Black Sea have been sung by Homer and Racine, Goethe and Pushkin, Chekhov and Mark Twain. However, the Krim-Tatars, its oldest inhabitants, have coined the phrase by which it is best known—"the green peninsula."

The climate of the Crimea is as mild as that of the Riviera. Silk acacia, cypress, magnolia, palm, mimosa, lemon and orange trees grow on its shores, and beech, pine and oak cover its mountain slopes. The steppe begins in the north and gradually rises higher and higher toward the south until it blends with the mountains on the coast. Sheer slopes of white and pink limestone mountains descend to the sea in steep cliffs, and headlands retreat into the heart of the peninsula, giving the coastline its many azure bays.

The Crimea has been, even more than the Caucasus, a way station for migrating mankind since the earliest times. It was settled successively by the Scythians, the Greeks, the Romans, the Goths, the Huns, the Genoese, the Tatars, and the Turks, all of whom have left traces of their civilizations in its ruins.

The Crimea has always rivaled the Caucasus as the most brilliant resort center of Russia, and since the Soviet government came to power its potentialities for cures and sports have been increasingly developed. The palaces of former tsars and nobles have been turned into hotels, sanatoriums, and rest homes. Many persons needing medical treatment are sent here by factories and collective farms.

[354] UNIVERSITY OF KNOWLEDGE

Courtesy Intourist, Inc.   Photo by Amurski
MTATZMINDSKAYA CHURCH AND TIFLIS FROM MOUNT DAVID
Historic church built in 1542, with the city of Tiflis in the background.

The Crimea is important industrially also, because of its resources of marble, iron, sulphur, oil, colored clay, and a soft yellow stone used in building. It produces a large part of the country's grain, fruit, and tobacco. The Black Sea fisheries furnish approximately twenty varieties of fish, the most important of which are herring and porpoise.

HISTORIC SEVASTOPOL AND SPLENDID YALTA

The principal points of interest to the foreigner in the Crimea are Sevastopol and Yalta.

Sevastopol is remarkable for the historic siege of the Allies during the Crimean War in 1854 and as one of the oldest seats of Hellenic culture. It played a dramatic role in the Revolution of 1905 as the scene of naval revolts against the tsars.

Sevastopol is picturesquely built on slopes descending to the sea to form a vast amphitheater around one of the largest bays in the world. It is a bright town of well-laid-out boulevards, clean streets, and colorful houses. A spectacular sight is that from the Marine Parade, which offers an unbroken view of the sea and of the northern part of the town, with its common grave for the fallen rank and file of the Crimean War.

In antiquity Sevastopol was the site of flourishing settlements of Hellenic colonists, and every year fresh archaeological treasures are unearthed beneath its streets and in its suburbs.

Visiting Yalta in the sixties of the last century, Mark Twain described it as "a splendid spot." Some thirty years later Anton Chekhov, one of Russia's greatest playwrights, moved from the windy steppes of the north to make Yalta his home until he died.

The Russians call Yalta their recuperating ground. Sheltered by the craggy walls of Ai-Petri Mountain, it has a record of sunny days per year surpassing that of the Riviera. It holds the Crimean record for number of parks, palaces, gardens and woods.

Four miles out of Yalta are the Nikitski Gardens, rivals to Kew Gardens in London as the most entrancing botanical gardens in the world.

Despite the fact that it is now traversed by a motor road, Ai-Petri is still a favorite ascent of mountain climbers. Many vacationers make the ascent to spend the night in the inn at the summit and watch the sunrise. On a clear day Asia Minor may be seen with a good field glass, and a fine view is obtained of the southern coast and part of eastern Crimea. A Greek village and a fortress of antiquity are located on Ai-Petri.

THE UKRAINE: GRAIN, COAL, AND 'BROIDERY

Stretching south from Central Russia to the Sea of Azov and the Black Sea is the Ukraine—a golden, storied country. It contains three of the Soviet Union's largest cities: Kharkov, Kiev, and Odessa. It is the home of the proud and fearless Cossacks. Gogol, one of Russia's greatest writers, was a son of the Ukraine. Ukrainian melodies were abundantly used by Tschaikowsky and Moussorgsky in their compositions.

Geographically the Ukraine is a vast steppe and therefore a fertile agricultural region. It is drained by two great rivers, the Dnieper and the Donets, whose basin produces the coal and iron which feed Ukrainian industries. In the endless prairie the peasant huts are carefully whitewashed or plastered with yellow clay and buried in the foliage of their gardens. The swarthy, handsome natives dress gaily in white embroidered blouses and high boots.

MODERNISTIC KHARKOV AND ANCIENT KIEV

Kharkov, 285 miles northeast of Odessa, the capital of the Ukraine, is an industrial center, due to its proximity to the Donets basin. Little that is old remains. Today Kharkov is in a fever of construction and here, more than anywhere else save in Moscow, the quick tempo of Soviet life is felt.

The new modernistic Palace of Pioneers—built by The Young Pioneers, a Communist children's organization—is Kharkov's most interesting sight. The city has also a new theater, accommodating 4,000 persons, a gigantic stadium, Palaces of Physical Culture and Industry, several museums of Ukrainian life, and a famous university.

Kiev, 400 miles north of Odessa, is the oldest city in Russia and one of the most beautiful in all of Europe. Ancient parts of the city are unspoiled bits of the Middle Ages. A thousand years ago it was athrob with the world's trade for eastern Europe. The Byzantines were enraptured by its opulence and splendor and called it "the second Constantinople." It reached its glory as the capital of the old Ukrainian state in the twelfth century. In the thirteenth it was captured by the Tatars who ravaged and ruined

Courtesy Intourist, Inc.

UKRAINIAN GIRLS AT THE MAY FIRST PARADE IN KIEV

The Soviet government stresses the value of various movements for the benefit of the young people of the nation.

Courtesy Intourist, Inc.

COLLECTIVE FARMING IN THE STALINDORF DISTRICT

The picture shows a huge modern combine harvesting a field of grain. This district alone sells annually more than 25,000 tons of grain to the Soviet government.

Courtesy The Art Institute of Chicago

LAVRA MONASTERY IN KIEV
This monastery is one of the chief architectural achievements of old Russia and was an important religious center.

it so completely that it did not recover for a hundred years. In 1654 it fell into the hands of Russia, and since then it has continued to grow in wealth and number of gardens and fine buildings.

The Sophia Cathedral of Kiev, built more than a thousand years ago, is a unique monument of world art. Its architecture combines Byzantine, Syrian, Persian, and Roman types. Another relic of the Middle Ages is the Kiev-Pechersk Monastery, built on a high bluff above the Dnieper. Strong walls surround the ancient church, built by Greeks, for the monastery was used as a fortress by the Cossack chieftain, Mazeppa.

Kiev rivals Kharkov as a center of Ukrainian culture. It is the home of the Ukrainian Academy of Sciences and the Ukrainian National Library, preserving the literature of the ancient Ukrainian language, which is still as much the tongue of the region as Russian. Its shops display the embroideries and other handwork for which the Ukraine is celebrated: elaborate blouses and dresses and brilliantly painted pottery and wooden dishes.

[360] UNIVERSITY OF KNOWLEDGE

Courtesy Intourist, Inc.

PHYSICAL CULTURE PARADE OF UKRAINIAN YOUTH AT KIEV
The paraders carry a huge picture on which there is a likeness of Stalin.

The city also plays an important economic role as a producer of sugar, leather, alcohol, yeast, flour, and tobacco. With a population of 500,000, it is the third largest city in the U. S. S. R.

ODESSA, "THE SOUTHERN PALMYRA"

Odessa, the Ukraine's window on the Black Sea, is so well planned and well laid out that it has been called "the Southern Palmyra." At the end of the eighteenth century merely a small Turkish fortress, Odessa has grown into a busy industrial center and important seaport. Its fine beaches and celebrated mud baths, cures for a number of diseases, make it a popular resort. Its opera house is one of the finest architecturally and one of the best equipped in Europe. There is also an excellent university.

If it had none of these, however, Odessa would still be immortalized by the pictures of its magnificent marble steps, leading down to the sea, in Eisenstein's notable film, *S. S. Potemkin*.

ACROSS SIBERIA

Although few tourists are able to make extensive visits to Siberia, a bird's-eye view of this virgin, unexplored country may be had by a trip on the Trans-Siberian railroad from Moscow to Vladivostok or the Manchurian border.

Besides giving a long view of Siberia, the Trans-Siberian offers a short cut for the round-the-world traveler. The trip from Moscow to Vladivostok requires nine and one-half days, reducing by three weeks the time required for the voyage through the Red Sea and Indian Ocean. The cost is also less.

Leaving Moscow, the Trans-Siberian heads across the steppes of eastern Russia toward the Urals, the gray mountain range dividing Europe from Asia. The Urals were first explored in the eleventh century by Russian traders and Viking adventurers in search of the gold, silver, iron, and precious stones which, according to Greek and Byzantine legends, abounded there. Modern science has shown that these fantastic tales underestimated the wealth of the Urals. Today these hills are foremost among Soviet Russia's richest sources of gold, minerals, and jewels. The Ural range is also one of the busiest hubs of her industry.

The train pauses at the capital of the region—Sverdlovsk, formerly Ekaterinburg. Since its founding in 1720, Sverdlovsk

COLLECTIVE FARMS
One of the great experiments of Russia today is the collective farm. Here can be seen large modern tractors at work on big scale agriculture.

has been an industrial town, and with the new exploitation of Ural raw materials it is experiencing a rapid expansion. Its factory for the cutting and polishing of precious stones, founded in 1765, is among the oldest gem factories in Europe.

From Sverdlovsk the train turns southeastward toward the great Siberian steppe. Siberia deserves better than its harsh reputation as the world's largest penal colony. It is a land of wild and vigorous beauty, with its great forests and its cold blue lakes and streams shaded by white birches.

VAST LAND

Having an area of over 5,000,000 square miles, Siberia is larger than all the countries of Europe combined. On the north it is bounded by the Arctic Ocean, on the south by the Altai, Sayan, and Khingan ranges, on the west by the Urals, and on the east by the Pacific. Rich resources of minerals, metals, and oil have only begun to be charted since the Revolution, and important discoveries are still being made.

Siberia is drained by three of the world's mightiest rivers—the Ob, the Yenisei, and the Lena, all emptying into the Arctic Ocean. With the opening of the new Arctic sea route these have become important trade channels. It is dotted with young industrial cities growing with the feverish speed of American frontier towns.

The first stop in Siberia is Chelyabinsk, formerly called the "Gateway to Siberia." Until quite recently it was a typical market town doing a big trade in raw materials raised in the surrounding countryside. The industrialization of the Ural region has changed it from a provincial town to an industrial city with important machine and metallurgical plants.

HALF-TAMED HORSES AND SPEEDING BUSSES

The next important station is Omsk, economically and culturally the chief city of Western Siberia. It is a half-European, half-Asiatic town. Buildings of concrete and steel are encroaching on the picturesque Kirghiz bazaars. The Kirghiz on their camels or half-tamed horses ride through the streets beside speeding busses. Omsk was founded by the Cossacks in 1717. Dostoyevsky, the great Russian novelist, served a prison sentence here and the "Dead House," the prison building described in his *Notes from a Dead House,* still stands.

From Omsk the train turns north to Novosibirsk, the capital of Western Siberia, a straggling frontier town not unlike the frontier towns of the American far west. The next important station is Tomsk, one of the oldest cities in Siberia, having been founded in 1604. The first Siberian university was established here.

HALF ANCIENT, HALF MODERN
Here we see camels drawing an American-made mowing machine in Western Siberia.

Courtesy American Museum of Natural History

CROSSING THE DREADED HOT SANDS OF CENTRAL ASIA

After Tomsk, the train enters Eastern Siberia. The first stop is Krasnoyarsk on the Yenisei River, now becoming an important port as the point of departure for voyages to the Arctic Ocean. From Krasnoyarsk the Trans-Siberian turns south and skirts the southern tip of Lake Baikal, a fresh inland sea 375 miles long, surrounded by mountains and cliffs. The train runs between the mountains and the water amid scenery as magnificent as that of the Swiss mountains.

The first station after Lake Baikal is Verkhneudinsk, the capital of the Buryat-Mongolian Autonomous Soviet Socialist Republic, and the juncture point of rail and air lines to Mongolia. The nomadic inhabitants of this region saw an airplane long before they saw an automobile.

The last important station in Siberia is Chita, a city famous in Cossack military history and the capital of the far eastern republic. It is a medical research center.

At Karymskaya, shortly beyond Chita, the Trans-Siberian line divides, one section running east to Manchuli, where it joins the Chinese Eastern Railway, the other going to Vladivostok.

The Vladivostok branch follows the Amur River, which has frequently figured in news dispatches as the scene of clashes between Soviet and Japanese gunboats. It passes through Blagoveshchensk and Khabarovsk, a picturesque shipping town on the Amur. Travelers may leave the train at the latter point and proceed by boat down the Amur to the Pacific.

The journey ends at Vladivostok, one of the busiest ports of Pacific shipping. It is a new city, founded in 1860, with both a Russian and a Chinese section. During the Russian civil war (1918-22) it was the scene of clashes between Red and White armies, in some of which American troops played a role as part of the Allied intervention.

HOT SANDS OF CENTRAL ASIA

Siberia is bordered by two of the most fascinating frontiers of the Soviet Union—Central Asia and the Arctic. In one an ancient civilization is being revolutionized in terms of modern technology, in the other a vast area heretofore considered uninhabitable by man is being reclaimed for civilization.

They are seldom visited by foreigners. But an understanding of them is essential to a complete picture of Soviet Russia. And in years to come they may become travel areas.

Courtesy Intourist, Inc.   Photo by Sterenberg

A MODERN POWER STATION IN ARMENIA

Central Asia, formerly known as Turkestan, lies east of the Caspian and west of Mongolia, south of Siberia and north of Persia and India. It is, for the most part, an arid land of desert and dry steppe walled in on the south and east by tremendous snow-clad mountain ranges.

The great migrations of Asiatic hordes which, from time to time, swarmed over old Europe, either originated here or passed through from the Far East—Turks, Mongols, Huns, Kalmucks, Tatars. It was invaded by Alexander the Great and was part of the empires of Genghis Khan and Tamerlane.

There are now five soviet socialist republics in Central Asia—Kazakstan, Uzbekistan, Tajikistan, Kirghizia, and Turkmenistan. The history of this region since 1917 has been principally a rapid evolution from ancient oriental standards to a modern civilization. Virtually the entire population was illiterate. Many of the races were nomadic.

THE STRUGGLE OF VEILS

One of the bitterest struggles raged around the liberation of women from the Mohammedan status of near-serfdom. Hundreds of Central Asian women have died in the struggle to cast off their long black veils and emerge from their mud huts to work in factories, attend universities and technical schools and become political and cultural leaders.

Agriculture has been collectivized. Because life here always has been almost entirely dependent on irrigation, it has been the scene of vast dam and canal projects since the Revolution, many directed by American engineers. Central Asia is becoming a vigorous rival to the American South as the foremost cotton growing region in the world.

Transportation, which until twenty years ago was chiefly by camel caravan, now centers about the new Turkestan-Siberian (Turk-Sib) railway which connects this region with the Trans-Siberian. Central Asia's cotton now has a swift outlet and the wheat and consumers' goods she needs are assured entry.

SAMARKAND AND OTHER STORIED POINTS

The principal cities of Central Asia are Samarkand, Bokhara, Tashkent, and Alma-Ata.

Samarkand is one of the most interesting and beautiful settle-

SAMARKAND

Mausoleum of Ismail Samanid, Bokhara. This ninth-century mausoleum is like the royal Bokhara rugs, regal and exquisite in design.

ments in Asia, as poets have testified for centuries. In its old city, still its loveliest section, are preserved the magnificent gardens and buildings, with their minarets and blue domes, which were built by Tamerlane in the fifteenth century when Samarkand was at its best. It is the burial place of Tamerlane, whose tomb is a superb example of oriental taste and luxury. Modern culture is represented by theaters, cinemas, clubs, and museums in the Russian section.

Bokhara is the third of Central Asia's great cities and the most oriental in character. The new Russian city has been built near the railroad, seven miles from the old, which remains unchanged—a flat-roofed oriental town surrounded by a wall of baked mud. "Holy Bokhara" was once a center of Mohammedanism and it retains its brilliant mosques set in narrow, crooked streets.

Tashkent, the capital of Uzbekistan, although not really an ancient city, has an oriental quarter of narrow streets, adobe houses, bazaars, mosques, and little eating places. The Russian section is spacious and well planned, for Tashkent was the seat of the governor-general of Turkestan in tsarist days. It has several museums, including a Museum of the Revolution which depicts the struggles of the people of the Orient.

Alma-Ata, the capital of Kazakstan, is the center of Central Asia's apple-growing region, an important station on the Turk-Sib railway and an educational and artistic center for the Central Asian people. The city has a splendid oriental opera.

CITIES IN THE ARCTIC

Along the ten thousand miles of Arctic shoreline from Murmansk to the Bering Strait, Russia is building a modern urban civilization.

The tundra is resounding to the blasts of factory whistles in raw, new cities, and to the chugging of tractors on collective farms. Thousands of pioneers are pouring into a land where since the beginning of history only explorers have dared to travel. The small Eskimo and other native population is being educated and trained for industry and agriculture.

Hitherto unsuspected resources of coal, oil, gold, and minerals are being tapped for raw materials for the new cities. Experimental agricultural stations have adapted almost every farm product but grain to the brief Arctic summer.

IN THE SNOWS OF SIBERIA
A wrestling match is about to begin between two natives.

The most heroic achievement of the Russians in the Polar region has been the opening of a sea route on the Arctic Ocean from Murmansk to Vladivostok—the northeast passage dreamed of by navigators for centuries. Over carefully charted routes, with the aid of powerful icebreakers, an increasing number of freighters traverse the Arctic each summer, breaking the path for an important world trade route.

With the recent establishment of a scientific station at the North Pole, the Arctic promises to become one of the world's chief meteorological centers. A minimum of errors is predicted by scientists for weather calculations from the Pole.

The principal cities of the Soviet Arctic are Igarka, Murmansk and Kirovsk.

Igarka, at the mouth of the Yenisei River, is the leading Polar port of Asia. It is a young frontier city, founded in 1932 to serve as the Arctic gateway to Siberia.

WHITE SEA PORTS

Murmansk, at the tip of the Kola Peninsula, is the greatest European port of the Arctic sea route. Founded in 1906, it has outgrown its pioneer period and is now a commercial and fishing center and the scientific and cultural headquarters of the European Arctic.

Kirovsk, south of Murmansk on the Kola Peninsula, lies in the heart of the Khibiny Mountains, a leading apatite-producing region. It was founded in 1930 to exploit this mineral base of fertilizer, a planned pioneering town which is developing into an industrial city.

South of Kirovsk is Karelia, a fresh, virgin country of coniferous forests. Lakes, rivers, and birch trees dot its landscapes. It has been reclaimed for trade and industry by the construction of the Baltic-White Sea canal, which opens it to European and Asiatic vessels plying the Arctic trade routes. Its principal city, Petrozavodsk, is a colony of Finnish-Americans who migrated to Russia after the Revolution.

CONCLUSION: RUSSIA AS A KALEIDOSCOPE

The Soviet Union does not offer travelers the rich cross-section of culture and history found in western Europe. But it provides a great picture of Slavic, European and Asiatic cultures; a kaleidoscope of almost all the scenic glories this planet offers; and, most unique of all, a chance to see a new world, a new form of government, and, perhaps, a new type of man in process of evolution. Only the future can determine whether soviet ideals will be achieved.

Courtesy Intourist, Inc.

DNIEPROGES DAM
This immense dam is one of the most spectacular and useful engineering feats of the Soviet regime.

BRITISH MALAYA

STREET SCENE IN SINGAPORE

THE STRAITS SETTLEMENTS, the four Federated Malay States, the five Unfederated Malay States, and British North Borneo compose the political entity known as British Malaya. It includes the Malay Peninsula, which extends southward from the continent of Asia to the Straits of Malacca, Singapore Island, Penang Island, Province of Wellesley, Malacca, Christmas Island, Labuan and the Cocos Islands, and the northern part of the island of Borneo. The estimated population is less than five million, scattered over a wide area of mainland and island territory. Singapore is the capital of the Straits Settlements, the most important division of British Malaya.

SINGAPORE

Singapore has been variously called "the front door to Hell," "the wickedest city in the world" and "a cesspool of iniquity." Ever since history was first recorded, Singapore has been a gateway to the east, the port through which the traders of India sent their

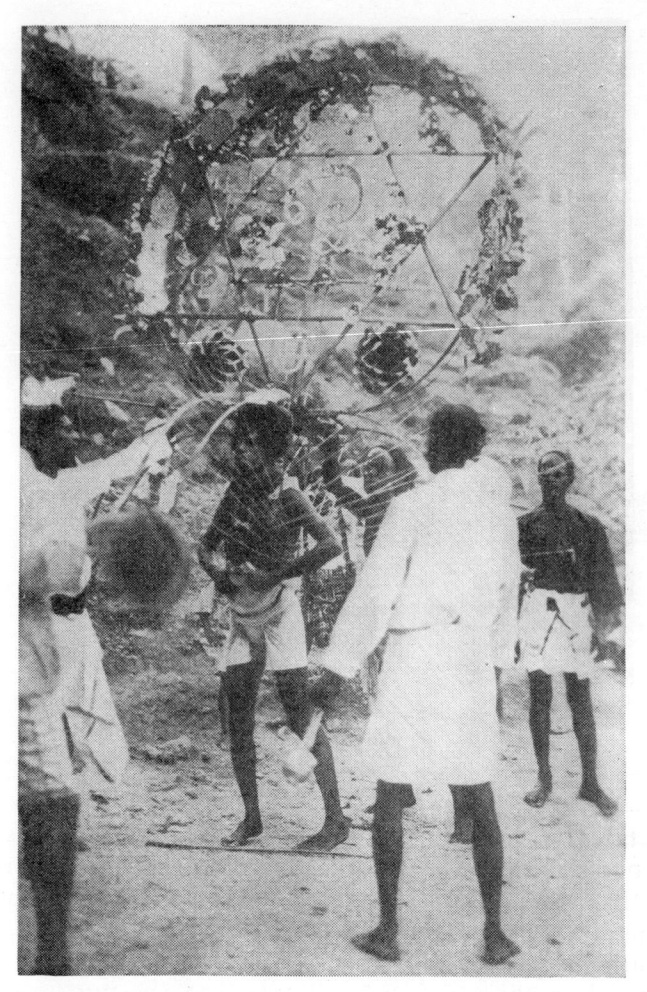

Courtesy Mason Warner

A HINDU "HOLY MAN"

These religious enthusiasts endure self-inflicted tortures of various types. This man's body is pierced with slender iron rods.

Courtesy Mason Warner
INTERIOR OF SNAKE TEMPLE, PENANG

goods to be exchanged for the products of China. Every year, more than 45,000 ships clear through the port, bringing sailors from all nations. It is because of them that Singapore's dance-halls, gambling dens, and saloons have given the city its evil reputation. For, here, along the waterfront are whites, yellows, black and mixed races attired in their picturesque native dress, just off the boat from a two or three months trip, full of suppressed spirits and ready for action.

Action, however, in Singapore is only for those who can withstand terrific heat. Situated only 87 miles from the equator, Singapore is hot, always hot, and sticky with humid heat because of the rains which fall almost every day. When the "Java winds" blow up in May and June, it becomes even hotter, for they bear more heat with them. Only between the hours of 8 to 11 and 3 to 5 should any sightseeing be attempted. A number of Chinese Buddhist temples scattered throughout the city are colorful and

Photos by Mason Warner

SULTAN'S PALACE, JOHORE

FUNERAL PROCESSION IN SINGAPORE

SCENE ON SINGAPORE RIVER

interesting as is the great Mohammedan Sultan mosque best seen from Bussorah street. Strolls through the different sections of the city where the Malays, the Chinese, the Japanese and the Hallams live separately also prove diverting.

SHARKS!

The daring ones also go bathing at Singapore's beach. The squeamish traveler merely looks on for he has been told that the wire screen which encloses the beach is there to keep out the sharks that infest the surrounding waters. Even a crocodile has been known to have slipped through the screen and venomous water-snakes are also to be found.

Most travelers make the journey to Johore, about seventeen miles north of Singapore. Here is one of the five Unfederated Malay states, ruled by Sir Ibrahim the Sultan of Johore from his capital

[378] UNIVERSITY OF KNOWLEDGE

Courtesy Mason Warner

TIN MINING IN THE STRAITS SETTLEMENTS

Courtesy Mason Warner

TIN MINING IN THE STRAITS SETTLEMENTS

city Johore-Bahru. The sultan's palace and the great mosque are among the main attractions of this little state which is connected with the island of Singapore by a narrow stone causeway.

The territory of Malaya produces enormous quantities of rubber. The surprising fact about this is that the rubber tree is not actually indigenous to Malaya. Back in 1877, twenty-two rubber tree saplings were sent from Kew Gardens, in London, England, to Malaya. Seven of them were planted in Perak, 400 miles north of Singapore. From that almost insignificant beginning grew up one of the largest rubber industries with plantations that now supply the world with almost half of its rubber. In the 3,000,000 acres of land now devoted to rubber planting, where there was once only useless tropical jungle, there is now a territory in which $400,000,000 have been invested producing $50,000,000 worth of rubber annually.

PENANG

Although Georgetown is the name of the Island of Penang's chief city, it is always referred to as Penang. As in Singapore, most of the population is Chinese and the wealthy among them, who

Courtesy Mason Warner

A STREET IN PENANG

have made their fortunes in tin and rubber, live in elaborate mansions. Most of the Malayans here, though, live in huts that are raised four or five feet off the ground with palm-leaf sides and long-grass thatched roofs.

Near Penang at Ayer Hitam is the great Kek Lok temple and monastery, one of the finest Buddhist temples in the world. Here are a number of beautiful gold, blue, white and red temples, pagodas, grottos and corridors that are well worth the traveler's visit to them. In one of the temples is a stone-enclosed fountain in which hundreds of sacred tortoises are kept. Animal worship is quite common in this land. One of Penang's colorful drives leads to the Snake temple, a Chinese Buddhist place of worship of the snake. In its small open-front building are hundreds of brightly colored snakes coiled around altar pieces, window ledges, lanterns and clocks. Visitors who dare are allowed to hold the snakes which are handled by the priests with impunity. At night the snakes come down from their perches and feed on the raw hen's eggs which are left on the floor for them.

A ricksha ride in Penang is an interesting experience. From the wharves at the waterfront with its tall ocean liners, Chinese junks, sampans and native boats with eyes painted on their bows, one is pulled through the narrow streets. Occasionally, the thin wail of a Chinese one-string violin carries through the stillness of the night. Then, suddenly, you are in the middle of a street that is noisy with people of all nationalities. Perhaps you might visit one of the Chinese theaters with its huge gong which is sounded whenever a joke is spoken to inform the audience that they should laugh. Of especial interest are the native markets which, in all oriental countries, are exceedingly interesting because of their color and the volubility of the shop-keepers and the customers. In Penang's markets especially is this noticeable. Interesting, too, are the portable restaurants which are dragged along on wheels by their proprietors from place to place.

BRITISH MALAYA [381]

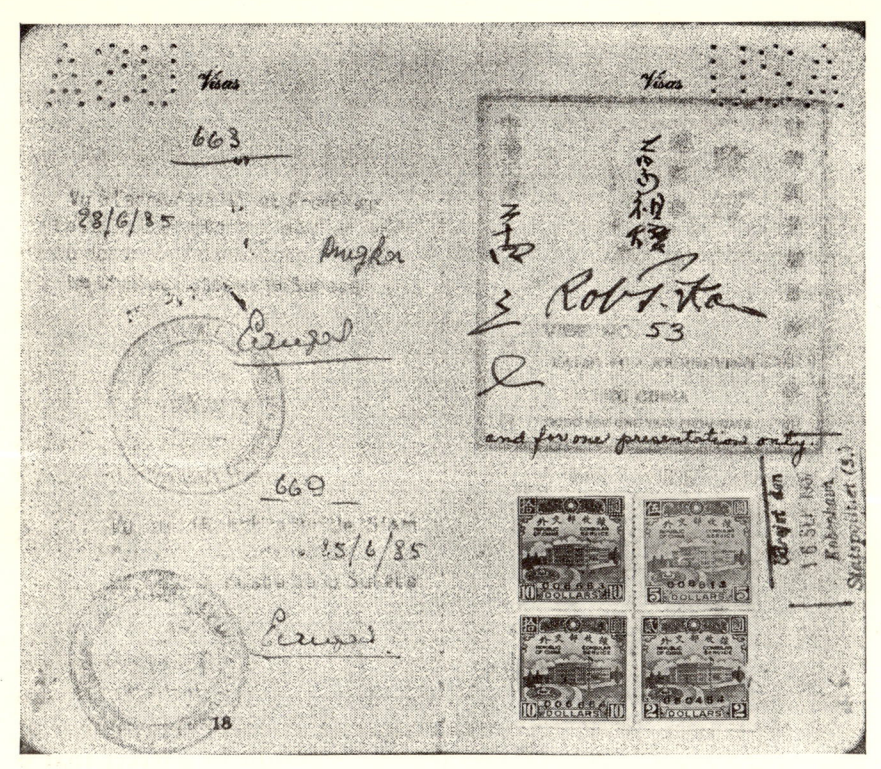

TWO PAGES FROM MASON WARNER'S PASSPORT (1934–1937)

This passport contains visas and entry stamps for Japan, China, Netherland East Indies, Bali, Straits Settlements, Federated Malay States, Siam, French Indo-China, Burma, Australia, New Zealand, Solomon Islands, New Guinea, Fiji Islands, Cook Islands, Society Islands, Norway, Sweden, Denmark, Finland, Poland, Estonia, and the Union of Soviet Socialist Republics.

DESIGNER'S NOTE

The design and typography of these three volumes of Travel were executed in the same style as the previous volumes of "The University of Knowledge."

The maps in front of each volume were especially drawn under the direction of the editor. The text is set in 12 point linotype Garamond with Eve initials at the beginning of each chapter.

OTTO MAURICE FORKERT
Director of Design and Layout